P9-EKX-267

The Kitchen Sink

Also by Albert Goldbarth

The Kitchen Sink

NEW AND SELECTED POEMS
1972–2007

Albert Goldbarth

Graywolf Press
SAINT PAUL, MINNESOTA

Copyright © 2007 by Albert Goldbarth

Publication of this volume is made possible in part by a grant provided by the Minnesota State Arts Board, through an appropriation by the Minnesota State Legislature; a grant from the Wells Fargo Foundation Minnesota; and a grant from the National Endowment for the Arts, which believes that a great nation deserves great art. Significant support has also been provided by the Bush Foundation; Target; the McKnight Foundation; and other generous contributions from foundations, corporations, and individuals. To these organizations and individuals we offer our heartfelt thanks.

Published by Graywolf Press
2402 University Avenue, Suite 203
Saint Paul, Minnesota 55114
All rights reserved.

www.graywolfpress.org

Published in the United States of America

ISBN-13 978-1-55597-462-6
ISBN-10 1-55597-462-7
2 4 6 8 9 7 5 3 1
First Graywolf Printing, 2007

Library of Congress Control Number: 2006929502

Cover design: Kyle G. Hunter
Cover art: John Schoenherr

Acknowledgments

The Kitchen Sink selects from the following books (by original order of publication): *Coprolites* (New Rivers Press, 1973); *Jan 31** (Doubleday, 1974); *Comings Back** (Doubledy, 1976); *Faith** (New Rivers Press, 1981); *Original Light* (Ontario Review Press, 1983); *Arts and Sciences** (Ontario Review Press, 1986); *Popular Culture** (Ohio State University Press, 1990); *Heaven and Earth: A Cosmology** (University of Georgia Press, 1991); *The Gods* (Ohio State University Press, 1993); *Across the Layers** (University of Georgia Press, 1994); *Marriage, and Other Science Fiction* (Ohio State University Press, 1994); *Adventures in Ancient Egypt* (Ohio State University Press, 1996); *Beyond** (David R. Godine, 1998); *Troubled Lovers in History** (Ohio State University Press, 1999); *Saving Lives** (Ohio State University Press, 2001); *Combinations of the Universe** (Ohio State University Press, 2003); *Budget Travel through Space and Time** (Graywolf Press, 2005); *The Book* (The Center for Book Arts, NYC, 2006).

Poems never before in book form were originally published in the following journals (by alphabetical order):

The Bellingham Review: "Some Leaves from the Permission Tree"
Beloit Poetry Journal: "'Off in the darkness. . . .'"; "Grahamesque"
Brick: "Bundh"
Crazyhorse: "'The famous Catalan Atlas of 1375. . . .'"; "Atmosphere"
The Georgia Review: "Versed"
The Gettysburg Review: "Completing the Things"; "Context"
Kayak: "Houdin"
The Kenyon Review: "Voyage"; "Whale and Bee"
New Letters: "The Western Frontier"; "Astronomy / A Pulitzer Prize Winner's . . ."; "Talk with Friends"
Nightsun: "Burnt Tree"
Ontario Review: "Fourteen Pages"; "The Song of Two Places"

* The copyrights to the twelve asterisked titles are retained by, and are in the name of, their original publishers as listed above. I thank them gratefully for their permission to reprint material from those collections.

Poetry: "Scar / Beer / Glasses"; "Human Beauty"; "'All totaled, the sunlight . . .'"; "The Too Late Poem"; "And the Rustling Bough As an Alphabet"; "Stomackes"; "Cock"

Poetry East: "Comparative"; "Buchenwald"

Poetry Northwest: "Units"

Pool: "1124 into Wichita"; "Stepper"

River City: "The Novel That Asks to Erase Itself"

Shenandoah: "Shawl"; "While Everyone Else Went Starward"

Slate: "Unforeseeables"

Third Coast: "'Assisted Living'"

TriQuarterly: "The Muse of Invention"; "Walleechu"

The Virginia Quarterly Review: "The Song of How We Believe"; "The English Rat"

Washington Square: "Emblem Days"

Thanks to the editors of the *Virginia Quarterly Review* for awarding their Emily Clark Balch Prize for 2004 to a group of poems that include "The Song of How We Believe" and "The English Rat"; to the editors of *Poetry* for awarding their Frederick Bock Prize for 2005 to "Cock," as well as to the Science Fiction Poetry Association, which nominated "Cock" for its 2006 Rhysling Poetry Award; and to Don Selby and Diane Boller at *Poetry Daily,* not only for recycling "Heart Heart Heart Heart Heart Heart Heart" and "'Off in the darkness hourses moved restlessly . . .'" onto their web site, but for their verve and numerous instances of kind attention. "Swan" and "Human Beauty" were broadcast on *Poetry's* "Poem of the Day" radio feature.

It has always been my way to submit work through the mail, not through personal connections. To that extent, the editors of the books and journals listed above—none of whom I knew before an original submission—deserve an extra round of my thanks, for their willingness to read honestly and openly in a world that so often works otherwise.

No computer was used in the creation and submission of these poems; and so some of the editors of the books and journals above have been especially accommodating during the production process . . . even the one who called me "a pain in the patootie." As for my insistent reliance on the typewriter over the computer: I will go down with this ship.

At the start of my book *Original Light,* I quoted from G. B. Edwards's *The Book of Ebenezer Le Page,* and I will do so again: "I must give it to Clive Holyoak he was a wonderful violin-player. I will never forget the way he used to rise up on his tip-toes on his little short legs to reach the top notes. It wasn't so much as if he was playing the fiddle as if the fiddle was playing him."

Contents

The soundless voice of the Rainbow People spoke to them, from no direction, out of nowhere, the words ringing in their minds. . . .

Listen closely to us, it said. Let us talk of the universe.

"It would be presumptuous of me to talk of the universe," said Boone. "I have no knowledge of it."

One of you, the voice said, has given thought to it.

"I have given it no thought," said Enid. "But there have been times I have pondered on it. I have wondered what it is and the purpose of it."

Then pay attention, said the voice. Listen very closely.

—CLIFFORD SIMAK
Highway of Eternity

"Off in the darkness hourses moved restlessly. . . ."

—A TYPO IN CLIFFORD SIMAK'S
A Heritage of Stars

We believed they were horses; and so
we saddled up, we rode expectantly
through the long day and into the night.
Then we dismounted; and slept; and still
they continued to carry us
—the hours. They wouldn't stop.
They carried us clean away.

A Prefatory Note

What's Not Here

Three hundred fifty pages, Graywolf offered me—and generously so. I couldn't see *how* I'd settle those dauntingly open plains. And yet within days, that sweep of pages was in danger of overcrowding. First, we determined that the book should include a substantial section of "new" poems. Then, of the pages left to accommodate the "selected" pieces, some were claimed immediately by lengthy ventures . . . a poem of eighteen pages . . . of thirty-four. . . . And so not only qualitative concerns decided policy, but also, more mundanely, the strictures of physical limitation. Clearly what was required were sensible precepts for wholesale naysaying.

The first decision: not to excerpt. This prohibited anything from *Opticks* and *Different Fleshes,* two early book-length poems; from *Curve* and *Eurekas,* two early long poems that each appeared as a chapbook; and from *Keeping* and *Who Gathered and Whispered Behind Me,* two early small-press collections consisting only of longer pieces. Sadly, the rule applied as well to more current work: for example, at forty-five pages, "The Two Domains" (from *Beyond*) is too long for inclusion here and not served well by only partial appearance. "The Book of Speedy" at nineteen pages . . . ? "From the Moon" at twenty-one . . . ? These, and more, found the entryway barred.

Poems—whether old or new—that have never yet been published in any format were likewise out of bounds. The same for poems that up until 2005 had only appeared in journals, but never used in a book.* There are many hundreds of these. (As I write this, I'm glancing over to a pile topped by the silver foil cover of *Stiletto #2;* inside it, a twenty-two-page selection of work that, simply, I couldn't consider for inclusion in *The Kitchen Sink.*)

My own writing aside, I wish I'd had room in which to acknowledge more of those lively "little magazines" that overspill my office shelves, those journals that originate from before the current era of desktop publishing, computer typesetting, and outside funding enablement . . . *Gum, December, Happiness Holding Tank, Road Apple Review, Quixote, Pebble, Green House,*

---

* With this exception: a single such poem—as a token gesture, and on principle—is included in each of the first four sections.

The Lamp in the Spine . . . small venues funded often out of one person's pocket and driven by private passions beyond one's resumé.

Here, a single issue of Jerry Parrott's *South Florida Poetry Journal,* 224 8.5 × 11 pages he retyped from his contributors' submissions and then had offset-printed and bound . . . and here, those lovely awkward issues of George Hitchcock's influential *Kayak,* not a one with its staples exactly centered, but all of them full of those crazy surrealist cut-and-paste collages with which he filled the margins surrounding the poems . . . a chicken sporting a chorine's legs, a fishing rod drifting on eagle's wings. . . .

Bits was hand-sewn by its editors. *Hanging Loose* was . . . well, it was loose, and stuffed in an illustrated envelope. Tony Sobin once described to me his all-night collating parties for the *Ark River Review:* volunteer friends and lovers hustling from table to desk to chair until sunrise, adding page to page until a copy of that issue was ready for stapling . . . then back to the start of the line. *Granite, Epos, Caliban,* the *Dragonfly, Umbral, Montana Gothic.* . . . The history of those titles (and their communities) is still awaiting its writing. And some stranger who bears my name is borne in all of their tables of contents.

Not always, of course, with work of distinction. But you couldn't fault his enthusiasm and dedication, his sheer love of the art, this "Albert Goldbarth" I find with a nineteen-page special section of his work in a 1972 *Pyramid,* a twenty-two-page special section in a 1975 *Midwest Quarterly,* a twenty-four-page special section in a 1976 *Little Magazine.* Who *was* this pixilated aspirant—this out-of-the-loop, completely unnetworked, wide-eyed, trusting licker-of-stamps-beyond-counting and habitué-of-mailboxes-at-midnight? I think of the reminiscence Edmond Hamilton—king of 1920s and '30s sci-fi pulp adventure—once offered: "I remember that I was so excited when I wrote that final space battle, and punched my little portable typewriter so hard, that the machine 'walked' all over the surface of my old flat-topped desk—and I sort of followed it, banging away as I finished my climactic scene."

Who was he? Kenneth Koch: "Sometimes I feel I actually am the person / Who did this, who wrote that . . . / But sometimes on the other hand I don't."

Whoever he was, that "Albert Goldbarth," he's seminally important to the book at hand—but has little representation. For a number of reasons, *The Kitchen Sink* favors works created from 1983 onward. Or, as a poem in this book observes: "In every day, some thing must die / for the day to keep on living."

What's Here

A few selected poems from 1972 to 1983 appear as "The Fossil of an Omelet."

Poems since *Budget Travel through Space and Time* (2005) are grouped together in "Human Beauty."

The largest of the gatherings—of poems from 1983 to 2005—is divided into two sections, the better to yield to the affections of friends who over the years have suggested that some of their favorite shorter pieces were sometimes lost in the shadows cast by nearby longer poems. For them, a separate selection of one-page poems appears as "The Rising Place for the Dough." The rest of the poems from 1983 to 2005 will be found under "Love and Cosmology."

However, poems within the four chronologically determined sections I've just described are *not* in original sequence of composition. (Louis Simpson: "For the truth is not in chronology [. . .] / Real time is inside one's head.") I've tried instead to reach a balance between the urge to consolidate like-minded themes and strategies, and the desire to be as various as that permits.

The recentmost piece in the book, "Off in the darkness . . . ," serves as an introduction; the oldest poem, "Field" (from 1972), acts as a coda.

Only a few times have I allowed myself to revise a single word or a single mark of punctuation since that poem's first publication. Occasionally in minor ways the texts of poems have been made consistent: "14" to "fourteen," "tv" to "TV," etc. But almost everything here is just as it was when first published.

Of many editors who have shown serial generosities to me—the books and journals that bear their mark are listed with vast appreciation on the acknowledgments page—I must especially thank the late David Citino, whose original ticket of entry to the Ohio State University Press allowed for seven titles with that publisher; Marion Stocking of the *Beloit Poetry Journal,* whose energy, welcome, and acumen have helped shape two generations of American poets and poetry readers; the guiding sensibilities behind the Ontario Review Press, Raymond Smith and Joyce Carol Oates; and three successive editors of *Poetry* (John F. Nims, Joseph Parisi, Christian Wiman), where twenty-seven of these poems first appeared.

That Fiona McCrae's Graywolf Press provides a much needed high watermark in literary publishing is no secret: I'd merely like to add my agreement;

and my thanks; and also my gratitude to Graywolf editors Jeff Shotts and Anne Czarniecki, paragons.

Last . . . to quote from a poem herein . . .

And: SKYLER, I'm
whispering suddenly, like a fifteen-year-old at the fresh cement

—at the air, at the dark, at the thin lunar light,
at whatever of this world might read me.

The Kitchen Sink

An Invocation
to the Muse

Shawl

Eight hours by bus, and night
was on them. He could see himself now
in the window, see his head there with the country
running through it like a long thought made of steel and wheat.
Darkness outside; darkness in the bus—as if the sea
were dark and the belly of the whale were dark to match it.
He was twenty: of course his eyes returned, repeatedly,
to the knee of the woman two rows up: positioned so
occasional headlights struck it into life.
But more reliable was the book; he was discovering himself
to be among the tribe that reads. Now his, the only
overhead turned on. Now nothing else existed:
only him, and the book, and the light thrown over his shoulders
as luxuriously as a cashmere shawl.

Library

This book saved my life.

This book takes place on one of the two small tagalong moons of Mars.

This book requests its author's absolution, centuries after his death.

This book required two of the sultan's largest royal elephants to bear it; this other book fit in a gourd.

This book reveals The Secret Name of God, and so its author is on a death list.

This is the book I lifted high over my head, intending to smash a roach in my girlfriend's bedroom; instead, my back unsprung, and I toppled painfully into her bed, where I stayed motionless for eight days.

This is a "book." That is, an audiocassette. This other "book" is a screen and a microchip. This other "book," the sky.

In chapter 3 of this book, a woman tries explaining her husband's tragically humiliating death to their daughter: reading it is like walking through a wall of setting cement.

This book taught me everything about sex.

This book is plagiarized.

This book is transparent; this book is a codex in Aztec; this book, written by a prisoner, in dung; the wind is turning the leaves of this book: a hilltop olive as thick as a Russian novel.

This book is a vivisected frog, and ova its text.

This book was dictated by Al-Méllikah, the Planetary Spirit of the Seventh Realm, to his intermediary on Earth (the Nineteenth Realm), who published it, first in mimeograph, and many editions later in gold-stamped leather.

This book taught me everything wrong about sex.

This book poured its colors into my childhood so strongly they remain a dye in my imagination today.

This book is by a poet who makes me sick.

This is the first book in the world.

This is a photograph from Vietnam, titled "Buddhist nuns copying scholarly Buddhist texts in the pagoda."

This book smells like salami.

This book is continued in volume 2.

He was driving—evidently by some elusive, interior radar, since he was
    busy reading a book propped on the steering wheel.
This book picks on men.
This is the split Red Sea: two *heavy* pages.
In this book I underlined *deimos, cabochon, pelagic, hegira.* I wanted to
    use them.
This book poured its bile into my childhood.
This book defames women.
This book was smuggled into the country one page at a time, in tiny pill
    containers, in hatbands, in the cracks of asses; sixty people risked their
    lives repeatedly over this one book.
This book is nuts!!!
This book cost more than a seven-story chalet in the Tall Oaks subdivision.
This book—I don't remember.
This book is a hoax, and a damnable lie.
This chapbook was set in type and printed by hand, by Larry Levis's then-
    wife, the poet Marcia Southwick, in 1975. It's 1997 now and Larry's
    dead—too early, way too early—and this elliptical, heartbreaking
    poem (which is, in part, exactly *about* too early death) keeps speaking
    to me from its teal-green cover: the way they say the nails and the hair
    continue to grow in the grave.
This book is two wings and a thorax the size of a sunflower seed.
This book gave me a hard-on.
This book is somewhere under those other books way over there.
This book deflected a bullet.
This book provided a vow I took.
If they knew you owned this book, they'd come and get you; it wouldn't
    be pretty.
This book is a mask: its author isn't anything like it.
This book is by William Matthews, a *wonderful* poet, who died today, age
    fifty-five. Now Larry Levis has someone he can talk to.
This book is an "airplane book" (but not *about* airplanes; meant *to be read
    on* an airplane; also available every three steps in the airport). What does
    it mean, to "bust" a "block"?

This is the book I pretended to read one day in the Perry-Castañeda Library browsing room, but really I was rapt in covert appreciation of someone in a slinky skirt that clung like kitchen plasticwrap. She squiggled near and pointed to the book. "It's upside-down," she said.

For the rest of the afternoon I was so flustered that when I finally left the library . . . this is the book, with its strip of magnetic-code tape, that I absentmindedly walked with through the security arch on the first day of its installation, becoming the first (though unintentional) light-fingered lifter of books to trigger the Perry-Castañeda alarm, which hadn't been fine-tuned as yet, and sounded even louder than the sirens I remember from grade-school air-raid drills, when the principal had us duck beneath our desks and cover our heads—as if gabled—with a book.

The chemical formulae for photosynthesis: this book taught me that.

And this book taught me what a "merkin" is.

The cover of this book is fashioned from the tanned skin of a favorite slave.

This book is inside a computer now.

This "book" is made of knotted string; and this, of stone; and this, the gut of a sheep.

This book existed in a dream of mine, and only there.

This book is a talk-show paperback with shiny gold raised lettering on the cover. (Needless to say, not one by me.)

This is a book of prohibitions; this other, a book of rowdy license. They serve equally to focus the prevalent chaos of our lives.

This book is guarded around the clock by men in navy serge and golden braiding, carrying *very* capable guns.

This is the book that destroyed a marriage. Take it, burn it, before it costs us more.

This book is an intercom for God.

This book I slammed against a wall.

My niece wrote this book in crayon and glitter.

This is the book (in a later paperback version) by which they recognized the sea-bleached, battered, and otherwise-unidentifiable body of Shelley.

Shit: I forgot to send in the card, and now the Book Club has billed me *twice* for *Synopses of 400 Little-Known Operas*.

This book is filled with sheep and rabbits, calmly promenading in their
   tartan vests and bow ties, with their clay pipes, in their Easter Sunday
   salad-like hats. The hills are gently rounded. The sun is a clear, firm
   yolk. The world will never be this sweetly welcoming again.
This book is studded with gems that have the liquid depth of aperitifs.
This book, *1,000 Wild Nights,* is actually wired to give an electr/YOWCH!
This book I stole from Cornell University's Olin Library in the spring of
   1976. Presumably, its meter's still running. Presumably, it still longs for
   its Dewey'd place in the dim-lit stacks.
This book has a bookplate reminding me, in Latin, to use my scant time well.
It's the last day of the semester. My students are waiting to sell their
   textbooks back to the campus store, like crazed racehorses barely
   restrained at the starting gate.
This book caused a howl / a stir / a ruckus / an uproar.
This book became a movie; they quickly raised the cover price.
This book is the Key to the Mysteries.
This book has a bookplate: a man and a woman have pretzeled themselves
   into one lubricious shape.
This book came apart in my hands.
This book is austere; it's like holding a block of dry ice.
This Bible is in Swahili.
This book contains seemingly endless pages of calculus—it may as well be
   in Swahili.
This is the book I pretended to read while Ellen's lushly naked body
   darkened into sleep beside me. And *this* is the book I pretended to
   read in a waiting room once, as a cardiac specialist razored into my
   father's chest. And THIS book I pretended having read once, when
   I interviewed for a teaching position: "Oh yes," I said, "of course,"
   and spewed a stream of my justly famous golden bullshit into the
   conference room.
This book was signed by the author fifteen minutes before she died.
This is Erhard Ratdolf's edition of Johann Regiomontanus's astronomical
   and astrological calendar (1476)—it contains "the first true title-page."
She snatched this book from a garbage can, just as Time was about to swallow

it out of the visible world irrevocably. To this day, her grandchildren
read it.

This book: braille. This one: handmade paper, with threads of the poet's
own bathrobe as part of the book's rag content. This one: the cover is
hollowed glass, with a goldfish swimming around the title.

This is my MFA thesis. Its title is *Goldbarth's MFA Thesis*.

This is the cookbook used by Madame Curie. It still faintly glows, seven
decades later.

This book is the shame of an entire nation.

This book is one of fourteen matching volumes, like a dress parade.

This is the book I'm writing now. It's my best! (But where should I send it?)

This book doesn't do anyth/ oh wow, check THIS out!

This is the book I bought for my nephew, *101 Small Physics Experiments*.
Later he exchanged it for *The Book of Twerps and Other Pukey Things*,
and who could blame him?

This book is completely marred by the handiwork of the *Druckfehlerteufel*—
"the imp who supplies the misprints."

This book has a kind of aurora-like glory radiating from it. There should be
versions of uranium detectors that register glory-units from books.

We argued over this book in the days of the divorce. I kept it, she kept the
stained-glass window from Mike and Mimi.

Yes, he was supposed to be on the 7:05 to Amsterdam. But he stayed at
home, to finish this whodunit. And so he didn't crash.

This book has a browned corsage pressed in it. I picked up both for a dime
at the Goodwill.

"A diet of berries, vinegar, and goat's milk" will eventually not only cure
your cancer, but will allow a man to become impregnated (diagrams
explain this)—also, there's serious philosophy about Jews who control
"the World Order" in this book.

This book reads from right to left. This book comes with a small wooden
top attached by a saffron ribbon. This book makes the sound of a lion,
a train, or a cuckoo clock, depending on where you press its cover.

I've always admired this title from 1481: *The Myrrour of the Worlde*.

This book is from the 1950s; the jacket says it's "a doozie."

This book is by me. I found it squealing piteously, poor piglet, in the back of a remainders bin. I took it home and nursed it.

This book let me adventure with the Interplanetary Police.

I threw myself, an aspirant, against the difficult theories this book propounded, until my spirit was bruised. I wasn't any smarter—just bruised.

This book is magic. There's more *inside* it than outside.

This is the copy of the *Iliad* that Alexander the Great took with him, always, on his expeditions—"in," Thoreau says, "a precious casket."

Help! *(thump)* I've been stuck in this book all week and I don't know how to get out! *(thump)*

This is the book of poetry I read from at my wedding to Morgan. We were divorced. The book (Fred Chappell's *River*) is still on my shelf, like an admonishment.

This book is stapled (they're rusted by now); this book, bound in buttery leather; this book's pages are chemically treated leaves; this book, the size of a peanut, is still complete with indicia and an illustrated colophon page.

So tell me: out of what grim institution for the taste-deprived and the sensibility-challenged do they find the cover artists for these books?

This book I tried to carry balanced on my head with seven others.

This book I actually licked.

This book—remember? I carved a large hole in its pages, a "how-to magazine for boys" said this would be a foolproof place to hide my secret treasures. Then I remembered I *didn't have* any secret treasures worth hiding. Plus, I was down one book.

This book is nothing but jackal crap; unfortunately, its royalties have paid for two Rolls-Royces and a mansion in the south of France.

This book is said to have floated off the altar of the church, across the village square, and into the hut of a peasant woman in painful labor.

This is what he was reading when he died. The jacket copy says it's "a real page-turner—you can't put it down!" I'm going to assume he's in another world now, completing the story.

This book hangs by a string in an outhouse, and every day it gets thinner.

This book teaches you how to knit a carrying case for your rosary; this one, how to build a small but lethal incendiary device.

This book has pop-up pages with moveable parts, intended to look like the factory room where pop-up books with moveable parts are made.

If you don't return that book I loaned you, I'm going to smash your face.

This book says the famously saintly woman was really a ring-tailed trash-mouth dirty-down bitch queen. *Everyone's* reading it!

There are stains in this book that carry a narrative greater than its text.

The Case of _____ . *How to* _____ . Books books books.

I know great petulant stormy swatches and peaceful lulls of this book by heart.

I was so excited, so jazzed up!—but shortly thereafter they found me asleep, over pages 6 and 7 of this soporific book. (I won't say by who.)

And on her way back to her seat, she fell (the multiple sclerosis) and refused all offered assistance. Instead, she used her book she'd been reading from, as a prop, and worked herself pridefully back up to a standing position.

They gave me this book for free at the airport. Its cover features an Indian god with the massive head of an elephant, as brightly blue as a druid, flinging flowers into the air and looking unsurpassably wise.

My parents found this book in my bottom drawer, and spanked the living hell into my butt.

This book of yours, you tell me, was optioned by Hollywood for eighty-five impossibajillion dollars? Oh. Congratulations.

They lowered the esteemed and highly published professor into his grave. A lot of silent weeping. A lot of elegiac rhetoric. And one man shaking his head in the chill December wind dumbfoundedly, who said, "And he perished anyway."

Although my eighth-grade English teacher, Mrs. Hurd, always said, "Whenever you open a book, remember: that author lives again."

After this book, there was no turning back.

Around 1000 AD, when the Magyars were being converted over to Christianity, Magyar children were forced to attend school for the first time in their cultural history: "therefore the Magyar word *konyv* means tears as well as book."

This book, from when I was five, its fuzzy ducklings, and my mother's voice in the living room of the second-story apartment over the butcher shop on Division Street. . . . I'm fifty now. I've sought out, and I own now, one near-mint and two loose, yellowing copies that mean to me as much as the decorated gold masks and the torsos of marble meant to the excavators of Troy.

This book is done.

This book gave me a paper cut.

This book set its mouth on my heart, and sucked a mottled tangle of blood to the surface.

I open this book and smoke pours out, I open this book and a bad sleet slices my face, I open this book: brass knuckles, I open this book: the spiky scent of curry, I open this book and hands grab forcefully onto my hair as if in violent sex, I open this book: the wingbeat of a seraph, I open this book: the edgy cat-pain wailing of the damned thrusts up in a column as sturdy around as a giant redwood, I open this book: the travel of light, I open this book and it's as damp as a wound, I open this book and I fall inside it farther than any physics, stickier than the jelly we scrape from cracked bones, cleaner than what we tell our children in the dark when they're afraid to close their eyes at night.

And this book can't be written yet: its author isn't born yet.

This book is going to save the world.

Love and
Cosmology

selected poems 1983–2005: I

The Far Perimeters

He was giddy and ecstatic. He went skating down a looping bridge of magnetic flux. He danced madly in the midst of a sputtering cloud of ions. He ducked his erratic way through the core of an exploding galaxy. He ran a race with the surging radiation that flared out of a nova. He somersaulted through a field of pulsars.

When it was all done, he hunkered down before a red dwarf and spread out symbolic hands to warm them on the banked fires of the star. The red dwarf, curiously, was the only luminosity in sight. All else was black, although somewhere far away there was the faint hint of high-intensity flickering, as if some great event were taking place beyond the far horizon of deep space.

—CLIFFORD SIMAK
Project Pope

The Talk Show

*In 1930, The Bell Telephone Company commissioned one of their
employees, Karl Jansky, to find out why the new car radios suffered from
static. Jansky set up radio antennae, and heard a steady hiss coming
from the direction of the Milky Way. Radio astronomy was born thirty
years later.*

—JAMES BURKE

A woman "heard angels." The paper says angels
sussurra'd her body, rang their praises daylong
through its reedy places, stirred her
smallest water. And elsewhere, Larry
"Dude Man" Chavez raises his #2 wrench
indifferently overhead on the C-track tightening line,
and feels something like lightning—only
there isn't lightning—beam to the wrench head,
branch down his arm, make all of his muscles
electric feathers, then exit his other arm out
its guttering candelabrum fingers and into
the frame of the Ford. It's stored

there. It happens. We all know it happens.
The cops and the hospital nightshift crew know
what a full moon means, and
if their decades of statistics don't cut diddlysquat
with you, here's someone being wheeled in
from a three-car smashup while the universe hums
its lunar kazoo, and adrenaline everywhere dervishes.
And statistics on sunspots, and suicides.
And statistics on lines of magnetic pull,
and conception. We're the few but beautiful
units of the first day of the cosmos
densed-up over time; when the lady I love

flaps suddenly in sleep like a wire discharging, it
makes sense as much as anything—bad dreams,
zinged nerves—to simply say *we're* where
the Big Bang ripples to the limits of a continuous medium,
flickers a little, kicks. I've disappointed her
sometimes; and so, myself. I've left the house then,
while she slept, and while my neighbors slept, as if
I could walk noise out of myself
through darkness, finally dialing-in
the talk show where the blood calls with its question,
and the "sky," whatever that is, whatever portion we are
of it or once were, answers. And

I've walked past where the university's planetarium
dish-ear swivels hugely for the far
starcrackle Karl Jansky more primitively
dowsed. It happens any size; that woman? picked up
cop calls on her IUD, the paper adds, in bubble-bursting
glee. Although if angels are voices beyond us
in us, everyone's umbles are singing hosannahs
under their everyday wamble and gab. I've
slipped back into bed some nights and clasped her
till I slept, then woke to her heart
in my ear, that mysterious sound,
on earth as it is in heaven.

Heart Heart Heart Heart Heart Heart Heart

*"Oh, many a night my cousins and I spent out fishing and sleeping under
the stars—or with the bugs, as we used to say."*

—A CHARACTER IN SEAN RUSSELL'S
The Isle of Battle

And that's the truth of it, the truth of the far perimeters
—the bugs; the stars—inside of which our little, loopy
human selves get lived; and lost; and led by rival vectors
of attraction way beyond our comprehension. Or not the whole truth,
no; the stars themselves are only showy speckling
on the ever-outward "surface" of an unknowable and invisible
veering-away; the insects? . . . symbolize the last of the apprehendables
before a faceless sub-ness starts, the micro without end.
No wonder we hold with such affection to the sky charts
of astronomy; to even *dilettantish* entomology,
its nets and pins. They make space seem to fit us:
I have a friend we found intoning one word scarily over and over until
she was lost, like a midge in a labyrinth: a mayfly in an oil drum,
out on the ocean, under the blown-open void.

"Self-inflicted injuries" as well. So she was locked up. And
she "came along," "progressed" in there, in finally understanding
how to master fear of what she called, as if it were her nemesis
and so had a campaign to wage, "The Shapelessness." For her, a certain
level of medication and therapy meditation "fixed her up."
For others, God: commandments and Heavenly hierarchies.
For others, anonymous serial sex: *anything* to act as a pattern,
anything to serve for rungs up all-too-empty air. And even
after she came home from the facility, she'd sometimes pick a sore
in her skin—her arm or her breast. "You see, the planet
is filled with all of these stunning potential jewels in its veins; but they need
to be dug out and given a form. That's how it is with beauty: it has
to be formed." The artful sore on her bosom, mauve and bright from damp
—in different light it might have passed for a brooch.

In early anatomical depictions—ancient Greek or ancient Arabic—
the world is still 2-D, and so we enter the cadaver as if
through opened doors in the thinnest chiffonier, of phyllo or rice paper
—here, our body's sweetbreads dangle like kindergarten cutouts on strings.
By the time of da Vinci, the tricky, miles-devouring perspective applied
to avenues of columns, or the sea, gets put to use on the sweep of our own
interior distinctions. The viewer now comes to see what the lover—spurned
or topsyturvily delighted—immemorially always knew: the heart holds
unlit mystery we float inside like spacemen lost to Earth. (So does the
    pancreas
and the intestines . . . although these organs don't play well in a poem.)
And when I said we found her "intoning one word over and over,"
that was (soon I'll tell you why) the word, her own nuts *om* of choice,
in which the sexual "tart" and the aesthetic "art" were also repeated
into a nonsense structure she was a gnat inside of, a fizzle of ash.

For some, the notion of "family." For some, to walk all seven of the Seven
Higher Righteous Paths of the Totem. Others, academic
rank. Creation science ["science"]. The fractal spread
of genealogical trees. If not for these, we'd have no guiding (check one)
)track)map)pole star)passion)overriding moral vision
)[add your own], and we'd be dropping through the nothing both
a major urban metroplex and a sesame seed are, under the rings
of their atoms. In a comic strip today, the phone starts shrilling;
the dog goes "Ruff Ruff Ruff"; the phone stops; and the dog thinks
"See? If you bark long enough, that thing shuts up." Yes, funny;
and pathetic. In one lovely eighteenth-century engraving,
the corpse's muscles from shoulder to butt are opened outward
like the petals of a rose: and we hold tightly to the ladder of ribs, for fear
of falling forever through this. For some, a sonnet's fourteen lines.

———————————

Xoana, *the shapeless primitive statues of gods.*
　　　　　—*The New Larousse Encyclopedia of Mythology*

And if you ask my friends: the god inside themselves has come unshaped,
like clay after rain. The newspapers say it; the TV. We
have lost the definition of that part of us. That wonder
is xoana now; that power, that knowledge: xoana now.
Distress over this isn't shameful. "After the lecture, I was left
alone in the autopsy lab. I idly lifted the heart. I started
to peel it: the pericardium came off like the merest rubbery breath.
And then another layer. Another. At the center, there was a tiny entire
mummy, and I unwrapped it. And at the center of that: a jar
the size of a molecule, with a heart the size of a proton inside it,
and inside that was the autopsy lab of a midwest university
where a woman who had just been divorced was lifting a heart
to the light"—the place where everything beyond the stars
and everything below the insects . . . meet, becoming the other.

22

1880

These women are alone—the one
whose stare is wide and level,
and the other one, who lids her look
and seems to see a separate world—in Renoir's
At the Concert. They could be named Pro-
and Anti-, they're so different,
although so tied to the rules of the same ocher palette.

 /O/

They're alone, in their elegant theater box, and lost
in the music, whatever the music is
that night, and lost inside whatever other place
the music takes them. But we also know

 /h, I dare say! Excuse me ple/

a century later, the hint of a man
in evening dress has broken through
Renoir's attempt to deeply purplish-umber him
out of existence. Infrared
confirms this, striking through the surface
like a paparazzo seizing on a hidden truth
and lighting it for all time: there's a man,

 /dn't mean to interru/
 /nchanting, my dears. I am suddenl/

or *was* a man, or the faint ghost
or the memory or the prophecy, but
in any case the *presence,* of a man
beneath the artist's failed layers of negation. Or

/istake? No. I refuse to believe
that Chance alone, as opposed
to a Knowing Destiny, has led me here toni/

it might be *they're* the ghostly ones,
to *him*—that they fade out and in like a radio song
in search of its clear point along the megahertz.

/misty to my eyes, don't
leave! Wait! I have much indeed
to tell you, only stay and listen to/

It could be so simple as this: the one who lids her gaze
is dreaming of a lover. Or it could be so amazing
as a spirit from the quantum (and therefore invisible) universe
sundering whatever extradimensional cambium layer keeps
his realm from our familiar, tactile spatiotemporal plane
. . . is it possible

/launched myself in search of, frankly
(my yearnworthy beauties, oh lovely jump-start cables
of my lonely heart) I was, I say, in search
of a different painting to enter altogether, and not,
if you'll forgive such indiscretion, this
complacency of Bach and rosy portraiture.
Listen to me, it's 1880! The telephone is invented!
By four years! Not radio yet, but—wait.
Not laser scanning yet, but—patience. Last year
Albert Einstein was born, and even as I stand here
in your lavish flesh-tone ambience (my twin flames
for the moth of my longing), Sigmund Freud
is a lowly and struggling neurologist busy
dissecting crayfish exactly the color of living brick

that the painter has given the walls here
and the plush of your couch! The world is about
to reveal its microconstituent self, and I was in search,
accordingly, of a painting by Seurat to enter,
all of his atomic confetti! Pardon my error,
I didn't intend to smack through here like an axe-head
from the back of the canvas. And yet, and ye/

Renoir *intended* this disruptive figure,
as a symbol of the unknowableness of existence?
Or, more likely, what emerges from its sticky wall
of pigment is a patron who was X'd-out
for withholding the artist's payment.
"Sister . . . do you sense somebody? Do you *cause*
somebody? When you close your eyes, I hear
a tiresome hum."

/isappeared, eh? Doused. But now
we have returned to one another, and it seems to me
(my pastries in the bakeshop of amour) that our various
sines and coefficients are in harmony again.
Come, join me. You especially, shyly veiling your eyes:
look up! I tell you, we have discovered seventy
chemical elements, Gadolinium just this year!
I tell you that a year from now Monet will begin
the rest-of-his-life seclusion at Giverny, where
his floating, atmospheric compotes of water and light
will serve, in part, to introduce
the field theory and particle physics
of Rothko and of Pollock! Do forgive
my brusque invasion of your snuggery, but
modernity is calling us! Quick,
before I fad/

We can see Renoir in the atelier,
we can sniff the fresh bouquet of oils and turpentine
on the rags. And now he's done for the day.
And on the easel. . . .
A woman, with her eyelids down.
Above her, a visual whisper: "a man."
Maybe he's someone not even born.
Perhaps he's dead. He's dead and yet
he's there, in the painted air. And she
can feel the weight of this close brush.

Spaces

Beneath the Dome that afternoon, she studies reproductions
of Medieval and Renaissance paintings, with accompanying text.
In the former, Jesus, Mary, plus glorious saints and angels
bearing halos as solid and clearly defined as hubcaps, all
appear against a flat, opaque (and often featureless)
background—in a sense, because this cast is more
important than the secular world, there is no secular world,
and they exist like figures painted on a wall, albeit
often a wall of gold and precious gems. But not much

later—say, the thirty years from Cimabue's Virgin
to Giotto's—scenes, like origami, open up.
By dozens of strategies that later will be codified
as "perspective," depth occurs: for the first time,
shadows; for the first time, railings running back,
with vases on them running back in recedingly smaller size;
and, for the first time, the deific is grounded in volume,
in an inventory: hounds and rabbits scamper
into "miles," into varicolored "distance". . . . She

wills the neuro-vid to *off.* It's nearly dusk,
and through the Dome's translucent blueness
she can see the two moons sweep around
like snake-eyes in the sky. And then the Dome,
by planet law, opaques. It's Mars,
a thousand years from now. She sees the fiery trail
of the evening Earthbound rocket
scrape its orange on the deeply purple night, and thinks
how many ways there are

to conquer space. And now she stores the paintings' images
somewhere inside her mind—this mind
that they say is more interconnected than the universe
it's a part of—stores them
alongside her riled-up childhood days,
the man who hurt her once, the man who *she* hurts now,
the baby whose bawling is tugging her attention away,
the layered shames, the fears, the glow, the dream,
the death of that dream, then another dream, and another.

Stephen Hawking, Walking

When I say that the orders "Bring me sugar" and "Bring me milk" make sense, but not the combination "Milk me sugar," that does not mean that the utterance of this combination has no effect.

—WITTGENSTEIN

I rolled myself down to the Thames,
The better to ogle the dames
is a half-rhyme I wrote and like
and remember now at the riverside
where the molecules of my feet
inside my feet are very definitely arranged
in the act of walking; and,
whenever I think of those insubstantial tentacles
of subatomic particles from the gold skins of these women
—streaming out of them into the humid air that rests
as thick as a Guinness-head on the water, and from there out
to the ionosphere, in the evermix
of the universe—*then*
the molecules inside my feet are positively dancing,
oh and negatively dancing, and nothing
courtly either: the boogaloo or the dirty dog
from a honky-tonk in some American mill town!
I love the skins of these women and I want them

in the way in which we all want abstract beauty,
as when an equation clicks its tumblers into place.
I trust that some of them may want me in this same way,
though I see one walks an infant in a pram
who thinks my face is a deflated balloon.
My face is a deflated balloon
And looks just like a protozoon
is another jingly half-rhyme of my happy composition.
I want the baby's tears! The baby is sponsoring
two quick licks of salt out into this rivery air

that's as yellowish-gray as the keratin in horn.
I love the river, and *its* nonstationary skin. I want to lick
those saline runnels up those saucer-of-sweetcream cheeks
to the wet pink cinch of their being emitted! And
beyond that?—the consummate darkness
of the living human cavity! There is so much
left to love. No wonder my long work at the blackboard,
and the chalk, and the hundreds of thousands of seabottom corpses
comprising the chalk, and the puffed dust
winking around my logarithms and cosines,
make me want to lick these golden women

feverishly to the origin-spot, and then to the other,
impossible side of the origin-spot: because this is my
chosen labor, because the flowering cosmos necessarily
once was a seed, and I would enter it
doing whoop-de-do and the bossa nova. Someone
tether me to the planet, then let me
love the tether, chewing my way through its leather,
float me, squeeze me out endorphins from the ozone,
milk me sugar from out of the fleshes of the dancefloor couples
spinning themselves to a rose, and let me dwindle
into a tendril of motes in the first and the last,
the ur and the nano, the pixel and fiche,
the sexual and celestial singularity of everything
the universe imagines through *us,*
its language. This

I've needed to tell you in words, though
in the molecules inside my head
I've thought it completely in numbers.

How the World Works: An Essay

That's my topic. How complex, Alhambran arabesques of weather
(seen computer-screened by satellites); and the weathering eddies on tiles
in the courtyards and intimate tryst-rooms and policy chambers
of The Alhambra itself: construe a grander pattern.
How the west wind whipples the osiers. How the slivery, eyeless
cave fish in Mexico slip through their fissures unerring.
In Nepal, a poacher reams a spoonful of musk
from that orifice near the urethra, holding—with his other
gloved hand—the deer's small death-kicks steady; and in
mid-Manhattan at 3 a.m., at Chico's place, the Pimp Prince
enters swimming in coke, with one new frou-frou dewy-cunted
acolyte on each eelskin sleeve, and he reeks of a vial
of musk. I'm singing the rings-in-rings song of the planet,
its milks, its furnaces, its chlorophyll links. One

suddenly clear blue afternoon (when I was eight) of the kind
Lake Michigan unhoards at winter's thinner end,
the sky: a child soprano's pure high-C struck after
months of ugly gutturals . . . a copper (as my father still
referred to them), a copper of the old school, beefy, easy, from
the one-foot-on-the-runningboard days of Chicago ticketdom,
stopped us *slam* in the midst of our shoreline spree, the flasher
calling all of Heaven's attention, I thought, to this misfortunate
secondhand dent-bodied Chevy. "Officer, have you had
breakfast?" "Why, no sir." And he wetted his finger and thumb
(he always did this with money) and from (as my father
still called a wallet) his billfold, a 5 (you could do it for five
in those days) sleeked on over. Later, educative and high on this
his mastery, he winked and told me that was how the world

worked. This was part of an interlocked system for him as
sure as the ecoconnectedness in the italic stance of a cattle egret,
the living shoulders it tweezes, lice that graze this egret's
feather-flesh, and dungbugs shitting the bull's more generous
shit back incremental and rich to the grasses . . . all
neat, clean, a perfect processional circle of textbook arrows.
So: you invited "the Boss" to dinner and used
the holiday silver and chortled at jokes that
were "a riot," and thus you "advanced"; you shmoozed
the waitress, and her service upgraded. This was a very clear
flow chart, and I sing the song of its unctuous functioning-well.
I was eight; I believed him. He believed himself. For
thousands of years, for that matter, the planet revolved
Ptolemaically, managing beautifully, thank you. Once

a woman I knew in my days of believing repeated sex
meant knowing a person, said, from out of some vaporous cranial
nowhere, "Do you think we come from monkeys, *or* little
enemas in the water?" and after the ripplings of pity and comedy
through me, I began the task of explaining the planet: I still
have the cocktail napkin that cartoonily shows Earth
axis-spit and pivoting, and that crudely rules a BC/AD timeline.
This was long ago; I'd like to apologize, now, for that
initial pity: once I saw the tiny beads of bravery she needed
to restring each morning just to face the next
dyslexic day, I understood—too late to do love any good—
the shadows she walked through the rest of us didn't. And
by then of course I'd also come to understand my father
wasn't sharp or slick but small in a way

that makes me tender toward him: one more anyone
with his salesman's satchel, and son, and wife, like counters
in some global game, "Advantage," tycoons and brigadiers play. Well
now he's *in* the globe, beyond maneuvering. I saw him
lowered; now he's part of the parfait striations I'm singing of,
part of the nitrogen/flywheel/hovel-and-palace totalityworks
called Terra—where the butterfly fish
at mating time, the vivid-hued and specifically-patterned
butterfly fish, fights rivals with its colors for weapons,
its cinnabars and its viridians, deepening, quivering, them . . .
while out back of Chico's, the Pimp Prince stands
his gaudy ground in front of a would-be usurper,
plumed hats, ostrich boots, gold neckchains,
one a ruby ring, one jade. . . . Oh the world

not only works but networks, rarefiedly, in
topnotch geewhillikers form. The ever-ravenous protozoa
in the rumen-goop of that bull I earlier mentioned, burbling
away at their cellulose walls . . . by one hashbrowns-surrounded
breakfast steak, they *are* connected to some soul-weary
salesman in 1929 pulling in to a roadside diner architected to be a
giant coffeepot on Pacific Highway outside South Tacoma.
Let the sign of that connection be the thready, heady
olfactory-waft of ant saliva the anteater rides like radar
unto its repast. And so there *is* a mode, an almost diagrammable
order, albeit on levels sub and supra while we sit around
in the dark with our luminous human desires confusing the
everything that they're a part of. Still we need
to remember, against our own small breakdown days. Once

after my father had died but before the family car was sold
I joyrode with a lady, one-handed wheeling us up
the curves past Lighthouse Point. A cop clocked our speed:
an hour later I was in custody—a shabby, crapped-up,
roach-infested custody—for attempting to bribe. It was
bad, but I was good, and it was brief. What's longer and
sticks with me more is being dropped off back at the car,
too tired even to feel defeated, somewhere on damp sand
miles from anywhere 3 or 4 in the morning. When
the engine wouldn't turn, that last indignity, all I could do
was sit stupidly humming—not singing just humming—
on the hood, and stare at the first gray rhythmic swashing
in-and-out of the water, sure that nothing ever does, or
ever had really, or ever would, work.

Ancestored-Back

*This is all the world, and in my sleep
there are older ones . . .
how many people I have been and how much
each of them has cost.*

—EMMA HOWELL

All ages are contemporaneous in the mind.

—EZRA POUND

Ancestored-Back Is the Overpresiding Spirit of This Poem

If only somebody would drill with a finger-long rig down
into my skull, and saw a tiny circle out of its bone,
so pools of acid antsiness and angst can steam away;
so all of the great in-gnarling, all of the bunched-up
broodiness can breathe; and so at least the day's
accumulated ephemera, its fender-bender squabbles,
its parade of petty heartache can evaporate in writhes
of sour mist—this spatting couple, for example,
in the booth across the aisle as I'm chowing on a burger
and their every more-than-whispered perturbation is,
this afternoon, a further furrow worked into my mind. . . .
You know I'm kvetching metaphorically. But literalist
Amanda Fielding, wielding a scalpel and electric drill,
bored a hole in her skull in 1970, filming that self-surgery,

———————

and zealously thereafter promoting the benefits of this
third eye, finally "running for Parliament on a platform
of trepanation for national health." The operation
was successfully conducted in the Stone Age (72%
of the skulls we've found reveal that the patients far survived
that crisis moment), and the Chinese medico Thai Tshang Kung
(150 BC) was said "to cut open the skulls of the sick
and arrange their brains in order." A Roman physician's
effects from the second century AD include a trepanation kit
in bronze, its tooth-edged bit and driving-bow
as finely produced as any machine-tooled apparatus
a surgeon in 1996 would wish for—when the bow unfolds
it's as intricate in its simplicity as a line of true haiku.
I've read a book whose major pleasure is its breathlessness

———————

in gasping at the ancientness of various devices,
flushing toilets(!) condoms(!) hand grenades(!)—the book
is a grove of invisible exclamation points. These
green glass beads like rain-splats on a leaf
—4,000 years ago. Bone dice, the same. The ribbed vault
in this early Gothic church is a masterly hollowing-out
of space—but houses of *literal* ribs, of mammoth bones,
were sturdy dwellings 15,000 years ago. Rhinoplasty(!)
soccer(!) odometers(!) "Butter" (a favorite sentence)
"spread everywhere, once it was discovered." Though we don't know
poot about the urgent stirrings in our own hearts
or the dreams irrupting nightly in our own heads,
we've been diagramming stars on plaques
of tortoise plate and antler, we've made sky maps,

from before we even understood the link of sex
to birth. And if our coin-op slot machines
can be ancestored-back to that Greco-Egyptian
contrivance of Heron of Alexandria (by which
a dropped-in-place five-drachma bronze piece
starts the portioned flow of a worshiper's ablution-water) . . .
if *ancestored-back* is the overpresiding spirit
of this poem . . . we *are* the progeny of stars,
we *are* their original core-born elements
in new recombination, densed and sizzled into
sentience and soul. I can't imagine the interior tumult
driving Amanda Fielding and her followers, but
I'm not surprised our smallest human units were created
in explosion, speed, and void. My friends

are not the kind to drill their heads and rid themselves
of troubles by decanting. Even so, I've seen them consider
their restless faces in the mirror and wish for *some* release.
Our daily dole of woe is unrelenting. In this burger joint,
in the Booth of a Thousand Sorrows across the aisle,
they're arguing still. Outside, the snow provides each tree
with a clerical collar—this couple is arguing. Outside,
the setting summer sun makes each tree a flambeau
—this couple is arguing, they'll never stop, their joys
have been prodigious and their anti-joy will balance this
or more, the hands with which they make their hard points
in the air are hands of oxygen and nitrogen and argon
older than dust or salt. It's midnight. How
emphatic we can be. How long they've been at it.

Second Thoughts

1862: Dante Gabriel Rossetti buried his young wife
Elizabeth Rossetti with a sheaf of his unpublished poems.

. . . and then of course the weeping: some demurely, some
flamboyantly. Those elegiac tears, if shed
enough, will alter a face and the person
behind the face. We all know that erosion

is a mighty thing, and even—for example—
the seemingly permanent, hard-black Mississippi banks
undo and slip south. In a sense, the delta
at New Orleans—the land gone silt, and rebuilt—

is the Mississippi's second thought. "My pet,
your wiles have altered my earlier obstinacy,
and the vision of you in your luxury stateroom beckons;
I *shall* join you for your voyage on the Gigantic

—what? oh. Titanic"—is a tragic second thought.
A happy one: when Skyler and I decided to try again
to "save the marriage." Now we're lazing in a pour
of Sunday-morning light as orangely voluptuous

as marmalade. A simile's a first thought,
then an equaled next. She slips back into sleep,
and now I'm reading about the night that shady London dandy
Charles Augustus Howell (1869) unshoveled the grave

at Highgate, broke the coffin, and looted her bone breast
of "the book in question, bound in rough gray calf, and with
red edges to the leaves," on eager orders from Rossetti
—who'd had second thoughts in seven years, desiring

to publish now a volume of his verses (1870, *Poems*).
Lizzie's death-stenched pages were saturated
with disinfectant by a medical practitioner "who
is drying them leaf by leaf"—and then they joined the world

of woven radish baskets, bobbered fishing skeins, and god dolls
in their second life as art on a museum wall; a world where
the "conversion pool" saw swimmers step in white robes
from its farther end, reborn to new religion; and the lumbering

land animals said *no,* and gave up legs, and so their legs rolled up
like stored-away and useless rugs inside them, and they returned
to the waters, and birthed and breached in the waters,
and made the waters their orchestral glory,

and spouted out their great Ionic columns of air and water
in the touch of the changing mind of Earth,
that's sunlit at times
and at other times darkened.

Invisible

The parents are fucking. The parents are discussing
whether or not the soul is ever in complicitous alliance
with the external world. The parents are arguing
garden green or *sand* for the bathroom
wallpaper (maybe you wouldn't be surprised how much
ferocity attaches to those differences).
The two-year-old is oblivious. The parents build
a hill of salt on which they writhe and slice themselves,
the two-year-old is crawling blithely through it
as if it doesn't exist. The crimson pillars
of sexual moan they raise throughout the house
are only empty air to him. (We all live in cities
to which we're unconscious, stride across
the warrens of the dead with less awareness
than the roaches in our shadows have.) In two years
they've been sensitized to wake at any rustle
from their child's crib, but slumber through
the plaintive lengths of sound the freight train
excavates through the thickly packed night.

_____

The giddy paleontologists are deservedly thrilled with this
impressive bone the size of a cannon;
and, right there at the site, with dust
the color of cow dung still in their teeth, ears, hair,
they break out their bottle of cheap champagne
and seven plastic glasses, and they toast themselves
and their Cretaceous souvenir, elated despite
the sun that kilns their skin and a wind that mourns
through the rocks like the call of a train,
a long phantasmal banner. Sun
and emptiness and a *T. rex* bone: that's what they see,
it's all we can expect these seven diligent men to see,
although they stand on sacred tribal ground,
in a city of gods, with timeless godly presence
all about them. They've defiled this land. The find
is theirs or isn't theirs: the law will decide,
which is also a vast, invisible architecture.

———————————

And finally the fossil is "jacketed" for removal
in burlap and plaster; in a single and finicky, levered haul
it's lifted 70 million years into the future.
I suppose that's loosely—very loosely—like
the transposition that a pharaoh and his populace believed in:
rising out of death itself, into the fields
of forever. Of course they expected even forever to be
familiar. Tombware isn't just symbolic
golden gaudery, but also simple bowls, stone knives,
and toilets(!) for the afterlife: as if
our body's systems necessarily imply a certain logical response,
and nothing else can be imagined. Yes—except
so many pharaohs *have* been untombed into a future
wholly alien to them. They watch the gawking
of museum-goers—less a kindred life-form than the offering-cattle
that once paraded past them. Also, mummies were used
to stoke the engines of nineteenth-century railroad trains.
We'll all be smoke, we'll all be pressed to oil,
all be recombined in a place, in a series of places, we can't guess
the laws of physics or periodic table of elements for.
We'll all be Mars, we'll all be rain.
Rain: the story we'd know, if only we understood
—in *our* world's terms—
the code of those tapping knuckles.

———————

Aerothermal photos, snapping subtle heat differential
from an airplane's height, have mapped dark smudges
of cities so lost, so underground/ . . . but
this is only an indirect way of saying a lover
recognizes absence in the slight signs left behind:
a relic intimacy the sheets still hold, a trilobite
of lipstick on a glass's rim. And what *was* in her brain
for their three iffy years of marriage?—what
alternative domains contained the shining, sky-high
spiderwebbish walkways of the twenty-second century, or possibly
the brutal dark of caves, with such insistence
that they finally seemed more real, overbalancingly
real, than this small suburban house? Somehow
he'll have to tell the two-year-old: the parents
are divorcing. You can stroke a head to sleep and still
not understand the universe an inch behind its eyes.
We *think* we "see" the stylized train of captured cattle,
lapis stones, acacia, pond ducks heaped in hummocks, eunuched slaves
paraded past a pharaoh's steady gaze in tomb art, but
our eyes are about as distant from his as they are
from a queen bee's polygons. Out the window a girl,
looks seventeen, is skateboarding, evidently
through a place her headphones structure: now she shimmies,
dips, leaps, lip-synchs, spirals, zigzags
past the pinnacles and deeps of a hermetic world.

———————

A train's been traveling through this poem,
and a bird is threading its way through the train,
and a berry is journeying through the bird,
is carrying the DNA of berries in infinitude,
back to the soil. It rains. The smear of guano
liquefies and enters the earth,
the home-of-homes, the alpha and omega,
the transubstantiater of bones. One day
I visit Waldheim Cemetery: my parents are here,
a little above the dinosaurs, a little below
the last spilled tangerine light of this August dusk.
They're here, with Uncle Lou, and Grandma Rosie, and everyone else
they were with on the surface, together again. It's a regular
retirement community down there, and I wish we'd buried them
the way the dead of Egypt were, with meaningful *objets,*
so that a klatch of bones could meet on every Thursday night,
and play with a deck of bone poker cards for a pot
of bone nickels, and laugh again at the same stale jokes.
That's all just fancifulness, I know: a way of saying things
that seems "poetic." But the dead *are* down there,
freed from time. And we can't see,
but they can of course,
the stilts
on which we walk through their cities.

Ancient Musics

Sumerian Votive Figurines

were meant to pray, unceasingly, on their owners' behalfs.
He thinks: they still might, even though the proper recipient
gods have long since gone to theology mulch; this faith is
stone and for the most part unbroken. Choired-up
this way—there's an even dozen he's studying—something
hushed and intercessionary *does* texture the air in a circle
around their geometricized devotional posture. Some were done
300 years apart, and yet a gentle uniformity attends these
stand-in men and women; he thinks of his own
world's fashions of 300 years ago, then shakes his head, because
what kind of halfass world-class Sumerologist *is* he, dizzy
at the edge of cracked conjecture when he should be adding up facts?
In any case, it's lunchtime: baloney-and-curry on white with
chocolate cream-filled Ooh-Oohs for dessert, and the mail is letters
from both of his kids. He shakes his head again, he needs to: Lou, poor
Lou, was nabbed two years ago by the FBI for harboring a stolen
circus elephant (the poop of which contained ten bags
of paradise-quality coke, though Lou persuasively argued ignorance), then
Becky (spouses always sensing the moment of thinnest defense
in one another) left on the day of his trial, left with someone
who styled himself (or so the script across the leather jacket blared)
The King of Venusian Blues, whatever that was (or wherever). Melanie,
meanwhile, couldn't be more jet-propelled successful; every week,
it seems, her company ("The Company," she says, like "Truth" or "Eternity")
eats some smaller companyette, and while she once was Lord Almighty
of its Alabama Xerox network, now she oversees
the "coastal-corridor/Europe conglomerate" for an empire of
"communications outreach" where, so far as he can tell from what
she patiently details, you can press a button in D.C. and, *whoosh*,
two blueprints, a bundle of money the size of a basketball, and, if
you want, a troupe of lubriciously spangled naiads tumbles
from a cloud of hi-tech pixie dust into a boardroom in Rome.

There are photos, from each, of the grandkids: Sonny
sporting a T-shirt tricked up with an airbrushed skull on fire
vomiting various barnyard animals; and Darlene
in a ballerina's tutu making her porky four-year-old's body
look, he'd swear, as if it just passed a very diaphanous fart.
It could make a man—what? guffaw? weep? or
see it's 5 p.m. by now and shake his head, and grab his lunchbox
(painted by Estelle to be an Assyrian sphinx) and head home.
Each day, five days a week, for seven years, he's exited this freeway
at BUBBA'S LAWN ORNAMENTS PAINTED OR PLAIN, and
nodded at the plaster hundreds grouped below its awning: gnomes
(whose bases reveal they're Lumpy, Dumpy, and Frumpy), fawns
and bucks, a contingent of Venus de Milos and several representatives
from the world of bare-shouldered flamenco danseuses,
bulbous-bottomed hausfraus with their bloomers comically skewed,
globe-helmeted deep-sea divers with overspilling treasure chests,
a number of Iwo Jima flag-raisings, artichoke-derriered mermaids
and their trident-bearing paramours, guardian lions, borzois
(he *thinks* they're borzois: *some* kind of italicized dog), assorted
Viking warriors and strikingly bonneted Indian chiefs
with feathered spears, and seemingly endless frogs and mice and turtles
wearing human attire—snoods or zoot-suits or biker garb. . . .
Okay then, pray for *my* people, he tells them.

Ancient Egyptian Canopic Jars

(she's learned now, as she sauntered with a light tick-tock of her spandexed hips down the dim Archeology corridors of the museum) were the vessels, stone or clay or wood, in which the fished-out organs of the dead would be stored, so brought like matching luggage toward Eternity alongside their eviscerated body. Okay; but why does she *keep on thinking* of them, even once she reluctantly steps from the museum (she was spending a solo lunchbreak there) and, on the way back to the Fitness Center, mingles inside this ragtag range of noontime lingerers watching a street musician set up?

This leftover hipster with bird-doo'd beret and slipping, clicking, splayed polymer teeth; this tangerine-dungareed woman with earrings the size of locker padlocks and LESBIAN OLD-TIME FIDDLERS ALLIANCE button niftily gleaming; this guy she's seen before with the . . . ferret? or mongoose? . . . an *ottery* thing, whatever, on a clothesline leash. . . .

As if she's goggled in "x-ray spex" from out of a comic book's backpage ads, she sees them as baklava-like layer-in-layer of tissuey *dermis,* with the living coiled sluice and fisting meat of their deepest linkages on display.—The "marrow fruits," her grandmother called those bloody bundles, or sometimes "swampgut roses"—chucking the tripe-pile out of a capon's rubbery purple-lipped rend.

The liver (Imset), the stomach (Duwamutef), the bowel (Qebehseneuf), the lungs (Hapy), each in its cylindrical container, each in the care of its individual sentinel-deity. What a neatly fourplex schema to make of our otherwise unmanageable interior! They even partitioned what we call "the soul," as Newton did white light: the *ka,* the *ba,* the *sahu,* and the *khu:* a world where spirit was composite, like a chord, or color wheel, and could be diagrammed!

Of course, she thinks, that makes sense in a universe whose basic rule is division of all of existence into the mighty and the not (you know: the high Nabobs, and the low Joes). Or maybe it sometimes *did* get interestingly blurrier in its distinctions: one of the placards said a mouse and a lizard were accidentally wrapped in with a mummy, one was found that held the leg bones of a bird, and often one "whole" mummy was actually chicanerously splatched together from several dismembered corpses, grab-bag toe-bones and pottery bitlets bridging any unevenness. And *then* what?—waking resurrected and shielding your eyes from the Glory with what you suddenly realize is not your arm but an ibis wing? This backroom crack-and-grafting is the Afterlife's genetic engineering, on the scale of platters of chicken ribs.

It's gods with the heads of crocodiles, it's women and men in the halls of Forever with cat femurs rattling inside them. It's all so lollapalooza circusy, it's . . . well, it's something like shuffling about this growing midtown crowd, this fractured expressionist welter of democracy, and she knows she'll never make it back to Jazzercise 1 on time, no, now she's loitering, connoitering, she's here amid muumuu, tutu, dashiki, tarboosh, babushka, wimple, shako, and sequinned tube-top, here where a man fine-tuning an invisible rocket-ship console in front of him nudges a woman as still as a marble icon, who models what seems a single perfectly gouged piranha-bite out of her forearm. Here, the dour, dough-jowled dowager's crowding the sleek *artiste* with hair dyed to look like an endive, who's holding a canvas that seems as if pinworms dipped in paint held orgiastic congress across it. And skins: the mineral-color of curry, the color of butter streusel, of oxblood polish! The freckles! The frizzled hair in the ears!

And now somebody festooned with a necklace as lush as a lei (but the "flowers" are fashioned of trash-can scraps, used foil, coat-hanger wire, madras-pattern wrapping tissue); and now the little boy crouched down like a picnic hamper; and now the little girl jitterbugging her sugar-rush out of her system; and now Osiris appearing amidst the crowd as the street musician carefully pours apportioned water into his homemade "hydrophone," and Horus the Hawk, and Isis, and Nut, whose plexus-wrenchingly beautiful naked body is the sky itself that shelters-over the world and over this street in the world where our own dear bodies no matter how frail are gathered, are stuffed with love and tumors and tremulous nodes, and the music begins, and each jar holds its own one whole clear note.

out of glazed polymer resins: "your choice of corals or blues" . . . The Ark of the Covenant out of sculpted whitefish, "with horseradish trim". . . .

She knows that from the pages of this inventively tacky catalogue *(The Testaments Shoppe)* a poem is waiting to be teased out, is metrically drumming its fingers. The Ark, the Big Banana, surely el Numero Uno in theophanyville, the chest (or throne) (or cabinet) of the shittimwood o'erlaid of beaten gold, and with staves of the shittimwood through golden rings and thus would it be borne; and here the Presence of the Almighty of Abraham, Noah, and Moses dwelt, the God, the Yahweh of the mountain peaks, Talmudic, unforgiving—dwelt On High, but also here, amongst the heart of the Tribes, and spake unto His people: something like an atomic reactor, she reasons, running gung-ho on transubstance. Something like light's, or infinity's, PA system.

And so the poem might be about kitschy secularizing: the Ark as plastic pencil sharpener (pencils, then, becoming those staves on either side, their shavings filling the smokily transparent-sided central box). The Ark as Q-tips organizer, tape measure, recipe tin. She tries to work it out in half-baked notational phrases, scratched-through, arrowed, nothing going right and the day escaping into the colors of dusk: plum, and a stain like muddy cognac at the horizon.

She tries to imagine the cumbersome weight on *her* shoulders, of wood poles holding the gravid, teeming housement of the Lord of All Creation, man and woman and beast did He create, and the fires, and the firmament. Surely their vestments included substantially padded shoulders?

They consulted it, under its gryphonesque gold cherubs, in personal crisis; they paraded it onto the field of war and, lo, the enemy hosts did tremble. Even when the shield-thumping Philistines sneak the Ark away in battle and bring it unto the city of Ashdod, there the Lord smote them with emerods (this she unmurks with her dictionary: hemorrhoids), and they commanded, let the Ark be carried therefore unto Gath, but there also the Lord grew wroth, and smote, "and they in Gath were afflicted with emerods in their secret parts," and so unto Ekron (emerods again) until they did return that mighty smiter of infidel flesh, with a tribute of "five golden mice" and (how they configured it representationally she can't guess) "five golden emerods."

Okay, but what was it *really* like?—when the Pillar of Flaming and

Darkness funneled back into its cube, and what was left was a kerchief's-worth of the dust of the plains, settling along with the flies on the open lips a sword tore out of a five-year-old's throat, and a mother hunkered over that useless pile whining *why* at the edge of the land of milk and honey.

She's seen that too, when the TV and bullhorns halted their whomp-whomp adrenaline-roiling jingoism, and what remained at the side of a toppled Harley was a woman dyed in engine oil and blood. Perhaps the poem is about that lulu of a step between deific infrastructure and the pitiful wobbly table of human affairs. Whatever, the poem had better get off its spongy butt and shake its fringed tatas a little: it's night, the lid's clicked blackly down, the creeping sleepies are on her.

And what *was* in it? A voice? A bomb? The wept tear of a god it requires four men to carry? It must have been so . . . *real* then, having God under your chin like a Stradivarius strung with peeled nerve. Was God the music pouring forth? Some scholars think the Ark held a meteorite. Does God have a "soul"? Could a meteorite be God's soul, dropped like a burning nickel, to Earth?

She witnessed an autopsy once, the bric-a-brac kidneys, liver, and heart lined up on the chest like garage-sale items; then what was the life-force, the spirit part: a diaphanous cockroach skittering through the shadows of those wares? What left the witches, when they salved their palms and soles with their concocted goos of elderwort and bristleroot, and flew? The poem might be about containment, about ideas of "in" and "further in," if she weren't closing her eyes now, if it all wasn't a haggis of crossed-out lines and a catalogue.

The Ark a "budvase of swirled lead crystal" . . . the Ark a "patented lock-lid airtight bagel bin" . . . The Torah Ark each synagogue has today, and the old men kissing it with their fingers, over and over, as if dipping into *poi* or *couscous*. . . . Dreams, and the Ark. Blankness, and the Ark. The chalk that draws on this blankness. The blossom, the out-of-the-body blossom, wafting out of a pulse-point on its etherically thin but sufficient stem: nodding over her, nodding simply with weight, or with an understanding assent, it's hard to tell, but nodding, glancing over those scattered notes and nodding, *Yes, this,* and nodding, *Yes, here,* and arcing over the bed, you might say as if in the sign of a covenant.

Etruscan

"xzm'g yv ivzw yb zmb nzm li dlnzm orermt."

Oh exkyoozay*mwah:* that's code. A simple one, a = z, b = y, etc. It means Etruscan "can't be read by any man or woman living."

Sex isn't enough. If it were, if our natural skin-to-skin congruence, flutter, and juice could be the key to cryptographic empathy sufficient unto an alphabet's unriddling, surely we *could* read these runic-looking nooses and tines inscribed around the silver cups, the ivory dice, the bronze sheep's livers with gall bladder (used for divinatory practice) of a people unashamedly given over to this same markedly carnal propulsion that drives our own small stay on the planet.

Tsk: they "do the thing," according to an outraged euphemistic Greek, "in public," and their banquets end in omnipartner, octopodish squirms. And see?—they've coupled for us in eloquent if sometimes faded murals done on marble, and especially in a terra-cotta that asks to be true to the flushes of conjugal holds. These pairs of wives and husbands stare at us with easy and voluptuary frankness through the centuries, in ways we'd *like* to think we understand: and yet the grapnels and cusps and moons and combs they've staved about their bases are a sentiment (sacred? salacious? we don't know) foreigner to our reading than animal spoor or the element-spectra of stars.

So this is the secret revealed in the days that dwindle, year-long, from the honeymoon: flesh is a separate language, and not a conductor of anything even vaguely approaching the conferral swappings of organized, public speech.

Although I know that there are ecosystems cycling invisible universe-units around, so that the elements of the periodic table are everywhere intricately mixed, I also know that the horizon of ocean and sky, to the everyday human eye, is a simpler, two-tone view: a solid layer of bluish-gray and its layer of airy meringue; the line between, the distance makes as absolute as the knock of our utterly flummoxed heads against Etrucscan stone.

We all know the story in which a scribbled *dearest* is—by the finalmost narrative revelation—"really" *deadest* instead; and therefore what we try for in our own domestic powwows is to not wind up protagonists of such a plot. But the going is scarily slickery and torchless. I can turn in bed to Skyler, in the moonslaw shaved through mini-blinds: Skyler asleep, and the thought in her skull is some transistor radio bubbling the aqua patois of drowned Atlantis. Said *I love you* then kaboom, conked out. Means what? *In the civilization Skyler, stated love was often*—then garbled. Put my ear to her ear: sea sound. Slide from bed. Late. Pace.

In my study there's a book: a limestone figurine, a goddess lifted by tweezers and thread against the grain of time; we know the pollen in the petrified shit of the lady who owned this holy doll more solidly than I can guess the dream-debris of the woman beseeching me sleepily back to her side. And no, our scholars *haven't* yet deciphered the upright fish and uterine doodles and bent-back shock absorbers of the *kohau rongo rongo,* "wooden speaking boards," of Easter Island—not even the board presumably addressed to the god of the "bright field," *Rangitea;* their distress is not within our learning, nor is their surcease from that distress. And we're still stymied by the ancient script of the Indus Valley, Harappa and Mohenjo-Daro, that land the hopeless color of untreated rope. And not even these Etruscan false teeth banded with hammerworked gold, as if a barrelsmith bridged them—they may say many a poignant thing, but not in words; it's "mlgsrmt" in words (code: "nothing").

I can't even unpuzzle the language the civilization Albert was using thirty-three years back, when it invented that code with the neighboring civilization Irwin Benovitz; isolated scraps of natter blow across the ditchburn and cracked tarmac of those years, but only that. I remember the names of two warrior groups, "the cool guys" and "the creeps," and of course "tits" over and over, followed by fits of giggles.

In fact, these "hooters" are highly mysterious still, to the civilization Albert's modern science. It's a good thing, too: they say, among the other brother-and-sisterly glyphs all men and women use to texture the come-hither skin of their lives, that what we've heard inside each other, faintly, stirring at the rim of being uttered (but always fading away), are the resonatings of what we call The Gods.

They say (as always in their overly flowery elocution) a version of this: *We come from the Anatolian steppe, the Polar drift, the Bright Field. There are signs we make, that we send through the Gates, that you see dimly. These are the Answers, these are the Thousand Answers to Things. And now we will tell you, now you shall know*

—(and then the text breaks off) and then a mote of dust of that baked clay's breaking-off flies up a tuft of muzzy vapor where the water of the far horizon translates into the air of the far horizon, there where they lie against each other, a layer of bluish-gray and a layer of airy meringue: two bodies, all night, coupled together in darkness, whispering.

The Reliquary

is silver lilted sibilantly around an enameled urn about the size of an old-time malted shaker; supposedly the kneecap of a saint is drowsing inside its gritty celestial packing, undefeated, marmaladed in there, awaiting the Mathew Brady powder flash of Resurrection, nodding, dreaming the former glories of leper-flesh persuaded into wholeness, of the shriving scream that followed each swack of the torturer's lash.

One bitter winter day, two people accidentally meet before its second-floor museum case: the woman from my "Ark" piece and a man from the crowd scene in "Ancient Egyptian Canopic Jars" are flimmering their first shy strands of a conversation together, the weather having ducked them separately (simultaneously) into these compliant halls, like a *shadkhen*.*

Ostensibly, they have little in common. She's a poet, one of those ditsy folk whose love is fixing *pixel, lubber, rutch,* and *cresset* into the same line. He's a CPA, his columned numbers rise for him as uniformly and sturdily as if lifting the roof of the Parthenon. Nonetheless, tiny, unseen, and unspoken spondees of attraction overflow them, and while I don't want to make what my niece with her chic bored look would call "a great big effing deal" out of either lust or effluvial waves of interconnection, destiny, star charts, etc., still the hall *is* charged with heartstuff here, in what, with a title like "The Reliquary," I thought would be a religious work.

And in fact, while they make sophsticates' rarefied versions of googoo eyes, the kneecap, in its swaddling rags and pneuma, is pietistically thinking "paternoster," "noumenon," "hierophantic," and the other bodacious concepts of an orthodox devotion. The knee is remembering the hamstrings and the plaited nerves that made of it a harp's case, or a zither's, for the glorying forth of psalm and lamentation, of jeremiad and forthright dulcet praise. The knee is bent in reverie on the nave's stone floor again, the way a forehead might be lowered to tap obeisantly, once, upon the sacred ground as the great mercurochrome smear of the sun appeared and a man therefore faced East in adoration and penance.

Ah, penance—! That calcium shell is adrift in its river of reenvisioned

---

* *Yiddish, for "matchmaker"*

iniquities: the singing, oops, no, the *singeing* of the nipples under the fired rods; the flail; the wheel; the bones of the fingers snapped in two like rabbit bones; the stake; the lance. . . . Adrift in doctrinal exquisitude. . . . Adrift in each of the few but madly vatic moments when someone's scaled-over eye or ulcer-pitted groin would yield to a fumbling human touch from which the healing sizzle of God Above shot electrically, like an eel; and then the blind rejoiced in sight as did the pained in the lifting of pain; and then a hush betook the crowd, in which The Word and The Way would be fulminated delightfully via a parable. . . .

All this may as well be the arcane speculation of another solar system, in the museum's contempo coffee shop. These two exchange the secret signals of love like freemasons meeting in a roomful of uninitiated slobs. The very air they sit in shines as if simonized. Look—she sees their individual coffee steams caduceus themselves around each other in erotic promise. The way she shapes her lycra! . . . How he burlily leans *into* a tough-put question, as if shoveling snow! . . .

And even so, the urn is with her: she thinks she can hear it, purring in *idle;* she thinks she can feel its transmillennial aura of ecclesiastical rapture. *That* part of her ponders away: if there *is* Resurrection, from what unguessed-at, astral-plane Goodwill shops and junktiques will the scattered skeletal units of saints be collected for reassembly? (If she rummaged those shelves would she come across, say, van Gogh's ear in a pile of nineteenth-century parts, its last heard word still ticking Time inside it?) She's read of one saint's ulna saved in a vessel of gold shaped as an arm, and of a saint's skull in a head-shaped reliquary of silver; but what of one of Christ's baby teeth, that creamily-teak corn niblet of a relic? And what of "the one true relic of Jesus' circumcision," knifed off smoothly, like a sliceling of cheese?—easily a dozen of these are containered-away in "curiosa cabinets" in European cathedrals: what are *their* jars like? . . .

It's as if she wants to take that kneecap inside her, the way they say a tree will grow around, *incorporate,* the foreign object. . . . Yes, but sometimes coffee steam outweighs the smoke that rose from Joan of Arc. Outside, the snow has thinned to one white thread unraveling the hem of Heaven. They hail a cab. They nail down a few Buds. They do most everything you'll guess by now they'd do, while the relic continues turning in place, in its tatters of drear, in an absolute faith it's the embryo that the Messengers of the Final Judgment will fashion back into a man; it can no more desist from fossicking theology than a star can stop its light. Its substance *is* an Earthly, ossified version of Genesis-energy that, two Testaments back, streamed forth originally from God's mind. Maybe this *is* a religious poem—though she wakes twined with Mr. CPA, a little groggily Bud-numbed, at the base of the downslope of fine sex.

Four legs, dáh-dah-dah that run in place in bed, she thinks; and, trying not to wake him, opens her bedside notebook. Scratches in it. Scratches out. She's been working all year on *Ancient Musics*—a kind of prose-poem overview of *spiritus* in its endless holy masks. If only all of the *dah-dah-dahs* could be completed. . . . Then: he rouses awake with a hungry look; and, his hand on her knee,

she closes the book.

The Gods

Enter ALBERT

Albert.   GOOD GODS!

—JOHN KEATS
Otho the Great

The Splinter Groups of Breakfast

1.

Not even nothing existed yet.
Emptiness, even, didn't exist.
And He-who-by-definition-precedeth-nothing
said—well, you know what He said,
in that grandiloquent King James way of speaking.
And there was light. From language—light.
And then the heavens, then the earth: a sequence:
a narrative. Fish; beasts; us:
a story. *The* story,
of God and of the power of the Word.
                                    But
at the same time—and by this, I mean
at the start of time—Nainema shaped
the forests out of his spit. At the same time,
Bumba vomited up the sun,
the moon, the stars, then "strained"
(a euphemistic translation of "shat"?)
out Ganda Bumba the crocodile, and Pongo Bumba
the eagle, and the rest: and "lastly, men came forth."
At the same time, Khepri masturbated
("I gave birth by my hand, I united myself
with my hand"), and Shu, the air, "came outward."
These are each
            the one true history.
There are thousands of one true histories.
And the God of the Winnebago Indians
wept, to form the waters of Earth
. . . from what I know of our lives here,
that's a *very* persuasive version.

2.

"Yeah, I know *him*. He sits at Dinah's Diner
every Sunday with his stack of books and notepads
like he's Jesus Christ deciding on whether he will
or won't resuscitate some poor dead dork;
meanwhile, of course, his acolyte—*excuse* me—
'girlfriend' needs to flit to other booths
for a scrap of human attention." And I've seen it
too: Elias self-absorbed, and Angie walking
down that long sprue of an aisle, helloing
gregariously to knots of eaters left and right.
I have my own opinion about that chemistry, but first
I want to say this week Elias is reading the *Scientific American*
for January 2001, the "Brave New Cosmos" issue:

*If the universe's acceleration is caused by vacuum energy, then the cosmic story
is complete: the planets, stars and galaxies we see today mark the end of cosmic
evolution. From here on, the universe dilutes and cools, and space will stretch too
rapidly for new structures to form. Living things will find the cosmos increasingly
hostile.*

But if one believes

*. . . acceleration is caused by the untapped potential of quintessence, the ending
has yet to be written. The quintessence could decay into new forms of matter and
radiation—protons and neutrons, perhaps stars and planets—repopulating the
universe.*

—"believes" of course being the key word.
As if now, in the new millennium, even
astronomy is a matter of whether
Wakonda chanted Existence into existence
or whether Izanagi and Izanami

"stirred the brine until it curdled"
into what we call our world.
Or Ea. Or Yahweh. Or Thunder Shaker.
The Turtle God? Einstein? "*Everything's*
a belief-system," says Elias. And what are *we?*
—we're *one* interpretation,
we're one *possible* interpretation,
of ways of universe-patterning. One night,

a few of us wandered out to the pasture—chatty,
catty, insouciant over ouzo and retsina,
and under a moon as full as the pinto rump of a pony.
"Oh yeah. Angie," someone said,
"the bitch queen. Ever see her
on Sunday at Dinah's?—whenever she wants,
she abandons her boyfriend, who sits there
stuck alone with a book while she goes around
granting audiences like the Pope to everyone else in the room."

3.

If speaking the light into coming
into being (as in "Let there be . . .") is somehow
more ethereally pure than, say, the firmament
as born from the saliva,
or the onanistic jisms, of a god . . . then surely
even purer—even more abstract—is when
the Indian "Divine Self" who "desired to produce
all kinds of his own One, with a thought
released the first forms."
With a thought: above
the need of any secondary mediation.
Isn't this the genesis
—the Matrix Egg, the template of all templates,
call it what you will, the Big
before the Bang—that's such a breeding place
of any-every-thing (including not-yet-things
and never-things), it's finally only
what *we* choose to see it as?—not history,
or myth, so much as somewhere we can read
our own psychology into sky and mist.

"I think it's *great.* He studies if he wants,
she sits with her friends if she wants, and they have this
silent assurance between them. Fuck, if only *we*
could be that happy in our relationships."

4.

A Fort Worth ball-cap manufacturing company, Pro-Line, was cited in 1992 by the Occupational Safety and Health Administration: it provided what was referred to as "inadequate rest room facilities for [its] female employees." That was the charge; the problem. Out of all of the possible ways to interpret "remedying the problem," the Pro-Line management decided to [select one]: a) ignore the O.S.H.A. findings; b) augment its current facilities to meet the required standards; c) fire its thirty female employees. The answer, of course:

is c, although that *might* not have been
your decision or mine, had we been consulted
by Pro-Line. And would we have seen the terra-cotta ram

from Mali, West Africa (1,000 years old)
as authentic or faked? (Its "glow rate"
under thermoluminescence testing is inconclusive.)
The slim Minoan "serpent priestess"
overseeing the bull-leaper games: ancient;
or forged? (The experts are divided on this.
At a panel last year, two of them threw shoes
at their opponents.) Or this warrior
on horseback, as a sunset turns the folds of his clothing
golden, thickly golden, like the runoff
in a pharaonic smithery at the end of the day:
is this the master's hand at work; or a skillful
Rembrandt imitator? (Two
well-funded art museum investigatory panels
disagree.) And the love your parents emitted
in great, rock-opera declamations for one another:
sincere; or was it humbug love
they purchased at the five-and-dime and memorized
while you were asleep? (The jury's still out

on this one: you can witness the various rival factions
sharply trade invective back and forth across
the holiday turkey.) God;

or evolution? In the window of the sacristy
each afternoon as the light achieves a certain degree
of slant, a lovely stain appears, an abstract shape
of indigo and rose; unless, for you,
it's the Virgin Mary, if you squint, and if your faith
controls your eyes. And Angie winks,
and Elias smoothes a page and doodles in its margin.
Or it's *neither* vacuum energy *nor* quintessence:
one respected group of maverick astrophysicists
believes that the varying-speed-of-light theory (VSL)
"remains a major challenge" to the orthodox cosmologies.
And Elias folds a note and scoots it across a plain
of eggs-over-easy greases, into Angie's hand.
They whisper, and the bones of Earth-Woman
turn into rock, her blood to springs of water.
They ignore each other, and Tepeu and Gucumatz
engender the three-fold Heart of the Sky.
They argue, and the universe tumbles headlong
over the icy edge of entropy, into a stasis
where its flames grow dark, and its interconnections fail
to relay the codings of life.
They touch, they stroke, and the universe wakens.
They touch, they stroke, and the universe
recalibrates itself; coheres.

The Nile

Elijah this.
The Children of Israel that.
And Moses. Moses in the bulrushes, Moses
blahblahblah. The doors closed
and the dark, fake-woodgrain paneling casketed us
away from the world for an hour and forty-five minutes every afternoon
in Rabbi Lehrfield's neighborhood Hebrew School. Here, as one,
the pious and the derelict chafed equally. The vehicle
of Rabbi Lehrfield's narrative drive was Obedience,
all the wonder in those stories was run down methodically
and left behind like so many roadkills. Methuselah
something. Somethingsomething Ezekiel. And Pharaoh
set the infant Moses in front of a crown and a plate of embers,
testing if this were the child it was prophesied
would steal his reign. And Moses
did reach for the crown. But the Lord set an angel to guard him,
who now did guide that hand to lift an ember, and so did Moses
thereby burn his tongue and lo would stammer all his life long.
Did I care? *His speech limped, but he lived.*
Did I listen? Every night I'd read another chapter
in those actionful shlock-epic books by Edgar Rice Burroughs,
the ones where Mars (Barsoom, the natives call it) is
adventured across by stalwart Terran John Carter, *Jeddak*
(Warrior-King) and husband of the gauzy-saronged and
dusk-eyed Dejah Thoris, Princess of all those red-duned climes.
It made more sense to me
than God is a great bush of fire. All the while
Moses stuttered in front of the Living Flame, I
silently practiced Martian. It was Rabbi Lehrfield's
Martian School for me the whole lackluster time.

Out of what we've learned to call
"deep structures," Lindsay Nichol, my niece, is pursing
the first of her organized sounds. They're . . . oh,
no words; but they take sure place in a pattern
as repeated as the crib bars, with a little
occasional lingual fillip
as decorative as the headboard's gnomish carving.
Slurp and gurgle, out of whatever
increasingly subatomic deliveryline of chevals
flashes the message of neural language-wiring on up
from meiotic gel unbroken to this nine-month-old
soliloquizer, Lindsay Nichol
is wailing, gooing, composing juicy musics, here
on the quantifiable, witnessed edge of a process that
starts somewhere magic.—Someone
pointing to a tree, saying: "tree," a heart, and: "heart,"
the first time; being with a word so new it's glass
not fully hardened yet, it's going to be a tree soon, or a heart,
but now it's rainwater, and the morning sun is living yolk in
      its skin. . . .
                In Moccasin County,
once, the night a full moon orb'ed the giant crosshairs
of a steeple, and any spirit-commingling was possible, and the line
between the Trinity and three tossed shots of cornmash likker
wavered in tremulous hoochiecoo veils of feeling . . . I could see
such language settle out of the air. They spoke in tongues. A woman
frenzied like a telegraph key on the sawdust-clumped church floor.
Galvanic bluebolts straight from Heaven twitched her limbs.
A man was shaking like sheeted foil. What they said was
clearly speech, although I didn't know the words
/M'lash k'HAB chebawby HEI-HEI-HEI ZH'BO/ was clearly
not a sloshy gibberish, but something
from the templates in the brain that give us English, only

singular and more shimmering with its source: a kind of
manna spangled over their tongues. If anything
I've also seen comes close, it's in films of some early
jazz guys jamming through the thirties, with the drapes
of cigarette smoke in those backroom clubs befuddling the stage,
and joy and concentration being the same thing, and
between their rumpled and utterly brotherly selves
a field I can only call "vocabulary" occurs and unites
and they play, in great asyncopated waves,
where the cells of the blood are notation,
where the nerves of the body are staves. . . .
                                                      I have this
daydream: squares and circles and triangles
floating out of the sky. My friends
are lifting them. Licking them. Taking intimate
oral pleasure off of these perfect lines. And after that,
nothing is ever the same. We're marked.
We've nursed on the "high structures" Plato says
precede the smutched units of Earth.

———————————

In my family, stories are normally softened
over the years.—As if a tragedy,
or even adrenaline-jetting celebration, any
abandoning of the blandest mean, was shameful.
By the time my life is secondhand
or third- explained to Lindsay, I'll be
anyone, and flatter than the nondescript stone marker.
Once I met my cousins Izzy and Rebecca,
only once—they'd come in for a wedding.
They were in their middle-seventies then, two crease-faced German Jews
from when a Jew in Germany meant you wore a number
dyed into your arm. And so I heard some stories directly.

"They were after me," he says. "I wasn't afraid
from their fists. But some had broken bottles. See."
He lifts his shirt. "I hid in a barrel. A barrel
of pigshit. Yes, really. It covered my head. In this, even
they didn't search. The worst part was the burning
against the cut, this pigfire, filthfire, eating my skin.
But then they gave up and I crawled out. It's a blur then,
really, until Becka and America." She says, "My mother
begged my sisters not to get into the truck. One was fifteen.
Meeseleh, she was only twelve. The driver told her, 'You
think you'll miss them so much, you get in too.' She
did, without a second's hesitation. In part, I think, to get them
all on their way before I was discovered in the haypile.
Well of course—they went up the chimneys, in the Camps.
Who knows what went on in those places? Twenty years later,
we were in New Jersey then and settled, a neighbor
gave me a little set of scented soaps, and I saw on the box
they were made in Germany, and—Izzy will tell you
it's true—I threw up. For a week after that, I threw up."
To reach America, they "did things" too—"not so nice,
if you want to know. These were not pretty times."
There are anecdotes of innocent German countryside couples
clubbed for their clothes. The irony is, they
reached their haven, Liberty lifting her torch high,
just when anti-German sentiment reached its peak.
"And so our accents—you know? For years
Americans beat us up in the streets." He shakes his head
as if the past could be shooed like a fly.
"So, anyway. Everyone's here for the wedding, a happy time,
now let's be happy." He hooks his arm around Rebecca's arm.
His speech limped, but he lived.

———————

God doesn't speak in the language of people
or need to. God speaks out of what first hurt us.
So of course, on the mountain, Moses understood
what was said by the fire.

I'm forty. I know, by now, my life, my friends' lives . . .
we will never wake to face some all-consuming
deific announcement. But I also know: hurt is inevitable.
Then: so is some Godtalk, sized to that hurt.

Now Lindsay's asleep, and quiet, quiet. . . .
Finally the long dark river of night
will deliver her crib to its tanglement
in the first pale reeds of the morning.

"The more you're meat, the less they treat you human," Kendall says
amid the general beer-tone party brouhaha. She's
just been hired as a hospital's Emergency Unit desk clerk.
"If you come in with a broken leg they'll talk to you
while setting it, explain things, chat. But
someone comes in mangled from a tractor toppling over and he's
just bloodied-up parts to assemble." This is all
new to her. She ledges out her lower lip in concentration.
"I suppose there are reasons." Later,
                              an hour maybe, I
see her hazily through a window. She's left the gaudy talk and
rock-&-roll, and walks by herself in the midnight yard,
around the substantial base of its guardian tree.
She's talking softly—to herself—or to some self-of-her
that's taken form invisibly out of the molecules of the night, and
walks beside her. Kendall's
musing. She's "working things out." Whatever

infinite hallways of pain and laboring tissue she's seen opened
in the bodies wheeled past her for the last week, these
are first inventing words to hold
small conversation with her. Moonlight's
whittled by the bough to a handspan conical shape; and
Kendall halts as if to press her ear against this
hearing-trumpet floating in the blackness, and be privy
for a moment to the murmurstuffs the electrons of Earth
exchange with the protons of Luna.
                                        Soon
she's back: she's wagging ass to some sperm-powered shout
in an early Rolling Stones hit. What I come
to understand, though, is that everyone—these
friends o' mine, my tender lads and lassies—needs some time
outside, alone, by the tree, in its Whispering Zone.
Now Casey leaves the very public hubbub for this quiet
domain, now Rita. . . . Some of them touching the bark
that's textured like the rope sole of an espadrille,
and some of them simply moving their lips in silence,
under stars that must be Cosmic Esperanto's
punctuation. "Albert, YO!"—I'm
                                        back in Stonesville,
avocado chip dip, argument, flirtation. When I look
next time, a fourteen-year-old boy is in the yard. He's . . .
a translucent fourteen-year-old boy. So shy.
So pained by anything in this world. No wonder
he's practicing Martian. "Thark," I hear him say
in a familiar cracking voice. "Tars Tarkas. Jasoom."
No wonder I love these friends I have now. When
I start to say a word of encouragement to him, he
distorts into a mist, he's air now, and my single gasp
inhales him. . . .
                        No wonder I love my people. We're
all woozy-eyed with partying by now, we're tired

empathetic heaps lounged out on the pillows. . . .
My sweeties, my grown-ups who have come so far, what are we
here in midlife, but
the scars of healing from where we once burned

our tongues on the Other Language.

A Continuum

Saint Isidore (born c. 560 AD) wrote, according to the Fortean Times, *"a 20-volume work encapsulating all the learning of the time, from theology to furniture."*

1.

Well I went went went to heaven, baby baby
—There was light in my head
(de DOOP, ba, de DOOP, ba, de DOOP de DOOP)
I say there was glory in my brain and in my breath
And in my heart, oh but instead
(de DOOP, ba, de DOOP, ba, de DOOP de DOOP)
*You know I just wanted your fine bodyyyyy*zoop!
Layin' by me in our bed
(de DOOP de DOOP de DOOP, ba, de DOOP de DOOP)

Well I went to the world of abstractions, baby baby
—I could float in the sky
(de DOOP, ba, de DOOP, ba, de DOOP de DOOP)
I say I was there with Truth and the Infinite,
With Thought, and with the Soul, and I could fly
(de DOOP, ba, de DOOP, ba, de DOOP de DOOP)
But I just wanted to be in bed with you,
Lovin' in J-e-r-s-e-y!
(de DOOP de DOOP de DOOP, ba, de DOOP de DOOP)

2.

Once you have a chair

you also have a theoretical chair,
an ideal chair, a spirit chair,
afloat at the top of the air,
a chair that can't be proved.
Would you sit in it? Would you

sit in it over the gorge a mile deep?
A chair that requires faith.

———————

It's like the word and its referent:
stone and "stone," for example.
Even "example." This
is a codependency we've made of them,
the concept and its anchoring thing.
They need each other
the way that "god" is there

in the icon; there by the chrismal;
there at the altar, nostrils flared,
inhaling our part of the contract.

———————

In the sky, what Plato said
are Forms. And they precede
our world. I suppose a cloud is a Form
for rain that cleans and scums and sinks inside
our own imperfect dailiness.
We might imagine thunder
and the sear of lightning, great celestial fracas,
as if something's being made
up there. A long night,
wet and violent. Then it's morning,
and quiet: we walk out to the fields

and in that great expanse,
where none had been before, from out of nowhere:
a chair.

3.

One tick—one putz's little sizzle of hate—
and the devotion of over seven thousand years is turned
to char and splinters. Who *did* bomb
the synagogue? That's the immediate question,
once it's ascertained no one was trapped inside,
thank God. You see?—"thank God." It isn't very long
before the second question: Does one's access to a god
disappear when the structures of that access disappear,
the *bimah,* the Ark that holds the Torah scrolls, etc.?
Well of course not; do we think that prayer
and revelation require wires, e-screens, sculpted columns?
No. And yet . . . the juju
is the otherworldly spell—the potent,
disincarnate Mystery itself—*and*
is the talismanic hank of straw and tail-hair and grave-clay
that the disincarnate lives in. There were rabbis
in our neighborhood as traumatized as any
of the members of the congregation—traumatized
and weak—who in the aftermath denied a possibility
of prayer (or anyway of *efficacious* prayer)
without the shaping space of an enclosure and its furnishings
to reinforce the frail, limping singsong of the human voice.
Let's say a woman's wandering around that sad debris
before the cleanup crew arrives . . . as if she needs to see
how total this destruction is—to bend, and touch
its edges—to believe
in anger capable of abnegating this much
of a city block; *it fit inside somebody's heart!*
Is there a physics somewhere that makes sense of this disaster?
Quantum Fester Theory 101. She has the monstrous urge
to slip her sandals off and run
barefoot across this plain of glass and shrapnel,

maybe *that* would make the lesson clear:
this chaos was *intended* to hurt. She wants to lift
a handful of these glass shards and these splays of wooden splinters
to her nipples, which are intensely alive now
—why? *is she crazy?* (maybe, the situation
is crazy), why? to ruin her own flesh
in an empathy with these—the *kiddush* goblets,
and the cantor's cedar lectern, and the rest—that have been ruined
but have no way to cry their suffering? Whatever
easy spin we give these fantasies of hers,
the bottom line is: they're intensified displays of what
would otherwise be normal, steady stewardship
of objects where her god lives: a *megillah* case,
the intricate *aron hakódesh* with its seraphim in bas-relief,
the chests in which the *siddúrim* are stored. Now, is the god
an equally viable presence in the rubble of these?
Or is it like Jeremy?—he was in her arms, all
eighteen years (plus seven months
of tumor-rampant hell) when, in a silent beat of time,
his waxy, bubbled breathing stopped
forever: something—*who knows what, but something*—
that had been in him, and *was* the "him" of him, was gone,
and what remained was just a stick of manikin.
She tries to puzzle out the linkage: God is holy:
so the word of God is holy: so the book (we'll say
the bench on which the word of God abides until called forth)
is holy: . . . is it? is the book *as object* holy? isn't that
idolatry? Yes, but when they close the book
they frankly kiss its cover. She remembers once when Jeremy was six
and they were in Georgia during flood time, they
were standing on a bank and watching couches,
loveseats, beds, the whole lost stock of someone's luckless
small-town furniture store go bobbing down the water. "Look,
Mommy," he pointed, "those chairs are carrying the river!"

4. A Song about Colonial Times

—also chayer, chaier, chaire, cheere, cheyre.
Not that the wealth of variant spellings
meant that their dwellings
were rich in these: most were spare-

ly furnished, "men and women
using stools or a bench ordinarily";
in the days of the Massachusetts Bay Colony,
after all, "chairs were not common

even in England." They look so serious
and practical, symbols of pi-
ety made of sturdy wainscot oak. To the eye
of the twenty-first century, even the most "luxurious"

have the hard lines of severe and
puritanical philosophy. And a large
percent of chairs for which we recognize the orig-
inal owners *were* used by the officially reverend:

Roger Williams, who, in a letter a
congregant wrote, was called "a godly minister"; Ezekiel
Rogers, reverend and owner of "ten chares"; Will-
iam Penn, our seminal Quaker; etc.

It's easy to imagine them sitting in wonder
and religious zeal so long, so lost, in such a hu-
man/furnishing symbiosis, that when they *do*
at last stand up, it might seem, in the chair's under-

standing, to be a kind of astral projection:
its sentience floating away. And speak-
ing of the Reverend Ezek-
iel Rogers . . . we must add that his selection

of "chares" was accompanied by "quishings" (that
is, cushions); in upholstery, there were velvet, satin,
plush, silk, serge, "and even sealskin"
chairs, *all* idea of comfort not

being completely disregarded as the century went
onward. Still, their sense of lush decor
was never that of the Roman emperor
Elagabalus, who "deposited his excrement

in pots of gold." No, not this breed; they
sat on wood the way they walked *among* the woods
of their new home, bonding with its amplitudes
and promise through the most everyday

of their objects: "And betimes I am aware
how the Eternal and the hosts of Heavn
do Speake or flowr or rattel me even
throgh a milking stoole, or my plain cheayr."

5.

Also, in 1673, the goodwife Faithine Winterthorpe, who fell asleep while laboring in the cider grove, was visited by an incubus, and it had its lickerish way with her, and despoiled her. And also, Thomas Satterfall, of the carpentry family Satterfalls, who lived with his father Matthias and sister Elizabeth in the house attached to the stables out at Mercy Hill . . . was attacked in June by a succubus as he slept, which is a fact, because his father and sister heard him cry in alarm, and because the Devil is ever awake and in command of invisible millions, and because his nightshirt evidenced the stain of that impure nocturnal encounter. And these are not the only instances, the histories are replete with carnal linkings in which one of the parties shows no literal carnalhood at all, but is a spirit.

Of the line between these disembodied visitors and the real human bodies with which they have sexual congress—whether this line is imaginary or actual, whether it's permeable or resistant—much has been written in annals theological, psychological, sociological. What's the line between the firing neuron and the thought to which it contributes? What's the line between the mind and the brain? Can we say that the brain is furniture for the mind? That words are furniture for meaning? Surely myth is the table on which a culture's various explanations rest.

A culture/epoch/zeitgeist *is* its furniture (and is also its dominant architecture); so are the people belonging to that culture/epoch/zeitgeist. It's a Weimar Republic man in a Weimar Republic time in a Weimar Republic chair; it's my friend Cole in the inflatable, transparent lime-green "Lounge-Around" that he bought one day as an afterthought on the e-shop site for Sidekix. (In her book *The Artificial Kingdom,* Celeste Olalquiaga refers to Walter Benjamin's concept of the "furnished man": exterior physicality—of *his own, specific, daily repeated* exterior world—"presents itself to his touch and ends up forming figures inside him.")

"The Wassily armchair, designed by Marcel Breuer in 1925–26 . . . is a structure of bent, chromed-metal tubing . . . recall[ing] a bicycle frame" (Witold Rybczynski); meanwhile, the honored parents in *Filial Piety* (China, 1100s, watercolor), easily sit, their legs crossed, on a rug. Bauhaus. Baroque.

The cluttery, bric-a-bracked front parlors of Holmes's Victorian London: shells and teacups and paperweights and robins' eggs and framed hair from the family's dead and china cats and taxidermied weasels in their thick, glass-front armoire. Whatever "semen" tells us, "jism" says another thing. Language is the furniture in which a sensibility arranges and comports itself.

The desk in the abbess's office is so plain, with such *intensity* of plainness, that it asks to be not only a mnemonic of her life's renunciations, but (against all hopes of modesty) an honorific one. And then again, as Jean-Luc Hennig claims, Toulouse-Lautrec "is said to have painted 'fleshy, common tarts on red sofas.'"

And what did the Puritan bed of Thomas Satterfall say, and was its public discourse any different from the nightmare things that whispered in the dark maze at the back of his mind? I don't know. But I know what I see in this statue of an Etruscan couple reclining together—two relaxed, contented parallel lines—atop a couch that's evidently been designed with just such a pleasant postcoital mutuality in mind. Among its many lovely implications, this: *there might be hope for all of us.*

6.

The denizens of Heaven have no bodies,
unless a "body" of light is a body. I say it isn't.
They're greater than human beings, of course;
yet less than vapor on a window,
less than trails of neutrinos. They're
the answer to the question: Void divided by Holiness equals?
Nothing inferior to this is allowed to stand before God.
And they *do* stand, or they circle
like rosy zeppelins, in Medieval paintings: necessary
artistic convention has given these ethereals a physical form.
And even God, who isn't "who" in any way
we'd understand that word . . . yes, even God,
the More-than-the-Universe . . . He sits on a throne,
with all that implies: stature, image, buttocks.

———————

God, in fact (if we can accept the ancient Jewish apocalypse story
The Ethiopic Book of Enoch as fact),
is far more human in appearance
than his radiant minions: "angels," I.P. Couliano says
in his study of "otherworldly journeys," "have no joints.
Only God can sit and the angels cannot." I used to visit
a basement lounge—the kind out near the shanties,
though the ritz and the cognoscenti were in attendance—and here
we all stood, we were grateful to be standing there,
to be there but also transported *from* there at the same time,
as the jazz pianist T-bone Rogers sat at his keys
with an easy, bluesy mastery of the room. I suppose
notation is a furniture for music. And I *know*
the women there were a sumptuous furniture for my eyes.

———————

As these painters have given Him "arms" and "legs,"
our language has given the same to the parts
of our furniture. Also "back." And "seat."
These terms bridge worlds,
they begin in our houses and end (*if* they end)
in the hymn-worthy mansions of Heaven
—and this association was here as soon as the word
was here: "chair" comes from the Latin "cathedra,"
and counts, as cousin, "cathedral." Though it's difficult
at times to remember this kinship with the numinous.
For example: chairs and even six-person benches
made completely from the joindered horns of cattle
and goats. Or the way the dominatrixes get paid
to use their slaves as human coffee tables and footstools.

————————

The first of the many McDonald's Happy Meal toys
that Jeremy received with his McNuggets
was a doodad from a merchandised cartoon called
Bobby's World, where the eponymous boy-hero sits
in the comfy hold of a purple pillowy armchair,
lost enchantedly in a children's book about
astronauts. But look: you can swivel him
out of sight on a plastic spindle, and up to take
his place is yet another Bobby, this one
in the futuristic-silver suit of a spaceman, with
a panel of rocket cockpit shown behind him. You
can turn the boy and the dream-boy into one another
all day, sweetly, seriously, until they blend
in the ecstasy of Ezekiel's flaming wheels.

————————

In the ecstatic visions of Gertrude of Helfta (middle/late
thirteenth century), she was admitted to the level of Heaven
where Christ waits with his "honeyed mouth"; he
escorted her into the "bridal chamber." This was no
apparitional tryst, but conjugal in the fleshiest sense.
And Swedenborg's Heaven, five centuries later, is neighborhoods
of houses: "like the dwellings on earth which we call homes,
they have rooms and bedrooms and courtyards," and
a wedding celebration there includes "tables with bread and crystal cups."
That was his idea: that it all went on, a version
of physicality went on beyond the grave, like the ditsy waves
of *I Love Lucy* through the universe after the television
is turned off—only solid, textured. This Heaven of his . . .
you can knock for luck on actual wood.

———————————

The drippy-nosed parishioners of a British church
in the thirteenth century likely knew less ease for their anatomy
than did Swedenborg's celestial beings. Even the barest
interior of a church included an altar (stone)
with canopy and frontal, a font (stone too),
a wooden bier, and a number of pennants, candles,
images of the Virgin and saints. "Conspicuously missing
were any benches, chairs, and pews; the congregation stood
[or] sat on the floor." Would any of them
have sprawled there on the cold straw
in a cold draft, looking hard-eyed and begrudgingly
at the silver vessel used to hold the bread of the Communion?
And it might be banded in ivory as well.
Furniture for the body of Christ.

———————————

"Angels"—what I read in quickly skimming through a poem
of Linda Pastan's. I'll say now: there are continuums
connecting the most striking pairs of opposites.
Marriage is only the commonest example. Or the body
of a hermaphrodite. Centaurs. Flying fish.
Mermaids. Sleep. Of course Jesus. In-laws.
But in this case it was the voice of Grandma Rosie,
dead now fortysome years, from when I was six or seven:
"Albie, finish your lox on bagel now. It's
time to go to *shul* and pray for Grandpa." Yes,
because *that's* what the word was—"bagels."
Those most shimmering elementals of all of Creation
were given an earthly link. Sometimes I think
I see them cavorting around the rim of that yeasty rink.

7. The Furniture Makers Have Three Patron Saints

Thank you for the shield-back chair and the ladder-back chair
    and the shepherdess chair. Thank you
for the look-chair with its padded rail, and thank you
    for the warming chair we scoot up to the fireplace
on bitter nights. For the bended-back chair
    we offer our thanks. The rocking and the easy.
For the folding, patio, lounge, and wingback,
    beanbag, arm-, side-, swivel-,
slat-back, comb-back, fan-back, banister-back,
    for hoop-back and for loop-back.
For recliner. For airliner. For those chairs
    in the earliest Mickey Mouse cartoons
that dance on festive, rubbery legs,
    we beam our thanks your way, for the chair
of the Pope and the chair of the slim-ankled bar girl.
    For the golden chair that clinked to the touch
of Midas's golden undershorts. And for the chair
    my grandmother died in painlessly,
with the slightly fearful but also expectant look
    of someone strapped in to a roller-coaster car.
And for the bones in us, that endo-chair
    born into a woman, into a man
—we thank you, Saint Victor, Saint Joseph, Saint Anne.

———————

Especially we must thank you
     for the interface between the beatific
and the ordinary, even the mundane.
     "The first recorded drawers were used to file
church documents"—you see? The realm
     of "deity," of "soul," and of "transcendence," here
alloying with an object of practical use. How could we *not*
     be agog at that marriage?—how
its evidence is everywhere; how "the formalized dress
     of the servers, the incantatory nature of their speech,
and the nearly liturgical cast of the menu" make
     a ritual of near-religious aspect for the congregated
under the sign of the Golden Arches, and haven't we all
     presented ourselves for respite
at the Counter and the Booth? And for the seater
     in the shape of a duck-billed hamburger
we thank you: let the kids play for a blessed while
     out of our hair. We thank you for so many variations:
table that's an emptied mega-spindle
     of underground telephone cable; cabinet of popsicle sticks
and beer cans. Someone's had a desk constructed
     to accommodate her new assistant kneeling in it,
out of sight, to attend to her intimate yearns; somebody
     else, a desk from which a gilded, gemmed ceramic statue
of the Virgin Mary pops up at a button's press
     as perky as a prairie dog. For these,
and all the "these" they represent, and for the nuptial bed
     Ulysses carved from the heart of an oak, its legs
still part of the tree and rooted down into that other
     heart in the liquid-iron deeps of the planet.
We thank you for ottoman, settee, chaise lounge, divan,
     Saint Victor, Saint Joseph, Saint Anne.

There's that story of the evil duke/count/empress
  and the evil bed: a guest too short
was forcibly stretched to fit it, and a guest too long. . . .
  Deliver us from such horror.
Please protect us from the bed of rancor,
  save us from the bed of glacial sheeting.
There are desks of such unboundaried, monstrous power,
  with such sheen, that lives like ours
are just the rags by which those surfaces are polished
  . . . please. Deliver us from these.
And from the judge's bench, release us.
  From the table in the light of the surgical cutters and probers,
yes, and from the slow chair and its slow time
  in the waiting room . . . deliver us
back to our ongoing lives, and from us
  ask for any gift for you or those in your protection.
There are chairs in rooms where the questions are asked
  with rope and a rubber hose . . . please
don't forsake us. From the spy eyes
  in the government's sleepless hallways of computer hutches . . .
please, deliver us. Please deliver us
  safe, on time, according to plan.
Movers of the human spirit,
  deliver us in your shimmering van.
Haul us, then install us in place,
  Saint Victor, Saint Joseph, Saint Anne.

8.

In just a few minutes the cleanup crew,
and dozens of neighborhood residents, and idle gawkers,
and shift two from the TV news, will break this
dreamy moment she's been given, of wandering solitary
around the devastation, of . . .
"communing" is the closest I can come to what
she's doing: every jagged fragment
seems to hold the screams,
the psalms, the devotional lilt,
of over seven thousand years
encoded in it, like the genome
woven into every cell. Here, look . . .
the pitiful crumbs of the main hall's tile mosaic,
so tiny and granular: almost the aerosol of a tile mosaic.
And here . . . the thick and heavy wooden platform
where the Torah gets unscrolled is now
a drift of wooden sand. *Well, what do I know?*
Maybe the dream of a heavy wooden platform is to be exploded
into particles so small that they can ride the wind
like spirits. (Yes, and maybe the dream of a spirit
is thick and nasty: it wants to be a bed.) And
here . . . she bends with fevered concentration. Here
are slivers of that very same Elijah's chair they used
at Jeremy's circumcision ritual almost twenty years ago.
(The chair proportioned to an infant, that he'd sit on
while the cantor intoned and the *mohel* readied the instruments,
and then he'd be lifted out of it, and—as the specialized blade
began its work—the prophet Elijah would sit in it next,
benignly overseeing.) As the chair was sized
to Jeremy when he was eight days old and living,
now that Jeremy's dead, is who-knows-where, these
small remainders of what might be called the corpse of a chair

seem sized to Jeremy still. She slips one,
toothpick-light, in her sweatshirt pocket. "Excuse
me, Ms. . . ."—those others start to invade the scene,
and she leaves. That's all. I wish there were something
more melodramatic to end with: that she
drops to her knees like a tree on fire and raves
until the flames have eaten her clean. *That*
would be a good one. Or a weeping
that's kept secret inside the cabinet of her sternum.
Even that. But no, she goes home,
and the years pass, as the years do
whether we're vigilant or not. And every Passover
at the *seder* with Scott and Michelline and Trishie,
at the part near the end where the door
is ceremoniously opened and the prophet Elijah
welcomed into the house, she slips
that sliver from its silver-inlaid memorial box and sets it,

a chair, at their table.

American Days

I live with my contradictions
intact, seeking transcendence
but loving bread.

—DAVID IGNATOW

The Open Road goes to the used-car lot.

—LOUIS SIMPSON

The Elements

The cool, dusk-blue of the shadows of these Dutch plums
is mixed with a quarter-thimble of gray that matches
    glints in the skins of the pears, the berries, the liver-paste.
If the dull swell of a herring on a plate picks up
    red chevrons meaning a candle (out of sight) is lit,
the crystal of burgundy weighting another corner is given
    a small red heart of light at its center so
everything, in shape and weight, is balanced, and
    the keen lines angled like stylized rain around
the base of the creamer say the same green as the stems
    that have been set like accent marks for the scansion of cherries.
In the back, in the middle, a hot loaf is broken
    for steam to rise in a perfect column of nearly
Corinthian detail, at the edges of which it thins
    in equilibrium with the night, as a breath might
leave a body and settle, composed and ubiquitous.
    I wonder if this still-life exists in the universe

---

of a wormy handful of rice. I wonder what the sense of time
    in which it was painted has to do with a year
in the dog cages. When a prisoner's released
    from one of those, he "walks" by sitting, moving his legs
ahead of him by hand, like huge quaint compasses.
    This group was abducted out of their homes and now will be kept
at an "interim camp." They face the camera with something
    in their eyes beyond despair. Before the film goes
to a New York–based reporter summing it up, we see
    a newly uncaged woman catch a doll
a soldier tosses her, then start to comb its patchy hair, and only
    hours later will we come to understand this
is her infant daughter dead of cold water and lye.
    I wonder, in all of science fiction, if there have been
two universes this discordant, or what it means
    that there can be a suffering so intense its balance only
exists somewhere in the next life. And

———————

I wonder if I should hate that painting, I wonder
if out of faith kept with the brutalized, I should revile
    the easy leisure with which another world applied its dedication
to a study of shadow lengthening under tangerines, I
    wonder if now we must love that painting more than ever,
its calm, its idea of order and abidingness, I wonder
    isn't this exactly the freedom for which we risk the cage
and dream of in the cage to keep us living, this
    aloof, light space in which the heft of a peach against
washed linen can grow important and exact,
    I wonder if I should burn a painting like that
and turn to the knife and the placard, I wonder if
    I should give my days to the completion of its housing
under temperature control, I wonder what we give
    our nights to, and how much our days define our nights, I
wonder until I sleep, and I sleep like a fresh bread
    cooling, reaching an agreement with the elements.

Effect over Distance

The six-foot indigo plumes of "the sacred necropolis bird
of ancient Egypt" rose from urns on either side of the stage,
and there were billows of an inky incense just as thick. . . .
Amaz-O the Grandiloquent, "beguiler of both royalty and the masses,
from the steppes of Outer Shaz to the salons of naughty Paree,"
was about to flabbergast the annual convening
of the Synagogue Social Society for the northwest side of Chicago,
in 1960, when I was twelve, and embarrassed of being twelve,
and embarrassed of my parents, who sat on my either side
like the upright plumes of the squarest, drabbest avian life imaginable.
He'd already been successful at scarves and rabbits
and an unbroken river of golden hoops—"And NOW,
I shall endeavor to READ THE MIND of an audience member
across this Emptiness Between Us!" I was sick with fright
then, feverish and clammy at once; for *I* knew I'd been thinking
of his slinkily-spangled assistant in her barely-there sarong
and snakey boots, and she reminded me, by easy links
in logic, of Miss Portney, assigner of *Ivanhoe* and *Silas Marner,*
whose tailored-over swells and winky fissures had me
imagining voluptuary excesses that were poignantly real
if (given my inexperience) sappily vague, and might be best
summed up by picturing the wallowing of a seal in sweetcream.
I knew—he was going to probe this rotten nethermind
of mine, and though he'd be too gentlemanly
to reveal my moral putrescence in public, still,
it was inevitable some tincture of his discovery, some
greenish O of weeks-old eggs, would float the air above
and give my budding culpability away, to these
assembled hosts of goodness. If it seems foolish now,
that fancy, I take comfort from the instances of similar belief
in dramatic effect taking place
across impossible distance, sometimes instances believed in
by the wisest and the most. We know Medieval scholars
placed their faith unquestioningly in "green vitriol." Listen:

"If a piece of a wounded man's raiment, stained with blood
from the wound, be dipped in water holding some of this
miraculous powder in solution, the wound forthwith begins
to heal. It matters not how far the sufferer is away
from the place where the bloodstained scrap is treated.
The patient might be in affliction in Marseilles,
and the piece of linen might be effectually operated on
in London." Of course. Even now, in travel, I'll suddenly
think of my wife back home, and know whatever
love or shame, whatever tangled fear or passion, is the major thread
of that etheric fabric—weaves a visible pattern
of cause-and-effect in the actual world. In 1728
the obdurate, carpenter father of novice astronomer
Thomas Wright of Durham, England, gathered and burned
the fledgling scholar's books; well, I know perfectly how
that conflagration smoldered over twenty-two years, eventually
becoming his pioneering vision of swarms of suns,
of flaming uncountable bodies, scattered
throughout "the endless Immensity." By the way,
Amaz-O read the mind of a tittering corpulent woman
named Minnie Pinkus, who must have been putty inside his
well-kept prestidigitorial hands—it was a matter of missing car keys,
furtively eaten extra desserts, and some implied
erotic transgression so insipid the audience needed to *will*
its fitful blush and laughter to the surface. She sagged back
into her seat aswim in sweat. So I was spared,
I guess, although those very easy links of logic fastened me
inseparably to Thomas Wright—for even once
we'd moved on to the floating globe, and the pocketed fish,
I sat there on fire, I sat there burning into the starry future.

Will the Real Shakespeare Please Stand Up?

The bar is called *The Duck Blind* and is decorated with decoys
—of which, antique models are highly prized: the verisimilitude
daubwork on those compact backs, etc., and the cartoonier
ones as well. A man in a back booth is saying
he's tight pals with the TV-producer community—would she
like to pose for a promo portfolio, over at his apartment?
Oh he's good, he's smooth as dental floss—but
lying, through those perfect pearly teeth. In fact he wants
to use the knife on her, like on the others, an inch
at a time, the face first, till they plead. And she's all

golly whiz, wow *would* she! as she nervously swizzles sloe gin.
She's a cop. Her "Nude-Lift Casbah Bra" is
wired for sound, and three guys monitor her in a van that
says (cop humor here) MAMMA REE'S STEREO SERVICE.
"Let's go then—ready?" The "beef-katoothpick" "snax"
they've rearranged ten dozen ways on their plates without eating
are gravy-dyed soy substitute, and from this screen
at the side of the bar, the President is mouthing like a carp
—if we could hear him, he'd be promising us he did or he didn't,
whichever we care to choose. And so my theme is deceit,

its intricate, dolorous beauty. William Henry Ireland,
eighteen, forgered—ballsily enough—two "new" entire
plays of Shakespeare's, plus contracts, autographed receipts,
a sheaf of love letters (bound in a strip of ancient tapestry
torn from the walls of the House of Lords), and a document
proving Ireland's ancestor once saved Shakespeare from drowning.
Guess if a committee of the era's most distinguished scholars
lapped it up like honeywater. Boswell dropped to his knees
to kiss these artifacts and claimed that, having
seen them, he'd die happy now. But happiness,

scant hours after, is "fiddling in Venus's
concert-hall" with a Miss Septina Withers, actress. It's
easy enough to picture him, a grampus operatically huffing
around some spongy nook, then napping, then ragging
her dried patina off his noodley member—why
avert our gaze from something so honestly pursued?—but much
more difficult to steadily look as he's penning his letter
home to Margaret, filled as it is with the sweet *bon mots*
of fidelity. Our resolve in this world gutters
like a candle-flame. And that knife-crazy serial killer?—I

———————————

invented him. The bar, though, is real and so
is the woman. She's home now. Because she's an amateur birder
she laughs at those decoys (they aren't antiques but slipshod
plastic things that look like hiking boots with bills)
and then, with no transition, she's weeping, she's drunk
and she's weeping: no serial killer, okay, but still he was
a class-A asshole jerk. She turns the TV on: the President,
rerun for the country's insomniacs. She shakes her head
as if to clear it, then switches channels: the President again.
Let's visit her. She would say: "brood parasitism"

exists among ducks, and five other avian species;
the European cuckoo, for instance, replaces the eggs
of the warbler or thrush with its own, and it will duplicate
egg color and design for the birds being suckered. True,
the victim may discover this deception, then weave
a new nest over the cuckoo eggs—but just as often
the cuckoo simply repeats its trick: we've found nests seven
layers tall, the real, the fake, the real, the fake. . . . *Now*
what's the President saying up there?—the soundproofed ovens
of Dachau? the vows to the Aztec and Sioux?

Units

We could say that Rembrandt was a greater painter than Kandinsky. We could
not say that Rembrandt was three and a half times better than Kandinsky. . . .
We could say, "I have more pain than I had yesterday." When we tried to say, "I
have nine dols of pain," we found we were talking nonsense.

—LESHAN AND MORGENAU

This is the pain you could fit in a tea ball.
This is the pain you could pack in a pipe
—a plug of pungent shag-cut pain,
a pain to roll between the thumb and the forefinger.
Here: *this* pain you could pour down the city sewers,
where it would harden, and swell, and crack
those tubes like the flex of a city-wide snake,
and still you would wake and
there would be more for the pouring.
Some pain believes its only true measure is litigation.
For other pain, the glint of the lamp
in a single called-forth tear is enough.
Some pain requires just one mouth, at an ear.
Another pain requires the Transatlantic Cable.
No ruled lines exist by which to gauge its growth
(my pain at three years old . . . at five . . .) and yet
if we follow the chronolinear path of Rembrandt's face
self-imaged over forty years—a human cell
in the nurturing murk of his signature thick-laid paint—
we see the look-by-look development,
through early swank and rollick, of a kind of pain
so comfortable it's worn, at the last,
like a favorite robe, that's frayed by now, and intimate
with the frailties of its body, and has
an easy fit that the showiest cloak of office
never could. In 1658, the gaze is equally
into himself, and out to the world-at-large
—they've reached a balance of apportioned

disappointment—and the meltflesh under the eyes
is the sallow of chicken skin, recorded
with a faithfulness, with really a painterly
tenderness, that lifts this understanding of pain
into something so accommodating, "love" is the word
that seems to apply to these mournfully *basso*
bloodpan reds and tankard-bottom browns. Today
in the library stacks, the open face of a woman
above this opened book of Rembrandt reproductions
might be something like the moon he looked to,
thinking it shared in his sadness. What's
her pain? her ohm, her acreage, her baker's dozen,
of actual on-your-knees-in-the-abattoir misery?
I don't know. I'm not writing this
pretending that I know. What I can say is that
the chill disc of the stethoscope is known to announce
an increment of pain not inappropriate
to being blurted forth along the city wall
by a corps of regalia'd trumpeters.
Who's to say what a "unit" of pain is?
On a marshy slope beyond the final outpost,
Rembrandt stares at the moon, and stares at the moon,
until the background drumming-in of the ocean
and the other assorted sounds of the Amsterdam night,
and then the Amsterdam dawn, are one
with his forlornness, and the mood fades
into a next day, and a woman here
in Kansas turns to face the sky: she's late
for her appointment. She's due
for another daily injection of nine c.c.'s of undiluted *dol*.

Remains Song

The penis is gone, the penis of even *Tyrannosaurus rex*
is gone, the hardest of them all is only oleo
to time, and disappears, with the tongue,
and the brain, and its beehive of thought, and the portentous
vaginal lips, and their promise: vanished,
enzymatically, molecularly: gone. Although

the bone that anchored the "penis retractor muscle"
is a small rib in the towering, vaulted, domed
cathedral of dinosaur infrastructure that
remains—and, by its telltale osseous presence, we
can clarify our muddy paleobiological guesses at
Cretaceous sex. The jazzman's breath

is gone, but the saddle of callus is still intact
on the cadaver's lip: a fossil of pain,
of fucked-up pimped-down pain, and of the rapture
when we're blown like smoke rings out of ourselves
at 4 a.m. in cellarlight and sweat until there's no
"ourselves," there's only a haze on the stage. The rapist

is gone, but his signature DNA remains in the bloody wads
beneath her fingernails. The physicist is gone,
but light remains, its relativity and speed remain,
confounding us anew like the thwack of a barrel stave
against our heads each morning. The marriage
is gone, but the baby is seven pounds, three ounces

and screaming its shitty little petal-pretty skull off
in the bedroom. When the atmosphere is left below,
the air still *sishes* out of the 747's overhead nozzles. Then
something goes wrong. The plane is an untranslatable scatter
of metal debris and burnt flesh; but
the black box is an eloquence. The flint tool

is proof of the hand that wielded it: the hand is only
so many atoms of carbon now, some water, and
a coppery ancestral taste when we're licking each other's bodies.
And the moment of conception, of the universe's
becoming the universe, twenty billion of units we call "years"
ago, is lost, although the scream of this,

the fire of this, the pattern, and the radial awayness, these
are life as we move through it daily.
As we move through it daily we're always, somewhere,
gone. House dust is 70%
shed human skin, and what we breathe in is a whiff
of the extinguished. Here in Dinosaur Hall

our detective hero is woefully bamboozled: someone's
stolen a famous thigh bone the size of a Greyhound bus,
and though this room is nothing but structured
evidential testimony to life-forms from millennia
back—and posed with the seeming immediacy of centerfolds—
he can't find one hard clue to a felon who's history

by only sixty minutes. Later that night, alone
at home, he lists the facts repeatedly. Of course
alone. You're happy, you're together, then something
goes wrong. He knows that now. He studies her empty
half of the closet. Eerily: aren't these hangers something like the wire
a museum dioramacist fashions a torso around?. . . . He

studies her porcelain coffee cup, still here in the sink . . .
her lip-print on its rim. . . . To him, her cyst was
extradition to another world. "Another world"—and
we're *its* archeology, its ongoing Ur or Assyria.
"She's with God now," the priest said—frowning, as if
God were a boy-toy neighbor she'd decided to run off with.

The Jewish Poets of Arabic Spain
(10th to 13th Centuries), with Chinese Poets Piping out of Clouds (and Once an Irishman)

1.

A brother or a sister poet is constantly over our shoulders.

—SOSHO

Gone, the last of the copcar sirens.
Gone, the final whine of a neighbor's midnight lust
for powertrimming his frowzy hedge.

———————————

I'm watching you sleeping.
Your lids have set down
their harps.
I'm watching the breath-flesh rise and fall;
                                        and
Judah ha-Levi is writing
There is no likeness unto your beauty,
The apple's shape is your breast's shape, oh
The apple's hue is your cheek's hue.
                            I'm thinking
about the wall a disagreement raises
even between two people who love; and even with bricks
the size of grains of dust, it keeps
their separate sides of the bed
inviolate;
            and
Judah ha-Levi is writing
My love could wash her clothes
In the pour of my tears. My eyes are hers
For well-water.
                I'm leaving
the bed, I'm staring—not the first time, either—

blankly out the window, at the Siamese-twin blankness
of the night, attached by where my forehead
leans against the windowpane; a night
like this, and Tu Fu wrote
I'm empty, here at the edge of the sky
—what Ku-t'ai-ch'ing called *idle grief.*
For hours, I'm a thinnest balance
walking the long insomnia-lines
of my own face, holding discourse
with the mirror, for everyone, asking it
those grayish questions of want and likelihood,
act and intent . . . the brief bare glances inside of ourselves
that the day won't allow
and the dark is ashamed of.
                    And these are the words
of Judah ha-Levi's I take back
to the pillow with me:
                    How shall I go through the narrow straits?
He may as well be writing it
in this room, it may as well be the eleventh century, anytime
sleepless, any century full of moons like dinner plates,
and any language, and any people:
How shall I go through the narrow straits?

—————————

And Wang Shih-chen (about 1700):
Now there's someone rapt in meditation;
It's midnight and still he hasn't gone to sleep.

2.

. . . phosphenes, the scientific word for the "stars" you see when your head gets banged and for the scenes that appear when you're half-asleep or when you meditate with your eyes closed. Between the ages of two and four, when a child can hold a crayon but knows little of how to draw objectively, he is most apt to draw things with a distinctly phosphene character. And this is about equally true of primitive humans who lived during mankind's childhood, to judge by the phosphene-like figures in some of the prehistoric cave paintings. . . .

—ARRANGED FROM GUY MURCHIE

Is this the story of Cain and Abel? It
could be, it's that early: this is another green day
(before the idea of "days") on a planet of scavengers and gatherers
at the cusp of learning hunting. Let's say . . . oh,
two million years ago, by potassium-argon dating. A man
—an almost-man—awakes in the unslaked chill of dawn,
beside his almost-woman. His face is bleeding, so
is hers, but they're alive: more than the strange-one is,
on the other side of the glade. *His* skull is crushed, and we
can match that indentation to the responsible
—to the specific responsible—antelope leg bone.
Here it is, in the hand of our near-man. Pain
is a flickering diadem in his head; he
closes his eyes,
                    the Ice Age cave walls, figurines, and wands,
scored-over with their star/wave/crisscross sacred doodles,
go by in a dream;
                    when he opens his eyes it's 192 AD
Wang Ts'an is writing:
One goes to war when the lord commands,
Such decrees cannot be disobeyed.
This frontier post brings nothing but sorrow,

On the road there are starving women,
White bones cover the plain.
And yet he still might lift his head from his paper and hum
a traditional melody:
Tenderly I think of my lovely one,
Clouds fly, I cannot forget her.
                                    So. There
is always the war. There has never not
been the war. It's simply more or less
legitimized at times. And
there is always this couple
at 4 in the morning, in bed, their asses touching
but their heads in different worlds.
Outside, the rumble then thunk of the garbage truck.
It wakes me for a moment
from my single hour's sleep, and through such milky
pinhole consciousness, the universe
floods in: its stars /
its waves / its encompassing crisscross.

———————

Then I doze back into my half of the pattern
a diner waitress would call out to the cook
(two-over-easy-on-toast)
as "Adam and Eve on a raft."

3.

Az men dermont zikh on dem toyt iz men nit zikher mitn lebn.
(If you start thinking about your death, you're no longer certain
about life.)

—YIDDISH PROVERB

All afternoon we watched the American bombs
and the Iraqi bombs, and counted the bodies; and, even so,
the television distances this suffering:
its final effect is about the size of a cigarette burn
inside us. . . . No wonder
we quarrel that night:
                              to hurt, to remember
we *can* be hurt. That's
part of it anyway—who could ever wholly understand
the vendettas of intimate partners?
No wonder so often we let ourselves be lost
in some interior fog . . .

———————

. . . it thickens
near the river. When he pushes off from shore
it's thicker yet, and soon it holds
his barely-room-for-two excursion-boat completely,
which is what he wants: to float there
for a while like a dull thought, in a mind erased.
Now he dah-dah-dahs under his breath. And now
he tries out some lines of a burgeoning poem,
"Flowers and grass appear far and hazy,
A crested loon flies into the current—
I ask myself what kind of man am I." Then:
"*Yah, yah,* I know jost vot you mean," a voice says in a Yiddish-inflected

Arabic. Well, Li Po startles: he thought he was alone in this mist but
no, he has a passenger barely visible beside him, who says:
"There is nothing for me in the world but the hour in which I am.
It lasts but a moment, and, like a cloud, is no more."
And Samuel ha-Nagid leans back, pleased with his phrasing.
Li Po is excited, he nearly drops the oar—now *this* is someone
he can talk to! "The river flows east,
And the gibbons cry. Men die in the wilds,
Vultures feed on human guts.
Sideways I look westward and I heave a long sigh."
Yes! Yes! His passenger nods in agreement!
"Man runs toward the grave,
And rivers hasten to the great deep.
I look up to the sky and its stars,
I look down to the earth and its creeping things.
The days of my sorrow are not complete."
A willow-dabbled bend in the water is going to deliver them
out of view, and Li Po is about to go breathily on
about cranes, or bamboo, or flowering plum, when: "Wait!
Wait!"—I'm running along the riverbank, pacing them.
"What about looooove?" I shout. They turn to me
with a look on their faces that says I've asked them something
so impossible it's even beyond
the speck-by-speck reflection
of *their* lotus-and-shtetl philosophy.

4.

It is tempting to conjecture how much love poetry was ever written by the Hebrews, and is now lost to us forever, because it was not regarded as Holy Writ.

—DAVID GOLDSTEIN

She: As the two scrolled sides of the Torah roll apart
  To reveal the scripture of the day,
  So you roll me apart to reveal the text of the night,
  My love, my lion-of-the-desert, my blossom.

And the stewardess is demonstrating the oxygen mask in America.
And the hotel elevator has no 13th floor in America.
And the mint is under the pillow of the freshened bed in America
And in Paris, which is America, and in Rome, which is America,
O and any day now in Zimbabwe. Come beneath the sheets
With me, Room Service will bring us a light California wine.

He: I went to see the flocks, and they were shapely on the hill,
  But not so shapely as you, to me, my gazelle, my oasis.
  I went to the orchard, and it opened up its sweetness for me,
  But yours is supreme, but yours is the privilege,
  My dove-of-the-towers, my almond.

"Pisa pallor," they said to our American ears, in Tokyo,
Which is America. There, in the pizza parlor,
Ravenous boys check out the ravenous girls, and also the other
Way around. There is no stopping American blue jeans or the wanting
Of what fills them to exquisitude, in Stockholm, or Lima,
Or Dzubovich, or on MTV, which is America, darlin'.

Both: The wrath of Adonai is great:
  The flood, and the dust, and the locust.
  But the season changes; the clemency of the seasons never dies,

It will last through even the tempest, even the fire.
Last night we were a storm,
We were a cloud as hard as a shield,
Its light was flung spears.
Let us wake into a newer weather,
My bulwark, my ewe at the delicate shoots,
My flame kept lit in the Temple.

And the genders are revving their engines, automotive and sexual
Equally, and cruising the downtown drags of our America, and love
Is being made on Bible School retreats, on toxic dumps, and love
Is in that hidden island tribe that just a year ago was Neolithic and
Now of course is America, boomboom music and Coke and freedom
And escrow and give me a kiss in the high school halls,
In the shopping malls, in the golden skyscraper walls
O of America.

Yüang-yang, mandarin ducks, are Chinese symbols
of "conjugal happiness." Chiang Ch'un-lin sees
Thirty-six pairs in a lovely pattern,
Together they bathe in the clear brook.
And for Yeats? "The Wild Swans at Coole"
". . . paddle in the cold / Companionable streams or climb the air"
(how?) "lover by lover." It's 1917.
Or is it 810? Yüen Chen is writing
As I sit watching the morning sun come up,
A flock of birds returns by twos.

5.

Returned from dream, I rested for a while
and wept profuse tears. . . .
                                          —HUANG TSUN-HSIEN

Then waking: rubbing another marquee
of phosphenes out of my eyes.

———————

Beside me, you're first lazily breaking
out of the gluey webbing of sleep.
And over us . . .
                    something . . .
                                    maybe the future
is here in the room above us,
is looking in for a minute—fondly?
could I think it's fondly?—not unlike the way
I'm remembering back to those lines of Samuel ha-Nagid's:
    Come out and see the morning light
    —A scarlet thread in the East!

———————

I think it's the future. At least, it's the future
we called "tomorrow." Here it is,
"today": one hundred cups of effort,
good intentions, small misunderstandings,
stretching away from the bed
and finally leading back to it.

———————

Who are they, anyway?—watching us
staring each other, watching us willing
the first emotional patch
sewn over our last emotional wounding.
I think we do it for them. The future always needs
the wistful story of disrepair and mending
to play out its pain in a handful of verses,
to heal itself in a handful more.

Sometimes the first of me given over
unto another day has been the skin
raised by the touch of your tongue
—the first, and the best,
of the compromisings
of self in a welter of others.

The traffic jam and the headlines are waiting.
　　Come, my pomegranate, my swan.
The memos and sirens and deals are waiting.
　　Come, my candle, my crown, my song.

Headlong into it—each of us is both
the herder *and* the herd.
As if just to drive our own shadows before us,
to market, is labor enough.

This Thing Larger than a Self

The most beautiful of pairings come from opposition . . .
Consider the bow and the lyre.

—HERACLEITUS

Wrestling with Each Other

When the President declares the war over,
the other wars aren't over. The dust
is still at war with the subatomic needles
of electrical charge that stitch the flesh together.
The light is still at war with the sour dark
in the toe of the shoe. The woman besieges the man;
the man, the woman. The white; and the yolk.
When the Holy Benevolent Tyrant of Tyrants says
the bloody crusade is ceased, the opposition of Eternity
and History continues. That's not funny; and can't you
take a joke. Reality; and "reality." It's dawn, you
wake: mind rises into the body like sun
above the horizon. Another morning.
Fire; and water. Hook; and eye.

———————————

It's raining, a light gray skein of it, and
she sees this as the house's being woven
ever tighter into a viable notion of family. She
wants a child. She hugs herself at the window,
repeating the feel of that tightening weave
and everything it means: a nest,
I guess, comes close as a symbol. Meanwhile,
the weather is ruining his plans
for hunting dove this afternoon. I love
these friends of mine, and with the priceless coin
of their marriage I can't choose sides. He
doesn't want children. All day
it rains. The stream; and the bank.
The rush of flood; and stasis. All day and into the night.

———————————

In this fourteenth-century Sienese *Virgin and Child*, Mary
is stolidly shapeless under her mantle, certainly
Her gold-leaf chest is breastless, is as flat as the panel
it's painted on—and yet the infant suckles,
from a small flesh-colored ball the painter's set
against the gold and purple cloth around Her armpit,
so it is and isn't corporeal, so it might be something
pliant and taut and mammalian, something as veined
as a ball of blue cheese, something soapy and nubbled,
or might be just the brief, begrudged idea of this
in the overwhelming gold holiness of the scene.
The ageless incompatibility. One night: "You
creep, you only want me for my titties." The next: "*Now*
what's the matter? *Look*—doesn't this turn you on?"

———————

When the emir waves his feathered wand, declaring
the border skirmishes at an end, there's still that line
in quantum physics where the particles of "our" "time" meet
the tachyons of "backwards" "time," there's still
conflicting powers in our voids and sines and serums.
When the pasha and the brigadier sign their treaty,
God continues needing feuding with Darwin,
cop with robber, rust with iron, "truth" with "subjectivity."
It rains; it sounds like a tommygun on the roof.
The earthworms swell and slither. And then, of course,
the early birds. When clan and clan lay down their swords
beneath the Tree of Truce, even so, one still is drawn
to that line by Dickens: ". . . misery and magnificence
wrestling with each other upon every rood of ground in the prospect."

———————

Mary, Mother of God and Secret Agent from Space, is
one scenario. Fantasy novels in which the Earth's
a war zone, and our species is the working-out
of another galaxy's battles, or another, eldermost
pantheon of dark deities'. Then every brachiate
dwindle or surge of our evolution, every noted
fascicle of devotion or gumption or dumbfuck luck
in History, is one more moving-forward
of foreign hostilities. Even the most benign of mornings
on the patio. Or we're warriors controlled by our genes.
Their needs. The tides of fortune, and the nucleotides.
The Cross. The cross look. Sun in the puddles
left by the rain. A man and a woman sitting down
to breakfast in that relentless machine.

I've weighted the game: she *doesn't* want a child,
it's dissatisfaction airier, slipperier than this, though
no less painful when it stabs or when her own reflection
stares back from the window filled with thick gray weather
inside her skull. He *doesn't* bag dove: I couldn't pass up
that mild bird with the olive branch
heraldically nipped in its beak. But
their distress is true. The rain and whatever
pall of contention it's come to mean is true,
and will return, with all of its fierce life
and erasure. It will be here at the end,
whatever the dialogue, it will have the last word.
It was here at the origin, stirring the mix.
The first sex on Earth was division.

Hegemony; and the subaltern. Particle; and wave.
The neocortex; and the hypothalamus. Honey;
bitter herb. Having spoken just now to both of them,
I set the phone back in its plastic cradle
as if it could explode. When every military wallah
lauds the ways of peace, the lamb beside the lion,
there will still be my two friends. My head
is feverish with their bicker, a simmer
of helplessness won't leave my brow,
and I lean my head against the cool,
the impartial, glass of the window—feeling it leach
this fever away, with the press of its clarity.
And, from the other side: the tapping,
the reminding, almost the arguing now, of the rain.

Roses and Skulls

"Jee-ZUSS, I just got a call from the crazy old bitch,
she bought herself a shotgun, a *shotgun,* now
if Vessie ever tries climbing back in the house she says
she's going to blow his balls off—look, I've got to go
sort this out for them, do you want to come too?"
I've only known Joan a week. A week. Now Vessie
does a crow-dance on my shoulder, and nutty Irene
on the other. A trailer they've painted in roses and skulls.
"I've never told you . . . when these things happen I
turn on almost everyone I love. *(pause)* Will you hold me?"

Really entering another's life . . . ?—is like you're walking through
the flat and familiar background of thirteenth-century paintings
when, with a sickening whoosh, perspective
gets invented; and the world, its saints (with halos
like those crimped gold-foil paper cups
for gourmet chocolates), its shitdump-guzzling swine,
its finches and beggars' bells and candelabra, *everything,*
is tumbled and sucked down the colonnade lines to a pinhole
on the horizon, as if a bullethole opened up in the shell
of a jetliner, and you're lost lost lost. Disorienting

switches in style, though, are nothing compared to switches
in worldview. If this "person" from a 1580 folk-art painting
steps inside this Impressionist day in a sun-emblazoned hillscape:
he's a "child," "childhood" having been invented by now. Or
move this houndsteeth streak of mountains, Romantically
rendered as glorious, back one hundred years: and it's
a bleak impediment to travel, only that. In Lucas Cranach's
Staghunt (1544), the splendid ladies of the court row out
to watch the great beasts disemboweled by dogs, an afternoon's
diversion: run *that* past your Sensitivity Workshop. Zapping

back-and-forth between two worlds accumulates
a dangerous static charge along the zapline, and is never
as easy as s-f adventures imply with their casual *pop*
of inter-time or -dimensional travel. Wife and husband
dunk each other lustily in the tub, then transact
business from it: this is a Medieval painting—master,
mistress, seven children, four apprentices, several poor relations,
and a scurry of servants live in these two hall-like, straw-strewn rooms
of a standard bourgeois house, where tables are also beds and
sleep six visitors at a time, *our* sense of "privacy" not

existing yet. For that, we need to enter this
mid-sixteenth-century Dutch home, brick and gabled, where a couple,
for the first time, is a "couple," defined by surrounding
intimate buffer-space. The architecture says this: *snug*
is Dutch in origin. Bickering. Planning. Waking
like two elements in suspension, in their own and conspired
suspension. Having "psychologies." Knickknacks. Pulling up
into the trailer court's lot: "Oh I didn't tell you anything about Angelo;
no matter what he says, *agree*." As if holding your own face woefully
in your hands at midnight isn't enough. Now holding this other face.

Burnt Offering

Rembrandt's friend, the physician Tulp, writes of "a distinguished painter (who) was under the delusion that all the bones of his body had softened to such a flexibility that they might easily buckle like wax"—his report dates this case of "melancholia" to the same months' gap for which we have no record of any Rembrandt work.

This is how we fought:
we clambered into his oil *The Slaughtered Ox,*
we had knives, no not exactly
knives but we loved each other and so knew enough
to cut deep. The ox was flayed, beheaded,
pole-strung to the four quarters. In it,
we went for each other, there were no rules:
the weapon we had was intimacy.
With the gore of it smeared on our faces.
With its red meat pustules jeweling our lips.
We climbed the monumental sternum tiers,
we reached the pit of it, the nave,
the lightless center the rectal-hole
and the fluttery phlegm-edged esophagus-hole
both bleed toward. Nothing stopped us.
First we skinned each other. Slowly,
in spirals, deliberately as a peach.
A meat peach. A blood peach. The fruit of an ox.
With its ribs like a Viking ship's.
With its mucoused trusses and bellpulls.
In that air where each cell's ghost stinks.
First we skinned each other and
then we shucked whole muscles off.
It hurt, it was good. We used our teeth,
it was tasty. We pulled long fibers out
and their tissuey skreeking was music.
In the hall of its chandelier seminal vents.
In its buttery ducts. In its chancel.

First we skinned each other and
then we shucked whole muscles off.
In its rendering troughs. With ox fat under our nails.
And then we went for the bones.

He
was melting. Inside. His bones were turning wax. He grabbed the worm-
holed, nap-worn cap and the wharfmaster's cape he favored, and left to walk
the city, to let its hard sights harden him. The wind today was brisk. Late
fall. A goosepimple blue snuffled up the good burghers' legs and under their
good wives' skirts. He watched a gang of teamsters push an overburdened
sledge up one of the city's steepest bridges—he wanted to sketch their curses
blossoming into the cool air like peonies, wanted to charcoal away at the
gait of the one throwing grease-soaked rags beneath the sledge's runners to
lube its ascent. He'd done the bridge before, the imperturbable look of its
stone. All the bridges of Amsterdam were stone. All public buildings and
churches and most of the finer houses were brick or stone. Yet the city was
built on a swamp. He knew that it could give in, any day, to that essential
softness. He could give in. He was melting, inside. If one of the little shitty
urchins chunked a stone at his back, he'd pour out, he'd tip like a mold at the
chandler's. This wouldn't do. He turned back toward the Jewish quarter, off
St. Anthoniesbreestraat—he knew some of these people. He'd feel at home.
A home is hard, his home is filled with true hard things, it has shape. A hall
of plaster casts of goddesses; the waist-high garden statue of a child peeing;
his chest of petrifactions and animal skulls; his gold helmets, the halberds
and pikes, the various crowns and chalices, his Japanese armor; his mobile of
the universe done in chalk spheres circling a lustrous cherrywood core. This
house—the family was friends of his. He looked through the window. A
small self-portrait he'd given them was framed on a wall. He looked at him-
self. He was scared. It was Friday. Their Sabbath was starting. The woman
in the window bent her lace-shawled head in prayer and lit the pair of ritual
candles. The wax. He was blinded. They found him curled like a dog on the

cobbles, chilled but otherwise robust, although he claimed his knees could
not support him, so wouldn't they carry him, please, inside, and then he'd
walk home, when the Sabbath candles were melted and he rehardened, then
he knew he could walk home.

———————

And slept.
And dreamed we were back
at Barbara and David's. In my dream,
as in our "real time" with them in July,
the lights went out. Three square blocks of St. Louis,
kaput. So all night, then,
by one wan scrounged-up candle
at the center of us, and booze-glow: talking,
what do you think of, talking, but you're wrong,
do you see, no it's women who do that, talking,
once I did, of course you see, until the border
of any one of us didn't stop at the skin and whatever
othercreaturely compound-mind we made, it
floated the porch itself beyond
the borders of being a porch, on the long black hours.
There was a moment—everything
was possible. I looked: or you looked: our bodies were filled
by burning candles, we sat talking around
a single communal bone.

———————

I wake, I see
sleep's paired us, leg
in leg—we're like a giant synesthesia,
making little sense together but making it,
making it anyway. By this I understand
the grief is burnt away again, we can be easy, truly
empty of it and easy, a while.
You murmur . . . something—not kissably yet, you murmur
like a tailor from a mouth that's gripping pins, but
meant sweet. Now we have to trust
such meaning. In the room where I keep
art-book repros, photos and postcards tacked, the thin
flat light of daybreak first starts recognizing its own deeper
self in his portraits.
                        This young ghetto Jew
stares out at the world in such a delicately poignant
trick of chiaroscuro, we can see that really he
looks in: to where his bones, the stacked moth
spinal column bones, and the colonnade bones of the legs,
and the hummingbird skeleton whole in the middle ear,
and the rest, are part of the mysterious shipment
everyone delivers, at last, to that great reliquary
the planet . . .
and then past his bones: to where
our daily dole of endurance,
complicity, clouded-over good intentions, and ability to hurt
and be hurt are cupped from their bottomless well,
these, yes, and something else, the kind of dazzling sadness
when a spring breeze whuffs the cemetery dust
across a girl's dripsugar pastry
fresh from the bakery, so both
are on the lips her beau licks greedily in the sunlight. . . .
This is also in the face of Thomas Jacobsz Haaring,
bailiff at the Amsterdam Court of Insolvency; and

in the face of Burgomaster Jan Six; and
in the finely grained, contained face of Margaretha de Geer.
How open,
        how soft,
must anyone be to see this and
record its velvety, mottled illumination? Or
maybe I mean how hard,
to stand the task? Or don't we live
where the two are one, and the fury of needing to hold them
simultaneously shakes us with such breakage,
we're ever crying to offer up
one or the other unto the gods, a flame, a waft,
we think will leave us
feeling some one thing purely. . . .
                A postcard
showing the Rapture is pinned to the corkboard.
Possibly you've seen it: helterskelter cars
with corpses at their wheels, and something
albumeny-white, as slinky as skinks,
steaming out of those marvelous bodies.

———————

Now you wake. Now you work. Now you lay yourself down.
Another day gone up like smoke.

Squash and Stone

Like so many men of his time, he was after a grand principle that would explain a universal truth. An element that he called "septon" was, he declared, the instrument of decay and the cause of most diseases. He lectured on septon, wrote papers on it and even composed a long poem called "The Doctrine of Septon," in which his doggerel blamed septon for cancer, leprosy, scurvy and ringworm.

—ON THE NINETEENTH-CENTURY NATURALIST
SAMUEL LATHAM MITCHILL, COLLAGED FROM
JOSEPH KASTNER's *A Species of Eternity*

And so it is, with the physicists' need
to find a simple, nonexclusionary Supertheory that gathers
the "weak," "strong," gravitational, and electromagnetic
forces into a single "field." And so it was with the marriage.
We wanted its failures in a single word
that ends in -ism or -phobia. One thumb to suck.
One wilted plant to mourn for or renurture.
Isn't it difficult enough, to be a "me" in a world
of daily half-price sales at the Chooz-a-Self?
We wanted the flaw in "us" to be a single, lucid wrongness
(that would require a single righting).
Of course we wanted this; the Supertheory is meant to be
completion raised to beauty,
the way the ocean is both the ocean and the sky.
I'd see her sitting in the kitchen some days staring
at a random still-life basketful of leeks and summer squash
as if this might comprise a read-out screen, a Ouija mechanism,
to the planet of The Single Reason. Once, she said,
she watched me in the dusk light try to squeeze a stone,
she said I really looked as if . . . she thought
of a film-noir private detective trying to make a suspect talk.
I remember a day when the mill across the county line
in Nestorville caught fire, and I wished the arm of char
it raised across the sky
would write some Answer, something brief

the way the elementary is by definition brief, and irreducible.
Give us our god, our needle.
Give us our theory, we thought to ourselves,
as if it were a Constitutional right. Give us our septon.

"A wooden eye. An 1884 silver dollar. A homemade explosive. A set of false teeth. And a 14-karat gold ashtray,"

says my wife, and then she looks up from her book
called something like *Cockamamie Facts* and tests me:
"What's their common denominator?"—right. As if
we still believe some megamatrix substrate (God,
or atoms, or Imagination) holds the infinite unalike dots
of *its* body in a parity, and daily life reflects this. As if
all of our omniform, far-post-lungfish, nuttier-than-Boschian
evolution, crowned by any ten minutes of channel-surfing
the news and (little difference) entertainment possibilities here
at the bung-end of the millennium, hadn't knocked that idea
out of our heads and onto what my father would have charmingly called
its bazoonkus. Common denominator—sure. And yet

it's Sunday night—my wife is reading in bed, with the grim
conviction that the work-week upcoming is going to be one
spirit-dead, hellacious spate of days—and so her mood,
her mind, increasingly assume the über-darkness of the night
itself, the way "industrial melanization" means those moths
in the factory districts gradually blackened to match
their new, soot/city background: and I see, now, how
the sleepless nun, and the lycanthrope in a skulking prowl,
and the warehouse watchman telling the face of his friend
the clock his griefs, his griefs . . . are all subsumed and
equalized into the night, as into a magpie's hoard: so
maybe some Ultracommodiousness, some Great Coeval, does

exist (it might be the Night, it might be almost any of our
pancultural abstractions) and welcomes us into its organizational
gestalt. If so . . . if so, it's more than *my* day's scan
of newspaper cullings and letters can ever rise above itself
to see. I learn someone's investigated the annual global methane emission
in cattle gas; that every seven years a god will fill the toad

attached to the tip of a ritual ribboned pole, and glow like a lamp
in its warty belly—then it rains; that only yesterday a girl,
eleven, was found with the name of a rival gang, the *Lady Satans,*
carefully cut in her thigh and rubbed with drainpipe acid. Somewhere
there may be a world where such as these are equally legitimized, but
not here in the thick and swirling mists of Planet Albert. So

imagine my confusion today at a letter from friend Alane,
who's sweet enough to read and like my poems, and praises
my "inclusiveness," and writes "I'm watching a man with nothing
below the waist on television. He's saying he can do anything.
He walks on his hands, he has a lovely wife. Now, *you'd*
know what to do with him. Me, I just shake my head &
take my hat off." I can't guess at how reliably the toad god
zaps the crops with rain—I do know that this faith
in *me* is wholly undeserved. And as for lovely wives . . . the answer
is: *"Those are the weirdest items tuxedo rental-shops reported
finding in pockets of suits returned to them this year,
a fashion magazine says,"* and with that

thematizing of what had looked like data chaos, she
turns out the light, and fluffles the pillows, and
starts her billowy downslip into sleep. And leaves me
wakeful—leaves me wildly trying to think of pockets adequate
to *everything:* The ashtree staff of the hermit
on his mountaintop for seventeen years. The latest Nintendo
epic, *Callow Drooling Wombat Warriors.* The doctors
cracking open Nicky's sternum like a matzoh—he was five.
The perfect wedge of a brie John found one dawn on his car hood.
Gunshots. Twill weft. Owl-hoo. Storm, and calm.
The poem as fit receptacle. Sure. Right.
I'll know what to do with them.

The Girl Who Married a Wooden Pounder

If they do not arrange a real marriage before puberty, then a substitute rite of marriage is absolutely required. . . . She can first be married to an arrow or a wooden pounder.

—MARY DOUGLAS
Purity and Danger

All morning, and then through the rise
and sumptuous fall of the god

across the Dome Above the World,
the village women have made of themselves

the difficult machines that the difficult
tasks of home require: one is grinding

at the meal-stone; another slaps
her washing at the small rocks

of the stream with such repetitive abandon
that her white cloth looks like foam.

Elsewhere, the men of the village are silently hunting
something with tusks, something with claws

they know can swipe the gut from a man
as easily as summer honey out of the hive. You

see?—where I live, all the wives and husbands
are hard things necessarily,

shaped to labor; so in this, mine
is no different. I admire the functional line

he makes against the sky—the rich
traditional curve of him

I've polished with my intimacies. Surely
we've all known intimacies? At night

each couple lounges in its private dark;
they bring their difficult selves to this thing

larger than a self. And in the dawn
we see our flesh has known

again, has taken in, and grown around,
and given back in kind,

some splinters of the other.

The Fathers

Earth, receive an honoured guest

—W. H. AUDEN

Gallery

When my grandfather stepped from the boat
they gave him a choice of paintings to enter. "This one,"
he said by a nod of his head. Why not?—for weeks
in the bodystink quarters of steerage,
the lice had run as freely as milk through his crevices,
and the only food was saltbread softened in engine water,
but here, in *The Boating Party* by Renoir, it's spring,
the light is floral, even cloth and skin
are really petals in this light, the glass
the wine is in is alive in this light, the men are easy
in speaking with women (he noticed, oh especially,
the women), their mutual fascination is another flower
filling the air, and the clusters of fruits
looked as shining to him as an orchestra's brass section
—when he peeked around the corner of the painting, in fact,
he saw a grouse was simmering in peppered cream
and that settled it, he sat down at a nearby table,
listening to the bright and empty talk, his shy eyes
staring at his waiting plate. A server appeared
and left. On my grandfather's plate was a boiled potato,
only that. But he was starving, so he ate it. He ate it
indelicately, with an almost sexual fervor, and then
looked up to see the family around him,
with their corded hands, with their faces like worn-out shoes,
were eating theirs, just that, with a root tea. He
was in van Gogh's *The Potato Eaters*. The room
was as dark as the tea. Outside, the wind was a punishing switch.
The talk was hushed and raw and familiar,
he was at home here, he was at home in the broken
light of the hanging oil lamp. When the meal was done,
he stepped out into the lane, he breathed the country dark in
hungrily, then walked. He needed a wife.
He needed a future. What did he see ahead,

when he squinted? He would barely understand
that man in Edward Hopper's *Nighthawks,*
on a distant corner, some depleted 3 a.m.,
was his son—who slides the dime for his java
over the counter, slants his hat, then heads out into streetlight
from the diner's unrelenting angles and planes.
He's lonely. It's 1942. He'd love to meet my mother,
someone humming a hot little tune
and pretty as a picture.

Coinages: A Fairy Tale

On May 1, 1947, when *airlift* barely existed, my father
lay down beside my mother. He wasn't my father
yet, she wasn't my mother, not technically, the late sun
played the scales of light on the lake at Indian Lodge State Park,
and *rocket-booster* was new by a year, and *thruway*
only by two, and *sputnik* waited somewhere
in the clouded-over swales of the future and, beyond it,
pixel, rolfing, homeboy floated
in a *cyberspace* too far-removed and conceptual
even to be defined by cloud. He stroked her. She stirred
in her veil of slumber—when was the last time
anyone "slumbered," except in a poem?—but didn't wake.
Not that he wanted to wake her: only to stay
in contact with this singular, corporeal thing they'd made
of themselves amid the chenille and gas heat of the room.
It would be night soon. It would be dusk, and then
the dreamy, let's say the oneiric, nighttime.
Macrobiotic would come into being, *fractal, rock-and-roll.*
The first reported use of *twofer, LP, fax* is 1948.
Spelunker, 1946, and *cybernetics, TV, vitamin B-12* were
newfangled, still as if with the glister
of someone's original utterance on them. Others,
say, the *kit bag* that they'd lazily left open near the radio, as in
"pack up your troubles in your ol' kit bag and smile,
darn you, smile"—were even now
half-insubstantial, like a remnant
foxfire glimmering richly over a mound of verbal mulch.
Wingding, riffraff, tittle-tattle: holding even. I'm not saying
vocabulary is people, or anything easily
equational like that—although surely
we've all known a generation going *naught* and *o'er* and *nary*
that disappeared with its language. How
was the pulse of *boogie-woogie* doing? *demesne? lapsarian?*
He looked out the window—as solid by now with darkness

as a tile trivet. Obsidian. Impenetrable.
He looked *at* it—or *through* it—or looked crystal-ball-like *into* it
at himself, and tried to practice things he'd been wanting to say.
Outside, in an invisible ripple, *eleemosynary* faded
further from the fundament of human use—and *farrier*
and *haberdasher* and *lyre* and *tocsin* and *arras* and *yore.*
When was the last time a liar dissembled, the cressets were lit,
the nefarious were vilified? My father said "Albert"
—that was the name they'd decided on, for a boy. He breathed it
into the night, into the turning invisible
bingo drum of give-and-take out there, where *radar* was new
and dynastic, and *transistor* was equally sturdy,
and *aerosporin,* and the brave new world of *Xerox* and *laser* and *virtual reality*
held initiating breath in abeyance, somewhere
yonder in future time. "Albert"—it had been his father's name.
My mother opened her eyes now, she was sprawled in a daringly brief,
but sensibly flannel, nightie—exactly
under the ceiling fan, that turned like the oars of rowers
who keep circling over some fabulous discovery below.
That's what my father thought: it was fabulous! *They*
were fabulous! And he was terrified,
too; he knew that over the dark hills in the dark night,
varlets waited, and scurrilous knaves, and goons and racketeers,
he knew the darkness spewed forth villainy and predation the way
a spoiled cheese frothed maggots—after all,
he'd searched out bodies in the coal mine
with a thin wood lathe they'd issued him for feeling through
the seepage, and he'd lounged around the poolrooms
where the ward boss and his thick, pomaded cronies
held their shabby court. By this, and by the other signs
a body ages into itself, he understood the emptiness
in everything, he understood it long before
neutrino and *pulsar* and *chaos theory* would be
the current buzz, and simply standing there

in his half-price Florsheim wingtip brogues he'd polished
to an onyx shine, he understood a man and a woman
clatter for the casual amusement of the gods
like pea gravel flung in an oil drum. All this,
and a sense of grandiosity, of flame and aching sweetness
in the coils of him, and of the Milky Way he'd touched increasingly
alive in her skin . . . all this, and more, was asking him, now,
to be brought into speech, on May 1, 1947,
at Indian Lodge State Park. He swallowed,
and was silent, and shook, until she saw
and asked what was the matter.
He didn't have the words.

The Poem of the Praises

Tho' always unmarried I have had six children.
—WALT WHITMAN

No plausible claimant has ever come forward.
—JUSTIN KAPLAN

My name isn't Lucius; I never grew up
to own the mill down at Spiritwood, where the falls makes the river a blue leg
slipping into the long white laces of a *danseuse;*
where the marl pit is, and the radiant amber and ember-red wildflowers
like powers, thrones and dominions putting on bearable form; I
never consolidated with Midas Mill Distribution, and contracted
later with Yancy Hobbs for the stream of half-price darkie sackers,
and later still negotiated the first use of the Edison illuminatory bulbs
in a three-county area; and one day I didn't think of all the days,
and run into the meadow rubbing my face in the faces of flowers
like a rooting swine until someone came to speak carefully to me and carry
    me home.
   My name isn't Rebecca; I never bore three children,
of which Matthew died of the yellow phlegm while still at my nipple,
but Columbine is a poetess of renown and my sweet Lionel Alexander
is the governor's aide; I didn't enter Henry's study
while he was at cards, and open the book of that jackanapes rascal
Darwin as Henry referred to him, and finish the book, and form
my own opinions; I didn't color my conversation with these
while serving the tea, for years, a deep brown veritable
Ganges of tea, and its steamy, pervasive weather; I never
bled, at my "time"; I never crocheted; I never rode Heat Lightnin'.
   My name isn't Nathan Lee; I never gave up
seminary studies for astronomy—and that way traded heaven
for the sky; I never took as a lover the famous but stumbledrunk
opera tenor whose name I cannot here divulge, though he
and I like the stars were of the same mold and burning in affinity; and
at night in the observatory we never disported and wondered which

of the glass—the telescope lens leading high or the wine decanter going
increasingly low—could take a man farthest.

My name isn't Patience; I wasn't a stillbirth; I
wasn't even a stillbirth.

My name isn't Hamilton; and I was never ten; I never
gobbled Grampa's Ladies Church League First Prize watermelon
entirely on the Fourth of July; and ran to the creek, to wash off; and
ran, I was as slick as a seed, and ran, past the burnt knoll, to the fields
where a mower whipped round at the charge of a wasp and his scythe
neatly severed my windpipe.

My name isn't Maysie; I wasn't released
at age eighteen from the orphanage, to be a kerchiefed gypsy phrenologist
traveling with my monkey (Kip) and my body in bangles and taffeta,
a life of coins and kisses I would never trade to be a Queen; and
all the better for seeking out clues of my parentage, here
in a hedgerow, there in the Chinese tea, wherever; I didn't find
my mother, a lovely colored woman the shade of a fawn's far underbelly,
of high rank in a Boston philanthropic society
dedicated to aiding her people, she had a room in a house
done up in sheaves of pressed African flowers and Mexican crucifixes,
and had that same excitement in her bones; I didn't find
my father, and who knows how many others' father, I didn't
approach an open window at dusk in that battlemarked slattern
of a house on Mickle Street, no; and if it happened, and
it didn't, I was thirty-six by then and he was ancient and ageless;
a candle was lit; he was writing; the hat he kept on was a crumpled
gray, the soft and shapeless gray of a dray-nag's muzzle,
his beard was that very color bleached by a shade; but the vase
was a fire of pinks and tiger lilies; he looked up from the page;
he didn't really see me, I could tell his eyes were still filled
with the page; and yet they said to me, *you are my child;* not
that it happened, it didn't; I left; a steady
current of people filled the street, alive and loud; his
eyes might have said it with just as much claim
to a hundred of them, in May, in Camden, New Jersey, in 1885.

———————

And now we have read the books they write about our father,
singing his praises. This is the phrase they use: "singing his praises."
We, who never existed enough in his life, have read the singing
of the praises that never existed enough in his life, and now
from where we abide in the spaces between things touching, we
would like to sing his praises too. An antimatter chorus.
We would like to praise his words, they are so comely
in acceptance of the world with all of its rank perfume that sticks
in the creases and glazes over by morning, his words
that took the speech of horse-car conductors and walkup girls and
gave it the indigo-iridescent louse-ridden cosmos-connoitering
wings it deserves. We praise the ink of his words, it
is blacker and deeper than outer space though it fits in its
6-oz. crystal. And we praise the squid, that king
of all insomnia—whose ink glands mean perpetual night
is a living thing, tucked in its body. That king of diversion,
whose ink is a dummyself hanging credibly sized and shaped
in the waters—guardianangel-, golem-, doppelgänger-ink.
(And wasn't our father's ink his public being?) And
especially we praise the squid of the deep, we mean the *deep*,
where the waters are black and ink would be useless, but its
is a luminous cloud, a waft of bright light, a lamé.
(And wasn't our father's? Yes—wasn't our father's?) Now
a dozen squid are folded over a clothesline while the fishers finish
stacking their gear. We praise their knuckles a day's work's
rubbed dull garnet. We praise the air of the Greek islands over them
and in them, it has more dead than the air of some other places and
more honorable dead (we've seen our father open
Homer; marbled paper should be praised, and the raised
hubs of leatherbound spines). For every death filling the air, the lungs
have one accommodating alveólus, and this is efficient, fitting
synergy and cycling, so we praise the human body, every subatomic
pokerchip in the vast halls of its house rules. We

can never sing praises too many. Of even a rhizome, a protein,
one bulbette of roe. We have been waiting
in the null-spaces, here in the Byways of Possible Combination
one pi-meson wide, and we want to tell you those spaces are nothing
but genesis song. Sing with us. Simply be silent and
hear yourself sing. We are going to praise the almost-nothing
colors of malt and barley, in their barrels next to the dried green peas
and salt cod. We are going to sing for every string of sudden stiffening
below a nipple that flies it like a kite, for every wire
in a radio that's carried the news of murder in alternation
with the lyrics of love (doo-*wah*), for the life of the bottom-quark
(in trillionths of a second) and the life of the tortoise whose shell
time buffs to lustre its emerald burls over generations of men,
we're going to sing these praises and nothing can stop us, please
join in, we're going to sing of the perfect angle the beak of the
bluetit makes in territorial ardor, of the chipped hand
of a satyr on a bisque Pompeian vase, then of the chipped foot
of the maiden posed in flight, and how the signalman who's motioning
a jetliner into its bay is an eloquent stylized da Vinciesque figure
deserving of place in a pottery frieze for future archeological tweezers,
and of the moon, and of the nematode, and of the star-nosed mole,
and of the rumble of the moving van, and of the flash of a knife that
flashes other knives into the glare like one fish flicking
a whole silver school on its axis, and of a single scale in that school
distributing light's Newtonian range, of spare change
jiving in a pocket like an *a cappella* group in a basement club, the notes
they hit, and of the rose, and of the word *rose,*
and of the streetmarket bowl of roses on his writing-table this
otherwise grimed-over day in the late spring on Mickle Street, the book
he's writing, the room around a book or even a single poem
that's through now though the song itself, the cellsong
and the sunspotsong, is never through, and
we will sing the praises of you
and you will sing the praises of us, too.

Powers

Whizzer, The Top, Phantasmo. . . . They come back sometimes,
now that my father comes back
sometimes. With their lightningbolts sewn
the size of dinner utensils across their chests, with their capes
rayed out, with their blue lamé boots. And he . . . ? It's
hazy, usually; he's a part of that haze. It talcs
his early-morning stubble, it muffles the worry
love so often set like candles in his eyes. And: "Albie . . ." / then
that smile meant kindly, but also to say it came from some source
wiser than mine / ". . . all this reading is fine. But there's a
real world." It wasn't The Streak. It wasn't Mistress Miracle.
With their antigravity belts, their bellcurve muscles.
Night. One lamp. While he read every scrap of fiscal scribble
that said the rent couldn't be met, and in the darkness
tried to fight that vague opponent with every poor
persuasive scrappy peddler's stratagem he had, I read
by flashlight under the covers: City Hall was being burgled
of its Gems of the World display, and Captain Invincible faced
a Mineral Ray (that already turned two bank guards and a porter
into clumsily rendered crystalline statues) jauntily,
his wisecracks by themselves could make a "mobster" or
that dreaded gorillaish creature in a double-breasted suit,
a mobster's "goon," collapse in the ultimate cowardly self-exposure
of "crooks" and "scoundrels" everywhere. The Dynamo
could will himself into a wielder of electrical jolts, and even
invaders from Alpha-10 were vanquished. Smasheroo's
special power was fists "with the force of entire armies."
Flamegirl was . . . well, flames. And flying,
almost all of them, blazoned on sky—a banner, an imperative
above our muddling lunch-and-shrubbery days.
With their "secret identities": Spectral Boy, who looks like someone's
winter breath (and so can enter "criminal hideouts" through keyholes,
etc.) is "in reality" Matt Poindexter, polo-playing dandy;
The Silver Comet, whose speed is legendary and leaves

small silver smudges on the page as he near-invisibly zips by, is
ironically wheelchair-bound and Army-rejected
high school student and chemistry ace Lane Barker;
The Rocket Avenger parks cars; Celestia is a bosomy
ill-paid secretary. It could happen—couldn't it?—
to me: the thick clouds part as neat as prom-night hair
and a nacreous flask of Planet Nineteen's "wizard elixir" be
beamed down to my bedside: I would wake reciting
a Pledge Against Evil, and set to work designing whatever
emerald star or halo'd eye would be incised on my visor, it
could happen, right?—I wasn't Me but
an inchoate One of Them. With their Wave Transmitter Wristlets,
with their wands, their auras, their cowls. The Insect Master.
Blockbuster. Astro Man. Miss Mystery. Gold Bolt. Solaris. . . .
They come back to me now, they ring the bedroom air sometimes
like midges at the one watt of my consciousness, and sleep
is entered with this faint token of sentinel benignity upon me.
Maybe because sleep also
isn't what my father called the "real world." And
he . . . ? Dead
now, with his stone, his annual candle, my father is
also a fiction. And so he appears
with their right to appear, from the kingdom of the impossible,
he appears in their midst, with Doctor Justice,
The Genie, The Leopardess, Meteor Man . . . he steps out
from that powerpacked crowd, he's thrown his factory-outlet jacket
sloppily over his shoulders, it's late, so dark now, and
he's worried about me. Someone may as well be. I'm
in pieces over some new vexation: hopeless in the drizzle,
perhaps, a flashlight clamped abobble in my mouth, and trying to find whatever
damage in the mysterious shrieks and greaseways of an engine
bucked me ditchside in the wee hours; or, with equal befuddlement,
staring damp-eyed at the equally damaged wants and generosities
awhirr in the human heart. And: "Albie . . ." / then that very

gentle yet censorious shake of the head / ". . . how many times
have I told you? Be patient. Never force your tools or materials.
Don't give up." At moments like this, that his blood
pumps through me, his blood is half of what actually made me, seems
as wondrous as Bob Frank "deep in the jungles of Africa"
dying of fever and being saved by—positively
thriving on—a transfusion of mongoose blood.
This was in 1941, in *USA Comics;* Frank returned to New York
as the Whizzer—superfast, in an outfit
the yellow of mariners' slickers. And Triphammer.
Ghost King. The Scarlet Guardian. Eagleman. Magic Scarab. The Wraith.
With their domino masks or their gladiatorial helmets.
The Mighty Elasto. Lady Radiant. Space Devil. Reptile Boy.
With their various signs of legitimacy: their pharaonic rings,
atomic lariats, stun guns, mystic arrows, tridents, with
such amulets as hinge the Earth and Heavens into symbiotic grace.
The Invoker: I remember, he kept two planets at peace. And Hydro-Man:
could turn to water (a dubious strength, I always thought) and once
he conducted a current that fried some miscreant, so rescued
a willowy flibbertigibbet princess. And Panther Woman: her golden claws
and sinuous inky tail were all the good that (successfully) stood between
a scientist "bent on enslaving the world to his crazed whims" and
the populace of "Center City," the first place on his list. And
Whizzer . . . I remember, once, Whizzer was . . . I put down the page.
The knocking. The landlady. He was shaking
in front of her. She filled the door. He had to explain
the doctor cost extra money this month, and he worked all week
on double shifts, he really did, but this one time
we didn't have the rent, we'd be late, he was fighting back crying,
who'd never had to say such a thing before to such a person,
I remember: he said it straight to her face,
the one good pair of suit pants keeping its crease in the closet
cried but he didn't, the long day's wadded-up tissues cried out,
and the bar sign blinking pinkly across the street,

the horseshoes of dust that collect on the house slippers under the bed,
The Little Taxi That Hurried and *Scuffy the Tugboat,* that sorrily stained
lame angelwing of an ironing board, the ashtrays and the aspirin,
everything yielded up its softness then,
the carpet was green and black, the light was ruthless,
his voice never broke and his gaze never shifted although
the universe did, because we would be one week late, there! he said it,
he said it clearly, to her and to everyone,
spent, and heroic.

The World Trade Center

Miss Cherry Harvest of 1954 is savvily bing-bedecked
in snug red mounds of endorsement. Miss Home Hardware
overflows a gray bikini-top (done as a wingnut). Miss
Asbestos Insulation. Miss Kosher Franks. The Aluminum
Siding Queen of 1957. "I was never so completely
cherished, or so much a dispensary of happiness, as that
night distributing candy samples and wearing the fabulous
sack that said REFINED, Miss Sugar Industry always wore. . . ."
In jade: Miss Lawn Fertilizer, a weedy fringe
over her goodies. In gold: Miss Beer of the Year. "I was never
so debased. All night, this gross parade of paunchy gawkers
asking to eat my donuts, or punch the holes out
of my donuts, or use their cream in my donuts, or put their
nuts on my donuts. Thirty years later I hate those people
still. And donuts." Miss New Paper Goods
in marbled corrugation. The Bow-and-Arrow-Fair Queen.
Miss Kitchen Appliances waving like the Pope, though with
a greater sartorial splendor than the Pope's, from her silverized
pedestal at the heart of an eight-foot facsimile blender and
when it's on, she pirouettes in facsimile of its power and speed.
The Cupcake Girl. The Hog By-products Lady of 1962. We
need to love them. If every present moment is only a choice
some moment planted in the past made, then we need to love
these seeds of us if we're to love ourselves. Miss
Railroad Boxcars doing her choo-choo shuffle,
Miss Poultry, Miss Dry Ice. And little foil-petaled
nougat-and-marshmallow come-ons for the kiddies. One
free packet of cleanser. A complimentary photo of yourself
agog in the per-hour arms of Miss Pool-and-Patio Barbeque
while her court of attendant Charcoal Briquettes in their smoky hose
and baggy ash-like swimsuits dances in back. We
need to condemn them. This is the clownshow, this is the horribly
misshaped idea of sex's functions, and this
is the wedding of physical loveliness with commerce, we

contain as possibilities, let bloom sometimes and
need to root out. Miss Midwest Pharmaceuticals Co-op.
Need to refute. To look at us looking at Miss
Electric Handtools Festival looking at herself,
and gag. "I loved the attention, I loved making everyone feel
good, and nobody took it too seriously, it was fun just
like a mardi gras, and why not, I guess you can say,
well, I loved it." Miss Home Furnishings bouncing her bosomy
sponsorship of "Comfort *plus* Affordability" to and fro on the
bosomy couch. Miss Styrofoam. Miss Nuclear Power.
"I'd drag home dangling trains of plastic pretzels
off my fanny, so humiliating, and after a night of stinking drunk
tycoons and their yes-men downing slabs of sirloin and champagne
I'd open the door on my mother feeding on tea and breadcrusts and
I'd slam down my lousy day's wage." Miss Phone of the Future.
Miss Potato Crop of 1959. "A lot of care went into it,
all of the papier-mâché croissants and bagels they sewed on, and all
of the themesong lyrics, which I helped with" (sings:) "I'm the Bakery
Queeeeen with the tender lovin' oven" (now a faraway glazed look
in her eyes:) "I'll
never be that alive again." Miss American Plumbing. Miss
Sporting Goods. We must look at them closely, every
lipsticked mouth a beet-red butterfly quivering over hilly
fields of décolletage. The Lingerie and Sleepwear Queen.
Miss Fireproof Camping Gear. Miss Lumber Exposition. We
must look at them wholly, culture-wide, cross-time, like flowers
in speeded film, so many gauzy tutus being donned and doffed
a day—if these are flowers relegated to another age
by evolution, still we need to preserve their most exquisite sherbet pastels
and their greatest butchercolor striations. Vibrant
delegates of their mute, assigned constituency: wood paneling,
doorknobs, freestone peaches, tractor tires, picnicware.
Miss Pet Food. Miss Circus Equipment. Miss Pickle of
1957, '58, '59, and '60. And where are you now,
Miss-Pickle-handing-out-gherkin-slices, the welter

of seagreen spinach-and-celadon confetti long swept away, and where
are you now, Miss Carpet Shampooing Institute, now what
doting grandmama or business mafiosa have you been
borne to by the rising tide of that yesteryear's foamy bubbles?
I mean it. People die, and these traces remaining
pain us, Miss Furs, Miss Radio Home Repair—where
did your idling taxi finally breeze you afterwards, and
what became of that ten-year-old in the thick black glasses
watching you whisk grotesquely but ineffably away
until his father said "Albert it's late" then they left too
and what's become of the one in his grave and the other becoming
the age of the one, Miss Memory-Up-In-A-Puff,
Miss First-Wet-Kiss-With-Its-Glory-And-Shame, Miss
Lexicon-Of-Woe, Miss Poetry-Firing-Over-The-Skin, Miss Confusion,
Miss Needlepoint Maxims, Miss Funeral Shovel, Miss Semenburst,
Miss Everything, Miss Spider-Of-Blood-In-Its-Bodywide-Web.
We hate you. We're telling you now: we're ashamed,
Miss Amalgamated Canning Concerns, Miss Taxidermy, Miss
Soybean Dealers. Miss Generating Stations with the tiara
of flashing lightbulbs in your platinum hair. Miss Guilt.
Miss Undeniably Breathtaking Tenderness. Miss Knife-and-Gun.
We value you, with incredible passion. Miss Loosened Burnoose
in the Deepening Desert Sunset, Miss Tonsils, Miss Lesbian Love,
Miss Verdigris Glimmering Beautifully On A Hull Though No One Sees It,
Miss Guava Bushelboys of the Tropics, Miss Beef, we want you,
come nearer, be ours, Miss Manmade Fibers, Miss Avocado, Miss
Charge-Built-Up-About-A-Lightning-Rod-Like-A-Vigorous-
Sweetheart-Imagined-Around-The-Dildo, Miss Penance,
Miss Tallow, Miss Fossil, Miss Radium Technology, come
hither, where are you, what's happened to almost everyone
we know, do you remember us from that evening
in the fog we'd bring like intermittent patches of forgetfulness
for the rest of our lives and our seeking, tell us. Do you
miss us? Miss Us. Miss You.

(1990)

147

Complete with Starry Night and Bourbon Shots

Morgan's father will be mailed to her,
they've said in a letter—now that every bequested
dole of his body has been banked away,
the residue in its factory urn will be mailed.
She says Stephanie sometimes wiggles her fingers around
inside *her* father, so the bone chips
clink against the fired clay, and I suggest
the final char of Bob Potts be sealed inside maracas;
"He'd like that," Morgan says, especially if the Texas
Sexoramas used him percussively, his favorite
country-funk group. What she'll really do
this June is scatter him into the air
of Mt. Palomar "because he loved his telescope." Let him
circle and settle, circle, circle and settle.

———————

He also loved his drink, but no one mentions
touring the Pearl Beer plant and surreptitiously adding him
to a vat. The stories are legion,
legend: for instance Bill English of English's Bar
in one clean squeeze deadeyeing a shotglass
off his pate. Though now that's decades gone.
When I met him even his *teeth* were grizzled
—up at the bar surrounded by all of the gleaming
palomino hotpants twenty-year-olds of Austin, Texas;
reading Kipling's *Kim* in the sonic boomboom rock.
I first ate pit-cooked cabrito at one of his parties,
lank and sharp and good. Then doing our names
on the lawn, from the bones—in the light,
and in the easiness, before anything like that seemed symbolic.

———————

The Wild West–style saloon doors of "The Hall of Horns"
(the Brewery's tourist annex) open grandly on its choice, thematic
gawkables: a map of the United States entirely
done from snake rattles; sturdy desks, and chairs, and armoires
completely or near-completely from antlers and hooves.
Also the monstrosities: the Siamese-twin calves
with braided horns, like a Swedish Christmas candle;
the calf with horns that horribly loop forward and enter
its eyesockets. Yes, and there were those Victorian museums
of human residue: the brains of criminals floating like compote,
the gold-cased tibia and jaws of saints. Our wonderment
can seize on something commoner than these, without
diminishing: a skeleton of an owl, and the ribs of its digested
fieldmouse suddenly tumbling out.

———————

Because he loved his telescope . . . he's being flung under
everything above, the whole night sky is called upon
to be his memorial marker. Maybe our obligation
is finding lines from star to star up there:
the new bones of his new, if metaphysical,
existence. Etc., etc.—sky and bones, the stuff
of sonnets. Some people like calling the heavens
star-complected, to some that's "precious" odium. Tastes
differ. My father was heavily lowered into the earth,
is earth by now, is the dry click of ants in the grasses.
Still, I think that they might meet at the horizonline,
Bob Potts and my father. Maybe they're having a metaphysical
quaff right now, remembering how one's son and one's daughter
divorced each other—one of the copious little deaths.

———————

Even microscopic radiolarians have skeletons, and this
alone can jolt our cogitation meters into the red
astonishment zone—what then to make of Morgan's parcel
flying through the mails? Not that comedy, say, or bereavement
are matters of size. And still it's the whale I think of,
washed ashore in 1564 on Nod Thwaite's property:
yes, the whale would do, as a unit for Morgan to measure by.
Thwaite cleaned each stave, and on a brisking autumn day
when his buffing was done, began to charge admission to that osseous
Parthenon. Hundreds took the tour. By night a fire
threw the vaulting into flickery relief. By day they clambered
their midget way among these ruins. I like them mostly
in the skull; as if a whale were dreaming of what it had been
before it turned from that and chose the sea.

———————

I'm sorry, but this gray vase bearing gray debris,
this poof and its stringbean pieces of bone, is no
Bob Potts in his cardigan flecked with pipe shag
holding court at The Cedar Door or Mulligan's.
No. This vase is Nothing; its contents, Nothing.
And Nothing can't be counterbalanced. I'm sorry,
there isn't a fact that can do it, there isn't
a richly glitzed-up fiction in the world, not God,
not no-God, there isn't a memory that means anything
to Nothing. And Morgan says, with a tender shake of her head,
"That man," as if he might have been some feathercrested
platinum-shitting prodigy, "was something."
Even without his eyes he was something, without
his legs, and in the final sour bubble of breathing: something.

———————

Because he loved his telescope . . . he's given away
to that emptiness now, he's sprinkled from a daughter's fingers
into the galaxy pinch by pinch. As physics knows,
and so as endless poems these days repeat, we're all
constructed of the particles of stars. The service
may as well go *dust to dust, and astra to astra.*
Not that any rhetoric really comforts.
Not that any glint of wit or thundered scripture
suffices for long. But since you've asked for a poem,
my ex, my sweet and troubled one, I'll give you this
attempt, complete with starry night and bourbon shots:
Here,
I'm lifting a beer
for Bob Potts.

(Etymologically) "Work Work"

1. Go-Part

Somebody's stuffing excelsior into the penis
of the museum's model aurochs. Somebody's snapping
hundreds of plastic halos into the ruffs of hundreds
of plastic Infants of Prague. Somebody's grading exams.
Somebody's sleeping with the Senator. And
the Senator's promising even more jobs,
more automobile assembly lines, and everything
that means to an edgy electorate. In the kitchen
tonight, my niece is also putting a car together,
out of equal amounts of concentration and crayon.
"This is the go-part here"—the steering wheel,
obviously. Green by black by red, it takes shape.
And orange hubcaps. She's chewing her lip.
She's driven all night by this labor.

2. Shazzut and Tyupat

Eno's fingers seem as fat as those Red Hot Mama sausages
suspended in brine in a gallon jar, but under my hood
they tweeze out various ailing gobs with the finicky quickness
of surgical pincers. He lifts some oily puzzle-piece into the equally
oily light of the shop, as if it might explain
gravity or antimatter. "Shahzzut," he explains to me, "tyupat,"
in the secret fraternal language of auto mechanics. He
sings to himself: no one has ever been so happy. He's
fixing my engine, he sings, he's polishing my shahzzut
as if it's the milktooth of a saint. "Man's work,
whatever its ostensible purpose, is, at any given time,
to sustain the universe." Tribals, "asked the reason
for ceremony X, say that if they missed one year,
cosmos, the world, would collapse." (Richard Grossinger)

3. Elementary

They weren't handed masks, no one knows why.
We're a pile of elements. No one knows why
they weren't handed masks: they were handed
their slop-poles, though. They were handed the poles
and ordered up the inside catwalk, three stories high.
We're a pile of dirt-cheap elements. They
were ordered up the catwalk, they were told to skim
the floating layer of fester off the top of this
three-story drum of by-product animal blood.
They weren't handed masks. The drum was 103 degrees.
And one was found face-up and one face-down,
caked into the fester by noon.
We're a pile of dirt-cheap elements, bought,
and toyed with, then tossed with the rest of the shit.

4. Easy Enough

In his book explaining quantum physics John Gribbin
writes, "It is easy enough for me to say 'Anderson measured
the curvature of particle trails and found positrons';
it was much harder for him to do the work." All week
that mundane phrase has hummed itself inside my head
like an abracadabra, conjuring up my father, alive
again, and in the makeshift basement workroom
each night totaling those colossal rows of figures in his war
against an enemy alliance: Rent and Food and Clothes.
It's easy enough for me to wring the sweet rag of nostalgia,
now that he's cold dark particle trails himself.
It's easy enough to ennoble him down there: adding,
juggling, adding, with the same bit lip
his granddaughter later inherited. *To do the work.*

5. Fred: One

That summer (I was seventeen), the powers of Midwest Mercantile
(Roosevelt Road at Jefferson), seeing my reedy body was no use
shlepping delivery crates, assigned me to Accounting, where
my reedy mind was more disastrous yet: I doubt if four
consecutive numbers fit true. One day in the wake
of a contretemps (with tire jacks and a boot-knife)
at the loading dock, Koenig was canned. Would I
pitch in?—meant tussling one unbudgeable sumo
of a crate in the unbearable sun and stares out there,
and just as I was believing death was preferable,
Fred Nelson (The Black Bull everyone called him) moped
on by, in one hand lifted my butt by my belt *and*
in the other the crate, then carried us both the length of the store
and set us like eggs on the top shelf in Wholesale Drapes.

6. Fred: Two

In August, Teaberry Polk—a sassy lassie
from the mending room, whose rump thumpthumped in walking
like a pair of bongos—married Fred Nelson. I don't know what
he did or didn't do, if anything, but on the honeymoon night she
went at his clothes in the closet with a kitchen knife, wildly first, and
then methodically, until his sharkskin suits and French-cuffed shirts
were a wall of ribbon, like some avant-garde "art project." Frankly,
I wish my old friend D. had been upfront like that
with my old friend Jack; instead, it was a long-drawn mess
of misread cues, with kids and sanctimonious tears: the acrimony,
alimony, lawyermoney scene. As for my own divorce
—I remember my mother shaking her head. "Oh Albert . . ."
knowing the heart too needs to be a practiced economy
". . . love, shmove. You have to *work* at it."

7. A Social Section

Begging for work. (An out-of-work worker.)
Begging—for work. (A beggar, "working.") Hat out trusting
in coins: and yes we like this one, but not his beggar brother
faking blindness; or the one who pushes this perimeter further,
sneaking purses; or the one so far he's past this
social seventh section, out of the frame of understandable
reference almost completely: slinking shadow to shadow
with hatchet-edge glint. The feral labor living beyond
/and off/ the labor of civilized lives. The drive home
and the back door jimmied. The girlygirl
peddling her honeyspread under "the viaduck" and why
the hell not?—her man be drown this last week
in a drum of blood at the rendering works. Somebody
profiting off this, somebody buying the Senator lunch, sssh.

8. Brewing

Of a favorite labor in literature I sing. Of Miss
Amelia Edwards, Londoner, braving savagery, vast sands,
and not a little of the alien dyspepsia, to the mountains
of Abu Simbel, the two Great Temples there
with their friezes and carven Colossi. It's 1883. It's
unthinkably ancient and new and amazing.
Her work crew ably swabs the face of the northernmost Colossus,
Ramses II, restoring its whitened splotches with coffee,
"swarming all over the huge head . . . Reïs Hassan
artistically touching up a gigantic nose
almost as long as himself. Our cook stood aghast.
Never before had he been called upon to provide
for a guest whose mouth measured three-and-one-half feet. . . .
Ramses' appetite for coffee was prodigious."

9. Bonding

What did I understand? Let's say I was five,
let's say it was Friday, he was bringing me
on the collection route, his salesman smile
in place like a sew-on bowling patch.
The dirty life-cycle of any dollar bill—did I know?
The wheedling and two-bit genuflecting he needed me to see
as professional courtesy—did I see? Did it "take,"
this day of belabored bonding? Was I wiser now?
Time's work is continental drift and the red-shift.
"Opera," "racketeering," "telecommunications"
—workworkwork. On the way home he thumbed a spare coin
at the upturned snap-brim hat of the harmonica beggar
we liked. "So play me a czardas." Well, *sort of* a czardas.
Wheeling me under the skeleton-knocking thunder of the rush-hour el.

10. Easy Enough

It's easy enough for me to wring the sweet rag of nostalgia
—not that bucketsful would make a difference now—
or diddle away at the self-set tasks of the poet:
~~planet-shaking~~ skeleton-knocking. "Oh, I've worked *hard*
before this, I once set lobster traps," you always hear
at poetry conventions, "but *nothing's* as difficult as
Selecting The Proper Word!" which is usually just bullshit,
such a bullshit it's not even *real* bullshit, which
weighs down a shovel until the trapezoids scream.
My buddy John once spent a summer hauling cattle,
including hosing the walls of their holding hangar
free of crusted draperies of shit. He did a stint
once in the winter too, and outside of Denver hammered
urine icicles off their pizzle-tips.

11. The Modes

Someone busy lawyering: she's torte, she's court,
she's paving over the planet with paperwork justice.
Someone pretending to play a plastic sax with her twat.
The modes of what we call earning a living are the deepness
of the universe in human compactness, and some of it altogether
free of wages: the tomb of the Prophet at Medina was cleaned of dust
by an elder "celebrated for piety and purity" who was lowered
"through a hole in the roof by cords, with directions to wipe it
with his beard" (Sir Richard Francis Burton). *That's*
the work for me! The work for me, each me believes, is
something like being beamed into a spaceship: instantaneous,
acorporeal. But "even angels," says John Donne,
"who are winged, yet had a ladder to go to heaven
by steps"—so, no, there's never an end to it.

12. An End to It

After he retired, after his trophy shelf of crummy
name-plaqued paperweights for *Sales Leader, 19(blahdeblah)*
was plastic'ed-over to keep it free of dust, my father
took up part-time work at a local Shop-Rite,
for minimum wage. He greeted streams of strangers
at the door with that smile he'd used for Metropolitan Life
for thirty-five years and couldn't retire off his face.
The rent wasn't really a problem now—my sister and I
were self-supporting—but every night he returned
to those heavy ledgers in the basement, they were *this*
world's Torah and bore repeated scrutiny, they were a way
of life, were *his* life. When they weren't, one day, he
closed the Book of Life with a slam the nurse's stethoscope
heard, and let them do as they pleased with his smile.

13. A Survey

My sister in labor. Labor unions.
Labor law. We can never escape it. The body
asleep is a bellows and a steadily hammered forge.
(Herakleitos: "Even sleepers are doing the world's
work, moving it along a little.") Labor-
atory. So "lab work" comes from (etymologically)
"work work." Skyler earned her pay as a med tech
for a few years; in the lab they had a machine
that shook up cans of patients' shit like one of those
automatic paint-can mixers, and one day a can
with too much gas exploded. You can imagine.
The stories! Alice the microbiologist.
Claudia posing nude. Uncle Lou one evening suddenly
losing his left thumb to the bandsaw.

14. Over and Out

Jack calls from Dallas. He says that city's
crime rate is the highest in the country and
last night his ex-wife saw three shadows
slink from a shadow, then enter another shadow,
waiting. Nothing happened—to her,
but this morning the papers are selling a woman's body
chopped in two. "I went to a pawn shop,
I bought a shotgun." It's something like
a 14-gauge or a 22-gauge—I know nothing about these
arsenal terms, to me it's all statistics
from the dark side of the moon. "So that's protection
aplenty?" I venture. He pumps it. My phone fills
with the sound of an Exxon oil tanker cracking in half.
"Oh it'll do the job," he says.

July 23, 1995

For some considerable time there has been a lack
of a general synthesis of ancient Egyptian funerary
practices in a form which would be suitable both for
the general reader and for students of Egyptology. . . .
It was with these problems in mind that this book
was initiated.

—A.J. SPENCER
Death in Ancient Egypt

Deer

The Captain [Chicago Tribune mogul Joseph Patterson] *had many burdens, and one of them was his pampered socialite daughter, Alicia, who in 1942 made up her mind she was darn well going to write a new comic strip for her old man's syndicate. Few strips were released amid noisier fanfare and greater expectation. Few proved to be such monumental disasters so fast.*

Deer was an ancient Egyptian princess who, when professors cracked open her sarcophagus, reawoke in 1940s New York City and proceeded to embark on a thriller-diller of an adventure involving gangsters, Middle Eastern brigands and a lost treasure. She had a boyfriend named Bruce and a pet falcon that had accompanied her on the immortal journey from the grave.

. . . Time *magazine ridiculed it as the worst comic strip in history. Mortified, the mighty Tribune-News organization pulled the plug on "Deer"—in mid-story—after just nine months.*

—FROM JAY MEADER'S CHRONICLE OF THE
TRIBUNE-NEWS COMIC STRIPS,
A Unique American Art: 100 Years of the Funnies

Gumshoes, shamuses, private-eyes, -dicks, ops are terms
in the hardboiled air of 1942. Their hellspawn counterparts
are mobsters, gangsters, Machiavellian Mr. Bigs or simple
gunsels: thugs and goons and their corseted cohorts, molls.
Not that the roles themselves are very different, ever: these
eternal *noir* and boudoir personalities are who a human being *is,*
if structured *in extremis.* In the Thebes of ancient Egypt, too,
as the wheel of flies and the wheel of Ra's resplendent solar travel
roll incessantly: "then did the pilferers descend, with clubs
and many a savage cry; and the guards at the fishery gates
in the name of Pharaoh did rout them." Though the ivy tower
ethereum-minds at State U may exquisitely fuss at the differences

defining Culture A from Culture Z, the wiseguy, streetsmart,
roll-with-the-pummeling-punches, opportunity-savvy,
Real-Life-As-We-Know-It Dwellers amongst us ease through any
interworld transition with nary a doubtful pause
of their one-two piston fists, with nary a flicker of their wary
mascara'd eyes. "She slipped him knockout drops in his hootch
—you know, a mickey finn" becomes, *sans* even the iffiest glitch,
". . . and did stir in his portion of wine the juice of the poppy."
A .45 is a "rod," a "gat," a "chattering roscoe,"
and brass knucks are "bucket dusters," and a blackjack is a "sap," some bubba
sucking a stogie wants to lam it pronto with the boodle
—and this is eminently translatable back-and-forth between
the juke dives sullenly clustered along the Chicago River and those
that hug the Nile. So when Deathless Deer and dreamboat
boyfriend Bruce are licketysplitting through the alleys
with a splinter cult of (evil) Egyptian priests hot on their tail,
the story is instantly and achronally recognizable. "Darling,
here!"—and they duck into the vent-shaft of the hospital

where my mother is a territory further claimed each morning
by the cancer. You could trace her name and her dates
in the thickening residue it's leaving
on the lining of her lungs. "You see how the needle fits? Come look,"
she shows me her IV hookup, "Albert, I know *you,* all right: you'll put it
in a poem." Even now—her final, frail days—she can't stop
helping me. It's 1995, she's seventy-eight, she's dying daily by the handful, and
she's helping *me:* the story of her unassuming and others-enabling,
meritorious life. My mother this pale paste in a garnish
of medical wire. Because we know now that this poem
is an example of Existence as a working synchronasium
—an endlessness of analog-points freefloating in Time, that
sometimes touch—I sit at her bedside direly keening
inside myself a version of an earlier people's litany:

When the shirts wore out, she still saved the buttons
Now she's a quiet moan; the orderlies sometimes hearken, sometimes not
Her husband came, her nipples stiffened into umber thimbles
Now the cigarettes of sixty years are refuse dumps inside her
She saved the buttons, the thread, the crusts of the bread
Now they study her chart, they confer, they say no
When she posed on the lion statue, she was twenty-three and electric
Now she speaks—it's like a voice from a pool of tallow
She'd have saved the hair from her shaved legs if she could, and found a use
Now they bathe her: hosing down an animal in its zoo cage
Every night she rinsed the black gunk from the dog's eyes, gently, patiently
Now she says: "Why won't God take me? Aren't I good enough?"
She saved: it became my college, she saved: my sister's college
She threw away my comic books, she played her nickel poker games
She carried the burning caraway seed of a dream inside her, like anyone
Now nothing will save her: nothing will save her

———————

—meanwhile, *here!* "and they duck into the vent-shaft of the hospital."
Deer of course is amply familiar with that fat, deep-teal noun
of a thing, a duck: she's gorged its dribbling meat, she's
watched them court and squabble in the marshes; having
seen them feed—a *plink!* beneath the surface—this forthrightly simple
Anglolingo verb is no great mystery; the vent-shaft, no great fright
to someone risen from a mummy case. The truth is, at this
chronospatial fold in the continuum, most of everything
has easy correspondence; the Chicago news is full of powermongers
not so different from these renegade, black-magic-practitioner priests
who have stolen ("heisted," *we'd* say, or "lightfingered") a slender phial
of the Elixir of Immortality from its proper, immemorial place
in the Temple of Ra. Deer's stolen it back—but barely; and
this zealous pursuit of Evil hotfooting it after Beauty and Good
is, as we see in the primary colors of the Sunday comics, broken
through the linkstitch of Sequential Time itself. And so
they're here now, in this hallway, in this poem, milieuxed
cartoonily in the kind of drama most of us only know
as a small and day-to-day erosion of the heart. Deer says,
"Our peril is grave. The Vulture Priest himself has chosen
to follow me into your realm." Bruce says, "So *that's* his moniker,
is it? Well, cupcake—he's sporting a mug to match."
The frantic minutes that they spend in stealth eluding this pursuit
go by for us as seven-times-a-week installments of a story
—in the Laundry Room, the Kitchen, and amid fantastic shadows
cast by the Gothic contraptions of Rehab and Hydrotherapy.
"Bruce, they are nearly upon us!" "We'll have to stash
our little item for now, and make our sweet selves scarce."
So: hastily picking through a locker labeled *Supplies,*
"Bruce darling, quickly! Pour it in this!"—"this"

———————

being my mother's next morphine bag. So, in this poem,
the Elixir of Immortality enters her bloodstream. Not that this
has anything viable to do with her suffering *off* of the page
—she bloats in parts and withers in others, and sometimes
seems to whimper at even the weight of the cotton sheet.
But there's that other world—of concepts, and of gods
whose job is representing concepts. Some days, one
corrupted node in my mother the size of an infant's thumbnail
logs in pain enough to vastly outbalance cosmology,
theology, ethics, and all of the gassier -isms. And yet, and ever . . .
there's that other world, of formulae, and liturgical chants . . .

     I saw Anubis walking the halls—Dr. Anubis, they called him here
He wrote his prescriptions: Death, take people as needed
     Anubis walking the halls—the Devourer
His stethoscope drank up every heartbeat it listened to
     I saw Horus, the Hawk, he was scrubbing up
The silhouette of his head on the wall: a medieval surgical scraper
     I saw Nut, whose arching body is the sky
And as the stars came out, the shrieks of the world grew louder
     Thoth the Scribe and rounded Hapy and stringtailed Sekhmet
The gods on break, the gods at cards in the cafeteria
     I don't want to know the stakes for that game
I don't want to know who won, who lost
     I saw Osiris, the Giver of Life, the Breather of Resurrected Life
Some rooms, he stopped at; only some
     Or maybe I didn't see them, but they were there
Like gin in the watermelon: invisible spirits, invisible spirits
     For all of the good the oncologist and his chemo did my mother
Let Anubis walk the halls, let Osiris walk the halls
     Let their always-was and never-ending fight be the explanation

———————

—meanwhile, the life of the body goes on.
Despite all of my poetry hokeypokey-and-parsley, the life
of the body—the cellular fundament, the clock—goes on
until its final electrolytic tick of time.
Decay goes on. The grain-by-grain dissolving
continues as formidably as the bud-by-bud *in utero* accreting-together
did. When my sister visits she asks if my mother believes
she'll be "in heaven—with Daddy." The slyly
fearful/wishful noncommittal answer: "I *hope* so." This,
in a voice like a sliver of soap disappearing in being used.
The following day my sister holds her hand
for hours, while whatever "self" is left of herself, inside of herself,
flutters like a moth in search of an exit,
wearily beats at the cancerous lumpgrown underside of the skin.
There is no magic elixir for this, no out-of-the-empyrean
deific intervention—no, there's only the pissy arguing now
with a clod of a doctor over what he airily calls "pain management"
(too little too slow), and the true heart-sundering moments
when her eyes clear and that twenty-three-year-old life-fixated woman
on the lion statue stares at me from out of this sunken-in form.
That's it. That's everything. That's the whole world today.
And as for Deathless Deer and her beau and their villainous foes . . .
I don't know, and I can't care; but I think I've done
what I wanted to do: they're out of the hospital,
out of the limbo of cancellation in 1942, I see them
turn a corner out of sight ("Scramola this way, kiddo,"
says Bruce) and they're bringing their rollicking caper anew
to the dangerous streets of America. I've given her a second chance.
(It's easy: she's not "really" "alive.") Now I turn back
to my mother's bed on July 23rd 1995.

A Cup

Toward the end, when the pain from the cancer
was a slag heap, was an active, growing termite hill of pain,
my mother asked God to take her out of this world.
For weeks He didn't respond. "Why—aren't I good enough?":
a sentence now like a wire in my heart that won't cool off.
But she kept asking, kept inviting Him into her room
among its stained sheets and its maze of useless tubes.
Her voice was only a dying teakettle on the empty
Siberian steppes. But she was insistent, and genuine.
Even so, it wasn't like the Vegas-wattage invitations

other places sent out. In the temple of Apollo at Argos,
one a month, a virgin, "she-the-chosen," lapped the fresh blood
from a slaughtered lamb, and then the god was in her,
and she prophesied. *And still, my mother continued*
her frail request for His alleviating presence. In the eighth
—the highest—tower of the sanctuary of Bel,
there was a spacious temple, and in it was a great bed,
draped in gold, and here the consort of that Babylonian deity
waited, naked: and then sex was like one two-pronged strike
of lightning through their bodies. *Nonetheless, my mother*

wouldn't halt the whistle in her thick, corroded lungs,
her imploration. Her signal—I'm ready. In a way, the whole
of what we are is either a sign for stop
or welcome. Mauling at his own face with a talismanic
Kodiak paw, and with it scoring lines like wet red staves
across his nipples . . . thus, the shaman—"the beseecher"—
re-creates himself to be *so* fiercely radiant in ritual abasement
that the gods can finally see, and they home in along the beam
he emits, they weight his head with a knowledge of heaven,
and this he brings to his people. *Yes, and even when compared*

to that *dramatic gouging-out of body entranceways,*
my mother persisted in tiny, and sometimes silent, whimpers
saying her preparedness. Some days I'd swear the history
of the planet was nothing but one enormous chorus of voices
singing a clamorous opera by Beckon and Woo. There's a petal
evolved to resemble a cross between a mink stole
and a landing strip, and this entices bees the way the slither
of the stripper's slowly, *slowly* skin-descending zipper
hypnotizes (hip-&-rump-&-thighnotizes) eyes that form
a single syncopated swarm of voyeuristic pleasure

in the darkened theater air. The salt lick calls the deer,
the sugar-water feeder lures the hummingbird. An elder
sits all night at the grave with a platter of grain and embers
—his antenna, his reception dish—and just before the dawn,
a throng of the ancestors whisper their wisdoms. Though the airwaves
must be very jammed, eventually my mother received
her answer. *What was left of her rose out of her,*
a little whuff of steam. And then the nurses tidied up,
as if it were all a matter of crumbs and rumpled napkins.
She'd been heard, I guess. It wasn't like a rajah

in his howdah at the head of a parade of temple elephants
shouting *look! look!* to the skies; still, it sufficed.
I've read a report on various pilgrims to Jerusalem: and
there, where the holy fires are lit, and the word
is the Word, and the grand mosques and the synagogues
send heavenward their pleadings for redemption on a huge cloud
of a thousand accumulated breaths, "an English woman
in the 1930s went daily to the Mountain to welcome
the Lord's return with a nice cup of tea." But
she meant it; she was steeped in it.

!!!The Battle of the Century!!!

the handbills shrill, in searing orange-crimsons. *Any* century.
There will always be these two opponents, circling for a throat-hold.
Call them Plus; and Minus. Call them Void; and Matter
(from before there even *were* "centuries," or any creatures
capable of notching an antler into a lunar calendar).
Sperm; and Ovary. Belief; and Doubt. Thrift; and Bounty.
Steady-state; and Ever-expanding. Curse; and Blessing. *Versus*
is the only engine possible under the physical laws of our universe.
Slyly hip to this most elementary of verities,
the carny barkers are briskly pitching the wonders
of that asterisk-heralded titular battle scheduled for noon
in the center tent, twixt Dragon Sam, the Great Exhaler
of Gouts of Amazing Flame (whose claim
was, he could "conflagrate to the length
of four bull elephants trunk-to-tail," and for a coda
"thrust a white-hot coal inside his fundament, as a suppository"); and
Liquid Dan, the Living Geyser, Fountain of Fantastic Feats
(and who, in fact, could down a hundred mugs, then spout
a grandly arching shower into a silver basin twenty feet away,
"and you will see this stream change into a series of rainbow colors").
Fire; and Water. The ancient story. And so
the tent can barely hold the crowd.
And isn't this—because it's 1800—just a sideshow version
of the clash between the Neptunists and the Vulcanists
at scholarly colloquia? Such contumely
heaped like buckets of rhinoceros dung by stammering men of letters
over one another's anger-reddened heads!
". . . will clearly demonstrate, for all time, and beyond *all skepticism*"
[here, a glare of poison spear-tips at his colleague with the whiskers]
"that the agents of geological change have been—since the Creation,
to the Present Day—the rising and recession of the Waters,
and the work of Rain and of Rivers upon the land.
As to the specious, vapid, dunce-expounded theory

of the primacy of" [forcing out a jackass laugh] "volcanic action
evidenced at all . . ." [*Rah! Rah!* and *Bah! go soak
your beanbrain in your Waters!* and *Tell them, Chauncey!*]
at which, the bewhiskered proponent of Lava and Magma leaps up
to the podium, as heated as his subject, and: "You demonstrate
the intellect of a tuber!" [*Huzzah!* and also some *Boo!* and a single
Let them go at each other with rowboat oars!] "The work,
the immemorial work, of the Fires . . ." "Charlatan!" "Pestilential lout!"
[*and then it all breaks down beneath the weight of assorted professorial
catcalls, thrown tomatoes, hoots, and mooshed-in noses]—*
Scene: A Farmer; and a Cattleman.
Monotheism; and Pantheon. Electric; and Acoustic. There will always be
the bringing forth of Light, from Dark, and then a cosmos built
on that division. There will always be two sixteen-year-old lovers
screwing madly, for the contrast, on top of a grave.
Scene: He's back at the house, from the pasture. There's
this moment in his day—the sheep are tallied-up, and penned;
the silo, locked; the children, safely, even quietly,
at their various indoors busyness—when everything seems to fit
foursquare in its own ordained container, and the sky is the color
a rose is, and the dusk against his face is like another face,
familiar, soft. And then—what does it? a kind of sound?
some reminiscent whiff?—he has an image of the cattle ranchers
surging over everything, and suddenly aversion is a sickness
in his belly, is *a taste,* and hatred roils through his forehead
from a place in him so deeply lodged in Time, there aren't solids yet,
or sentience, and protein wars with protein.

———————

There's nothing. Then there's something. In terms of narrative
this is a rudimentary plot, this is The First Plot. Then
uncountabillion years go by: the story is the same now,
but the players are gods and primal monsters:
"Nothing existed, there was nothing," says the *Popol Vuh,*
"and in this nothing the Creators waited, the Maker,
Tepeu, Gucumatz. They planned the whole creation of everything,
arguing. . . ." Yes: *arguing.* For energy requires
a polarity, define it how you will. When two millennia go by
it's 1939, and *Marvel Mystery Comics* #1 is on the stands
and introduces its credulous adolescent audience to The Human Torch
(whose body is that, essentially, of a Superman flambé;
who hurls his fireballs—like snowballs, see? only fire—
with force enough to burn through steel, and can ensnare
the nefarious crimelords of his day in webs of fire,
or trap them in barrels of fire, etc.; who's solemnly sworn
to use his combustible powers "for justice!"; who can fly, because
"the combined blue and red flames made The Human Torch
lighter than air," a surely physics-revisioning concept) AND . . .
to The Sub-Mariner [as in *marinate,* not *marine*]
(who is really Prince Namor of Atlantis, undulant son
of the subsea royalty, ocean-breather, and commander
of the waves to do his bidding—and by extension, waters
everywhere—as well as his endless subservient conscriptees
of true fish, shellfish, and the occasional ocean-dwelling mammal, and
who can fly because of tiny wings on either heel).
Each premiered in a separate sock-and-pow adventure, of which he was the star,
but unlike calls to unlike, over barriers
of distance and time, with the undeniable inner pull
of gravity or magnetism: Matter; and Antimatter.
Cops; and Robbers. Done; and Meant-to-do. By July of 1940
the two are sparring with a grim, persistent hydro/pyro-inevitability
that so far—with lapses and revivals—has lasted over fifty years.

The ill-tempered Namor could *never* be lazily plotting any aqueous mischief
in his "self-appointed castle, the Statue of Liberty," *without*
The Human Torch, on serendipitous patrol above, besieging him
with fireballs, their snakily prehensile tails of cartoon-red
across the cartoon-blue of the New York skies. "I'll douse you yet,
you raging hothead!"—with a shaking fist. They made a holistic system.
Point; and Counterpoint. This hectoring, from a single issue:
"You flaming fool!" "You water rat!" "This is the end of you,
my little glo-worm!" "Here! I've got you at last, my fine
water-moccasin!" "Fire-bug!" "Water-bug!"—shibboleths
by which they know each other in a world they both find alien
(after all, they're both a super-brand of freak) or almost,
almost like the babytalk of lovers, or the weird, parodic
babytalk of lovers when their lust and loathing grip the same
whipped nerves: "Come on, you big fish!"
"I'm coming, Flame!"—and they're indistinguishable.
Continuing that interrupted sentence from the *Popol Vuh:*
"They planned the whole creation of everything, arguing
each point until their words and thoughts crystallized and became
the same thing." Though I earlier fashioned a comic scene
of rivalrous exchange between the Neptunists and Vulcanists,
the partisans of each were sober men engaged in sober labor
over years of thought, and of scrupulous fieldwork—the nascent labor
by which our comprehensive twentieth-century understanding
of geologic change was formed. To imagine these seasoned scholars, volleying
their invective—! "It is indefensible. . . ."
"Even a child would laugh at such impoverished reasoning. . . ."
Finally, posterity wedded them.

For forty years, my mother lay down at my father's side each night.
Now ten years after his death, we lay her there again.
If "her" is a viable construct, under the circumstances
—or "there." And what about "self"? And "who"? For instance,
to "who" did my sister talk, those several gray and rainy minutes
after the shovelwork was done and the dirt was level?
You can say a dozen different things, and none of them will change
the biochemical fact, the noise we are, the silence we become.
No matter *what* the question is, the real answer
is death. So: 2 + 2 = death. The major export of Fill-in-the-Blank,
and who did I see you with last night, and the number of feet in a mile:
death death death. It's surely the answer to where
we go in sex, the way our concentration
on the body—all of its anthers lit like Vegas,
all of its cellar kitchens spooning up a funky musk-alfredo—
pulses suddenly, and empties us out of our "us,"
out of our "here," and into some free-floating "where"
so atemporal, we could be motes in the sun
of Sumeria, or the dander of the twenty-fifth century
thermaling over the rocketports . . . wherever, it's the unguessable place
—if "place" is a viable construct—that my mother went
as the nurse held her wrist and the tiny molecular fuelpile
finished its countdown. This is vague,
I know, but no worse than the rational alternative
that traditional Science offers us: the swarming
entomology necropolis, then a redistribution
back to the world as combinable protoparticles. Okay,
swell. Or Religion: those delicate human-headed *ba*-birds
hovering over the chests of the recently entombed
in ancient Egyptian art are charming images, equally so
are the willowy ectoplasmic shapes escaping like bouquet
from uncorked wine, in Medieval and Renaissance scenes, but . . . none of it's
going to comfort my niece as she walks from her grandmother's funeral service

dutifully to the waiting limo. None of it means
a thing to the skin she lives in. On the homemade bier they carpentered
for Dragon Sam, a circus-poster artist painted perfect scroll-like flames
around the panels, as a tribute to his famous, florid talent,
but this, as always, is eloquent more of our need for ritual
than it is of our understanding of what's "beyond";
the mourner's Kaddish we said in that afternoon rain, we said
for ourselves. And when it was over?—I lingered
as the limo's windows misted and its engine purred pure silk.
I listened, hard. Two voices fought for attention. "The Emperor
Q'in Shih-hunang-ti was buried with life-size terra-cotta figures
of an army of over 1,400 warriors (including a section of cavalry
with chariots). It's amazing here, in me, where your mother is
now. There is no death here; only the dead, which is different.
Only the bones: the stopped batons. Only the music
written for scarab-shears and petroleum forming. I'm the one weight,
and she's a part of that weight. Look down—" and the other voice
broke in, "Look up." I did: the sun was like a gold yolk
being folded into gray dough. There were morphing shapes,
as usual, whatever I wanted: continents, fantastic beasts,
continual reorganization—"Everyone was here at the first,
and is here at the last," this voice said, "and then here at the first
again: do you understand?" "No, no; look down, and breathe
the nearly carnal richness from between a mushroom's pleats. . . ." And so
they vied this way, they wanted me, as if the shitty penny
of belief that I could offer were the universe's treasure.
—Each, beseeching allegiance.
Earth; and Air.

Radio Pope

Meet and rejoin me, in the pensive Grott

—ALEXANDER POPE

Here come the oddballs, the goofballs, all
of the shuffle-gaited in mien or thought,
pariahs scratching their pants up
into their cracks, the slow and equally
the insolently speedy, here they come, the weirdos
and wackos of our own genetic plasmpool,
lolloping with two left feet and four eyes
over their acreage of spilled drinks,
here they stumblingly come,
the shunned, the ones with the black shades drawn
like high schools during air-raid drill,
so no stray light will give itself away
no matter how zealously it burns in there,
and it burns in there, by night it burns and by day.

———————————

I thought he was fevered, I did, the first time
that I saw it. I was five, and I'd been fevered
with the various speckled ailments of being
three and four and five, and always he'd see me
through these with the mumbled love
and chin-chucks of a clumsy affection I later
learned to think of as a monumental tenderness
some sculptor began in stone but then abandoned.
(Once, I remember, he kissed my cheek pretending
it scalded his lips.) And so I thought: yes, now
he's running a temperature too, *I'll* need
to care for *him*. In minor ways, I cared for him
the next eleven years. Oh but it wasn't a fever; or not
that kind. He'd found another radio.

———————————

Some are lustrously umber-and-ebony tortoiseshell
in that 1950s plastic made to be as deep as La Brea
and withstand howitzer practice. Some are set in cabinets
of walnut as finely tooled as the coffins of oil magnates.
"Gemchest" (1928) is a rich metallic blue,
its grill a mythic Chinese waterbird in diecut silhouette,
while "Snapper" (1950) simulates the look of alligatorskin
in crazed black plastic. Some are leathered. Some
are louvered. You need to know the language.
Breadboards. Beehives. Tombstones. Some are elegantly
peaked cathedrals. Some are chorus girls with lightbulb boobs.
"Globetrotter." "Coronet." "Space Ace." "Egyptica."
"Whisperette." "Transitone." "Duchess." "The Gypsy."
"Rhythm Baby." "Synchrophase-400." "Little Miracle."

He'd found another *radio* . . . *sputter* . . . *crackle* stone
"as Gigantick around as the Head of an Ogre. And I
would very cheerfull deem it a Peruke-stand—but
the Veining at its *temples* and *jaw* is Glittering
to such a degree that it needs be commodated
to my Grotto"—Alexander Pope. The year is 1740.
". . . encrusted," says Peter Quennell, "with Cornish diamonds,
branches of coral, lumps of amethyst, crystals and quartzes,
'fossile' specimens, coloured Brazilian pebbles, knobs of ore. . . ."
Now Pope is dancing on his bandylegs around this
fresh addition, "as rowzed as by a cowslip wine." And
now he lifts it to his ear, then stills: as if his own
excitements were invasive, and could tease some dreamy
murmur out of the lithic core.

Not to mention the "novelties"—a stations-bearing
schooner-in-a-bottle; a plastic wiener slathered-up
in plastic mustard, and blathering FM jazz or AM news; two
versions of an equestrian Hopalong Cassidy (Topper rearing
in one; one, not); an elf; an elephant; a treasure chest
with gold doubloons for dials. . . . His favorite was *so*
plain, though, it resembled a toaster won at bingo,
a silver-sided "Melody-mate" he used to listen to
with her, all lovey-poo, and who-knows-what: I maybe
began as a lull between two 1952 top hits one night.
And what did he *think?*—some mystery pemmican
of a dead wife might be rattling around inside
its snags of tubes and wires, waiting to be moistened back
to life? He collected sixteen of the things.

And Raymond Chase's collection of 1,370 bricks.
"I like bricks and I find bricks fascinating. So I joined a group
of other people who like bricks." They meet twice a year
—the International Brick Collectors Association.
Lovers of the Stinking Rose (for garlicphiles)
has 3,100 members. And the Miniature Book Society
(definition: under three inches high). The Werewolf
Research Center has thirty members, who meet annually
at the WolfCon ("This is a dangerous business,"
Executive Director Stephen Kaplan says). And yes,
the Matchbook Society (1,500 members; Evelyn Hovious owns
five million matchbooks). And the sugar-packet collectors.
Saddlebags. Fishing lures. Marbles. Sand. (*Sand?* Three hundred members.)
And yes, the radio clubs. And yes, and yes, the radio clubs.

In Kansas, in August, the sun is a solvent.
The land peels back like cracked leather, and
around its edges a chaffy, yolky promise of gold
billows into the air. I'd sift the fields for arrowheads
(a steer skull once, I lovingly becrayoned) while
he'd deftly finagle the tag price on some yard-sale
"Listenmaster" or "Never-Static" ever lower.
All the year, we'd weekend down to every Babel of junk
clumped teeteringly between Blackwell and Waco, but
summers opened up the whole of his Rand-McNally foldouts
into enterable adventure—the Road! the Beckon! and
then the inevitable pulling out of the blazing late-day sky
to sit in dinge, in a den of like-minded folk
displaying their beautiful boxes of ghosts.

———————————

Here come the jokers, the jackoffs, the jerks,
the festive wearers of lavishly tasseled fezzes,
here they come, no *more* and no *less*
than the owlishly bespectacled, the labsmocked
and the bibliocentric sent by Fate to weight this otherwise
soapbubble planet in studiousness,
and by their garb, and by their jargon, they know
their own, by nametag and by intricate ritual handshake,
here come Dykes on Bikes and here come Moms Against Bombs,
the clans, the banded-together, and by their squirting
pinky rings and by their prayershawls, similar spirits
hearken and conjoin, and be they rabbis, hey or be they
flingers of cowpies, each seeks mirroring in peerage, don't they now O
reader of poetry, O fellow reader of poetry?

———————————

ca-thunk ca-thunk ca-thunk—in Muncie, Walter Berkoff
froggied out his mouth and imitated the sound
of coconut halves doing radio hoofbeats: *imitation*
imitation hoofbeats, wow! I remember so much. . . .
In Tuscaloosa. Sheboygan. The floor is linoleum
under "throw rugs." The mood is frivolous but the room is
dim, as if they need to play at being illicit, as if
they need to pass their radios around the room like
samizdat. Conspiratorial. Hunted. One (well, twelve
or so) of a kind. I'd be the only child and, most times,
the only girl in a world of a dozen sweet and
stogie-smokin' men. The singlest thing inside a scene
of singularity, I'd waken on a ledge of seven clunker
radios set in a row. The aroma of fat Havanas.

————————————

"Some Men, like Pictures, are fitter for a corner
than a full Light. . . ." "Solitudinous" in his *Grott,*
amongst "Spars Minerals & Marbles," of course
he came to praise the ways of those
who shared his passion, as well as those who donated it
forms. The Prince of Wales donated six urns.
"A length of Roman ruin from the Reverend Mr. Spence."
"A man not only shews his Taste but Virtue,
in the Choice of such Ornaments . . ." (so) ". . . in this sense,
the Stones may be said to Speak." Red Mundic.
Pieces of the Eruptions from Mount *Vesuvius.*
Brain-stones Snake-stones Blood-stones Flints.
"A fine and very uncommon Petrifaction come from
Okey-hole in *Somersetshire,* from Mr. Bruce."

————————————

because the first
>   of anything is
>   separation
the knife   at the cord   (or
on another level
>   the Expulsion
>   from Eden   one life
>   large)
we meet   we meet
>   in assembly
>   as if to counteract that
severing
>   and the greater
>   one to come

And Cowboys for Christ has 83,000 members.
Even the Brotherhood of Knights of the Black Pudding Tasters
has 2,000. The American Gourd Society: 2,500.
The National Clogging and Hoedown Council claims 846.
Of course the American Fancy Rat and Mouse Association
consists of only 150, but quantity isn't the point
here. In Toronto, in 1972, eight people convene
"to attempt to construct a ghost." For over a year,
eight "sitters" weekly meet and concentrate, creating
"Phillip," who raps on tables or sometimes tilts or
even overturns the tables—this, on call and in front
of credible witnesses. "Phenomena produced
do not seem to result from one individual." No, "they
seem to require the presence of at least four of the group."

Some *never* worked. Some gargled dots of megahertz,
but then a pure effluvium of story or song
—the wireless wonder in all of its warmed-up glory—
warbled forth, and these they'd gather around
like Druids at oracle stones. Or if one fizzled
in the middle, someone pitched in with a credible rendition
of *The Shadow* or *Amos and Andy* or *Lum and Abner.*
Rico Beazley did an amazing Kate Smith. "You have a good face
for radio," goes an old joke, and he had, it glimmered dully
in their circle like a twelve-pound ball of suet, although
his singing loaned it beauty. And some specialized
in Orson Welles; or FDR's "fireside chats"; or
. . . endless minor passions. City-states of individual need
within the confederacy.

—————————

I swear he could spot the sexy hunched-up shoulder
of a Deco "Grantline 502" or a "Tune-about" peeking
one inch out of a nine-foot pile of Chevy axles,
castoff baby carriages, and cans of crusted slop.
My eye got sharpened over time too, like a dull gem
polished endlessly at a lapidarist's wheel until it shone.
We had canteens, a compass . . . darlin', we were
mobilized for radio the way another lesser species might be
all paraphernalia'd for sex or bear. By day
we baked like clay in the sun; or raced long clouds
that brushed the tufted horizon like freight trains. And
by night I'd doze asleep beneath the broadcast moon,
the full blank moon where all of the planet's stations
overlap into a perfect white static.

—————————

Where does it start? Can we say that it starts
in the pre-Australopithecine dark
of the caves, between any two people who "talk" without seeing?
Does it start in 1865?—Maxwell is developing the theory.
In 1887?—Hertz is sending the first waves. Or Marconi
(*'n cheese,* I always thought as a child)?—that's 1899.
But let's say it's 1912 right now and a young man,
David Sarnoff, in a room on Nantucket Island where he works
relaying messages for American Marconi, receives
the impossible news of the White Star liner Titanic. Later:
I have in mind a plan of development which would make radio
a household utility, in the same sense as a piano or a phonograph . . .
What is it about the first-stated burst of a vision that makes us shiver?
. . . the receiver can be designed in the form of a "radio music box". . . .

———————

We were in a diner, sinking our fleet of oyster crackers into the chili,
when he rushed out: two humongous shitkick dogfaced types
were pitching radios out of our backseat into their flatbed.
First he just watched, stunned. But at the tenth he ran
straight at them like a pebble slingshot into a wall. A tooth
was gone and an ear torn by the time I hustled over—I was
eight—and stood in front of him and crossed my arms and told them
"That's my daddy." They stopped. They goggled. They could have
mushed us both, but laughed instead, dusted him off, and marched
us into the diner, treating us royally to apple pie and malts.
A year later, I came home early from school: he was in bed
with a lady, a stranger. "Scramola," he told me. I was hurt; but
it helped, remembering: the vital tenth of those radios, that so
shook him, was a "Melody-mate," one of the ones where my mother's
     ghost lived.

———————

Here come the skinheads, the deadheads, everyone
swastika'd and flaming-skull'd and all-cap tattooed
FUCK SLUTS or possibly DUKES OF SCUM
by razorblade and dimestore ink; their breath stinks
like their boot toes; and their boot toes, like
the blood running out of your ass. Here come the saints,
the pained-and-sunken-cheeked-but-shining,
in their aureoles like fingerprints
left by the late-at-night touch of the Lord Almighty;
solo in their suffering, the saints go marching in,
at last, in a cluster like fresh white bottles of milk.
Here come the Wobblies, the Mugwumps, the Commies,
the lobbyists, the DAR Grand Matron in her silver rinse,
the Kleagle in his eye-holed sheet—preaching at the minions.

Once or twice he slapped me—*hard*. But I was
half-hellacious hundreds of times; and so I figure that more
than evened out. "Sheesh. *You're* a dilly," he'd tell me
after, rubbing cool Noxzema into the sting. They always ask me
now, do I regret my "wayward" childhood? I'll tell you
this: it got damn claustrophobic at those meetings, like being
inside the clammy hold of a body cavity, when suddenly
all of its dental fillings picked up morning farm reports or swing.
A little idiotic, a little . . . "wayward," okay, sure. But I'll say
this, too: I was nine in 1957, I spent my time around
their simple, driven love; and in a nation readying
for serial assassination, breaking of the public trust, and endless
bouts of indignity, rancor, and pigjaw greed, I witnessed
this innocence flowering too, with malice toward none, in the corners.

"The Ostrych will swallow & then Regurg. his Stone
—Obtain one? Also today a handbill—that a *lithophagus*
Soamey Williams will swallow Iron & Flints; & Stones
the smallest of it being the size of a Pigeons Egg, and
in his Stomack you may hear them rattle as if in a Sack"
and then, of course, "—Obtain one?" Pope,
in a letter. Pope, and his network of curiosa fanciers,
gardeners, archeology esotericsts. Toad-stones.
Brindle-stones. Stones from a *(Spewed)* Volcanoe.
Shark-stones. An alabaster Pan. A Gem, I hear it
is from a bird made All of Gems. "Obtain one." Yes,
and in the Old Myths, weren't there stones that talked,
that transmuted metal,
that knew things? Orient coins. Saints' ash. Whyte coal.

Not to mention the ancillary ephemera of every stripe,
like yellowing copies of *Radio News* and *Radio Digest;*
manufacturers' catalogues; a Melvin Purvis
Secret Service Agent Scarab Ring in its chintzy shimmer. . . .
Such small scraps, for such large longing! In
Des Moines, on my eleventh birthday (I remember:
Ray and Jeri Wexler had frosted and candled a gutted
"Super Sound"), Dick Ortle treated us (once
again) to his sincere rendition of Veronica
"Big Band" Donahue's "Sorry Blues" as three big
trucker-looking collectors wept, at that voice
as clear as a thirteenth-century highlands stream. I cried too, not
at the beauty so much, but at how *important* it was
to him, out of all the world. Now *that* was sad.

They concentrate; the air gets densed; then . . . *rap* / and
rap / and "Phillip" "exists" or doesn't "exist," depending
on your philosophic stance and if you aren't sure,
the GRS (Ghost Research Society) *is* (or isn't, but isn't
with an openness) as well as the Society
for the Systematic Documentation of Paranormal Experiments,
the Psychic Science International Special Interest Group,
the MetaScience Foundation, the Psychic Detective Bureau,
or PROTEUS (Project to Research Objects,
Theories, Extraterrestrials and Unusual Sightings), all
of which are concentrating, as much as the accordion collectors
and aficionados of windmills or thimbles or striptease are,
and the air gets densed with group will, and whatever "is"
or "isn't" out there, rouses itself, and responds.

———————

"Lissome" : did I say that I was "lissome"? I was
butter—I was butter *on fire*—desiring being "lissome,"
a term I'd read in the pages of *Radio Romance*. There was a boy
in Fort Smith, Arkansas, whose wiffled grin and man's hands
made my skin leap up like a crowd in a burning theater,
though the crowd didn't *want* to leave—it *liked* this burning,
oh very much. *That* was a month! That was a gala month
in the milo at night—and then I was on the road again with The Radio Pope
my Dad, and my love my true love was a blue electron
spinning in our rearview mirror. I *raged*. On my eleventh
birthday fat Dick Ortle sang "Sorry Blues."
On my fifteenth birthday Dick Ortle was *still* singing
"Sorry Blues." They were dedicated to sameness,
and I wasn't the same. I was "lissome" and "lorn."

———————

X happened; Y happened; then, incredibly,
C happened!—all of it, done, and gone, and completely
sacrosanct from the besmirchy touch of the present.
In fact, the past is perfect. Roughly lived
until it's a tatter stinking with use, the past is still
the paradigmatic virgin. We turn our faces its way
with 10,000 forms of amazement. Now a man
is reading a scholarly work on Alexander Pope
(200 years ago—more!) who's in his garden fondly contemplating
his antique urns and statuary relics
—perfect. Even ruined, they're perfect. He fusses
with their placement, cants his wig at a rakish angle,
whistles, fusses, fusses, whistles. Ah—especially
ruined and forever ruined—perfect!

———————

"Jeepers creepers." "Geez Louise." In a long-outmoded
Magnavox model, somebody's saying "banana oil" or "daddy-o,"
and blowing rings from a Chesterfield, driving a new DeSoto.
The brio of uniformed Western Union boys
on their zip-by bikes. The *shish* of pinochle dealed.
Sousaphones. Brogans. Stove-heated curling irons.
This radio is a crate, is a shipment
of diner-counter mustard pots (with those small wooden oars
to trowel it thick, and a notch in the lid for the oar).
A porkpie hat. A watch-and-fob. Resort marimba music
punctuates the darkness over the moonlit lake.
It's anytime, it's once-upon-a-time. "Bunk,
brother—don't feed me that hooey!" And later:
"Not there. *There.*"—in a softer voice.

———————

This happened in Terre Haute, on August 16. I was
sixteen too. It happened at a Midwest Old-Time
Radio Collectors Jamboree at Norm and Deedee's house.
Their son-in-law was home and drunk and followed me
out to the car and pushed me down to the gravel and
bunched my skirt up over my waist and punched me
bad, in the belly. I'd been carrying a rare vacuum tube
that shattered, and I raked its jagged glass edge
over his face, and ran. I was safe back in the house.
And where had my father been, my Paladin Daddy who *I*
protected dozens of times? I found him in the basement
slumped like a rag doll over a "Melody-mate," and
never to collect another shred again, in this world.

                    I sold each of the stinking radios.

———————

This is, I think, a fine, a *salient,* place at which to leave him:
Pope is in receipt of a bucketful of *petrifacted ferns,*
they look like molds for the making of faery ladders.
Every spore-hung rung of them, miraculously detailed!
They arrived as a happy gratuity with a linen-wrapped basket
of Jersey shells, a gift from Aaron Hill, and this
confluence of affinities is—as much as the sought-for
specimens themselves—a good reason *the Rhapsode rises up
in my Pip-squeak Carcase today and crows!* Lord Bathurst,
Baron William Digby, Martha Blount . . . his weave
of kindred spirits, ever tighter, ever more fantastickall. Yes, this
is a fitting place to leave him, jigging with meticulous steps
around the bucket, composing a letter of thanks in his head
. . . *which I have found most grottofying . . .*

———————

The Bauergoths from Kokomo showed up, and
Eddie "Transistor" Frink, and Tito Stein who
cracked his knuckles annoyingly during the sermon part.
Me?—I was calm, and catered-to, and didn't need
convincing by the pastor's sappy parables: my whole life
I'd been taught that the juices of human existence
swim the air as wavelengths, so if *that's* what he intended
I was preconvinced. And I was busy imagining a future
of floral kitchen curtains and boys. Good-bye
to the highway! Good-bye to the back rooms stacked with trash!
I lived with cousins then, but that's another story. There
were many stories, many boys, and many nights with them, and more
than once a dream: something, I don't know what, but something
is left behind on a highway and I'm frantic at the loss.

———————

The stars: incendiary. The stars: far back in time.
Our lives on earth: a matter of heavy daily plodding.
Our loves: a matter of daily plodding. Sometimes
our loves: incendiary. The stars: a fire
sent through time. Our dreams: a matter of earth
and a matter of stars, in mixture. Our loves:
as if propelled by burning dreams far back in time.
The stars: a fire sent through time, and turned to language
on earth, by radiotelescopes. Our lives on earth:
receivers. The stars: transmission devices. The burning: a message
carried through our heavy daily plodding. I imagine
two people wake, in the caves. They can't see
one another. They "talk": the stars,
the dreams, the dailiness, the love. And it begins there.

———————

MEMO

To: M
From: Sam
Re: Your positioning A.a.
     Truly—*Australopithecus afarensis* is
simply your best work yet! They look
as if they might grumble, and snap off some
unwary 10-year-old's finger at any moment.
T. says choosing an arm-linked male and female
gives an impression blah blah by the fossil record but he's
a dried-up fuck of a fossil himself, and speaking
of pairing: I'm arriving at the symposium
by 5 o'clock, and bringing hunger for dinner and you.

I delivered a powerhouse paper at the colloquium
in Rome, if over 200 requests for offprints are a gauge
(and, later, an NEH grant) though the first loose wave
of applause was as thrilling as anything. Let me explain:
my work is constructing museum diorama models
figured as accurately as possible from paleontology
evidence. For prehistoric reconstruction, interpretation
is necessary (were there eyebrows? no one knows) and
wearying. The work is lonely. Accuracy (say, capillaries
in eyeballs) is exacting. Twice a year we meet, for papers
and for parties. Internationally belaureled dioramacists
jet in from every major scholarly nook on the globe. We call ourselves
The Institute; by what frayed thread are we kept
from being one of my father's radio clubs?

```
        d found another radi
                        time is entropy
                fields for arrowhea        is
breakage
                alabaster Pan              is
        recombina
marimba             sputter
        crazy                   frag
                crackle
ments get through
                        "Sorry Bl
the receiver can be designed in the form of
        hunger for                        utter
                                radio
```

_____

I'm not saying this really happened.
It happened, though. I was alone
in the lab. You have to understand: I was surrounded
by faces hanging from the beams like wheels of cheese
in a dim-lit European grocery. Grabby Sam
who *is* a dear had made me a gift of a human skull
I'd set as appropriate decoration on my desk, and
in a weird and idle mood I started doodling on it,
coloring it—with crayons, you know? . . . and then everything
flooded me, *everything,* the fields, the meetings, the smell
of the Buick's upholstery, and a voice streamed out of the skull.
My father's voice I hadn't heard for sixteen years. And
it was blurred, but if I concentrated, I could tune it
clearer. *Lost it* . . . (concentrating) . . . *Here it comes.* . . .

_____

Here come the covens,
the enclaves, congregations, unions,
packs, gangs, rallies and leagues,
the amalgamated thises-and-thatses,
those who measure their cohesiveness in angstroms,
those who reckon it by the thundering trumps of the seraphs themselves,
here come the amassed abused, here come the schools
of their tormentors, here come the encongressed
and societal, the loyal orders, the camps and committees
of every displayable suasion, both the bug-eyed and the blind,
here come Aladdin Knights of the Mystic Light
(1,000 listed), "dealers, collectors and users" (it *says*
"users") "of Aladdin lamps" as if enough might
rub, and wish, and so quicken the cold and lifeless.

————————

It only happened that once. I'm not insisting
you believe me. Everything quieted. He said my name.
He said my mother's name. He said,
in intermittent stretches of reception clarity, many things
and most of them cliché—*It doesn't stop, it thins
but it doesn't stop,* I remember. (Is this
what I *wanted* to hear, so heard?) It doesn't stop,
although it doesn't exactly continue: it's more
like a joining. He told me the hell with the pouters and naysayers,
go ahead, love it up, tussle it, rumple its skin
while you've *got* it! That's what he said, in a voice like a powder.
He said he was waiting—not "him," not "waiting," exactly. More
like a joining—an organization, a worldwide organization, and
one day I'd join it too, he said. There wasn't any rush though.

————————

The Rising Place
for the Dough

selected poems (of one page) 1983–2005: II

12th-Century Chinese Painting
with a Few Dozen Seal Imprints Across It

The tea has given way to plum wine,
and still they're talking, animated down to points
of fire deep in their pupils—two scholars. "Look,"
one motions at what's outside the sliding panels: landscape
where the purling of river leads to foothills,
then to the tree-frowzed mountains themselves, and
up from there. . . . The sky
has opened. Out of it, as large as temple gongs
yet floating as easily as snowflakes, pour
transistor circuits, maps of topiaries, cattle brands,
IUDs, the floorplans of stockades, cartouches,
hibachi grills, lace doilywork, horsecollars,
laboratory mouse-mazes, brain-impressions, all of it
sketching the air like a show of translucent
kites in blacks and reds, a few beginning
("Look, *there* . . .") to snag in the treeline, or hover
above the whorling bunched rush of a riverbend. . . .
"You see?" says one with a shrug and eloquent
tenting-up of his eyebrows, "You *see?*"—he's
too polite to declaim it in words.
They've been arguing if The Other World exists.

The Invisible World

A little bit of mass is worth an awful lot of energy. For example, one gram of matter, converted into electricity, could power an entire city for several days.

—PAUL DAVIES

This might explain ghosts, or ESP: the stuff of us is worth more
in the invisible world, as a source of fuel. It surely explains
why the universe is a field of here-then-not-here laws
and nano-warp and slant, half-state existences that's larger
than all of its solids combined; and why our moods
are a turbulent current the body can rarely swim against.
Even in sleep, the bonds in the brain are fire the size
of a galaxy's suns. Even in death, the brain is not a stone:
it hums in the earth, it does its ceaseless isometrics in the bellies
of dismantler-beetles. A *stone* is not a stone: it's the moon;
or at least it's a moon-equivalency, in its subatomic potential.
And the moon?—is seducing the ocean into cresting higher,
out of itself. And the land?—it could explode from the ocean's
teasing it, for night after night, with the foam hem of her flamenco dress.

An Explanation

They say this really happened, in the Church of Eternal Light:
a penitent dropped to the floor wearing nothing but sweat, she
spasmed like some snake on an electrified wire, she uttered
angel eldestspeech, and then she disappeared—they mean
totally, and at once. First the entire tarpaper room gave a shudder,
and then she disappeared—at once, and totally.
Nobody understands it. Well,
maybe I understand it. Once, in eighth grade, Denton Nashbell
had an epileptic seizure. Mrs. Modderhock squatted
above where he flapped like something half a person
half a pennant, she was pressing a filthy spoon to his tongue.
I've remembered him twenty-five years now. And—that woman? she
was the universe's tongue the universe
swallowed. That's as good an explanation as any.
Once, in sleep, you started a dream soliloquy,
the grammar of which is snow on fire, the words are
neuron-scrawl, are words the elements sing to their molecules. . . .
—I threw myself across you.
It wasn't sex this time. I just wanted to keep you
beside me, in this world.

The Initial Published Discovery

In another poem, I chronicled my descent
to a level of shadow and intermittent fiery light.
It was a world of emptied faces—almost sucked out,
as if eggs the weasels got at had been turned to faces.
Wanderers and their hunched-up stalkers,
mutterers to angry private gods . . . that's who I found
down there. I was talking about
our dream life—our subconscious—but a friend said
that she thought I'd meant the New York subway system,
ha ha. Nonetheless, I give to the neurobiologists
this first identification of a mechanism, somewhere in the brain,
I call "the turnstile." It allows our passage
into the depths. And what's the morning
—what's the clear new start—if not our exiting
back into this life through the same round gate?

Vessels

(Alexander von Humboldt)

In Caracas, Venezuela, in 1800, one can listen
to "the latest modern music"—Mozart, Haydn—
over sweetened ice, and Humboldt does, but once the rainy season
ends, he's off for the obdurate forests of the Orinoco,
and all of their grim amazements: streaming lengths
of anaconda, surly crocodiles, and vampire bats that hover
like nightmare hummingbirds over his hammock . . . yes,
but the greatest jawgape amazement is surely a human,
Señor del Pozo of Calabozo (a dusty
cattle-trading station), who, with no guide
but the treatise on electricity in Benjamin Franklin's *Memoirs,*
"built an electrical apparatus almost as good as the most
advanced design in the laboratories of Europe." Marvels
so often select unlikely vessels. Any alive enough

soirée should offer the example of a troll-like shnook on the arm
of a luscious hotchahotcha beauty, or the former diner waitress
with her petro-sheik amour . . . and then the tsking disbelief
of the envious rest of us. But shouldn't we *know?*
When God / His Son / His Virgin Wife decide
on a Message of Ultimate Importance for All of Mankind,
do They relay this through a group of visited
presidents, sultans, queens, and similar potentates?
Do comets spell it out, over Rio, Tokyo, mid-Manhattan?
You know. One day in a one-burro scatter of ant-swarmed shacks
in Mexico, or clutch of huts in the Urals, a mute, retarded girl
looks up from the torpor of street dogs to the sky
—and speaks. She's eloquent now with the Word, and the Way,
and the air in her wake is electric.

Some Things

I'm tired of writing about the gods,
those causal winds we snap in.
Tired of reading their signs in the entrails
when the guts themselves, the fat swags
of an animal, are eloquent enough.
And: if-the-universe-is-expanding-what-
is-it-expanding-*into* . . . I'm tired

of all of it, I'm weary of every gasleak
of abstraction. Conscience. Self-determination.
Omniscience. Lassitude. Free will.
The ancient rabbis fasted, prayed
and fasted, finally they were Spirit,
flew through air, *were* air, were air
on fire around His throne, and

still returned to an umber mug
of cabbage soup in the morning.
Checking the goat in the pen; she
birthed the night before, her vulva
one engorged carnation
with paprika-spots of blood. I may
require theophany after too many

things, but for now give me things.
For now, they have the power of liturgy
off a cuneiform tablet—absolute and hard.
The sixth-grade class once left "a thank you note
for Nick at Twin Donut." It goes like this:
We saw the deep fryer, the oil, the kitchen,
the rising place for the dough.

Desire Song

The graspy heart, that lobster of ours that
wants, and wants, and is evolved to lust
for one grain shat by a swallow in flight
as much as the whole packed four-story silo.
There's a cloud across the moon tonight
like the skin boiled milk gets
cooling—slightly blue and slightly wrinkled.
I want the glass of warm milk from my childhood
carried up to the crib by a living Grandma Nettie
with her hair still singed in odor
from the frightening tines of her old-fashioned curler,
yes, and I want the moon
in its entirety, the moon through the windshield
detailing Phyllis's breast for me the first time
it was more than a wish or a centerfold
peeked in private, yes, I want the moth of faint veins
holding her nipple, the coruscations it made
in stiffening, casting complicated shadows within itself
not unlike the moon, which I want,
and that '63 Chevy we parked in, which I want,
and the father who loaned it to me that night,
who I want waiting up for me, walking the planet
instead of being one more battery slipped inside it,
powering the rest of us, who are sweating our sheets
with our wanting. Michael tells me:
in the slammer—call it what you like, the pen,
the hoosegow, the big house, call it shit city—
you want *anything* from outside, and
a used-up tube of lipstick or the one-eyed spaniel's water pan
can hold the same desire a limousine does.
He's seen kneeling men lick cell bars
for the salt a visitor's palm left.
Think of the rib cage . . . think of the lobster
clacking inside its trap.

A Photo of a Lover from
My Junior Year in College

Or the Earth: one half in sun,
one half in darkness.

The planet can be its two selves at once.
Not us; we're either asleep, or awake.

We're either walking over the countless graves,
or in them. Here, or there.

We rarely pay attention to the moment of transition.
Blood, being oxygenated. Love, when it's still just chemicals.

She has one of her arms in an arm of her blouse,
and the other one wonderfully not.

The Rocket Ship

He hasn't thought about it since he was twenty-five,
and—here it is! in a box, in the attic, and still shrill
in its candy-red and deeply mango-yellow 1950s plastic,
carefully molded into the astrodynamic silhouette
of "the future": all those "solaratomic" fins
a spaceship evidently would require in the year 2000.
Now he's fifty-five . . . and, for a minute, as he lifts it
to the window, the air of the attic really does become
the cat's-eye swirl of gases that's the atmosphere of Jupiter,
and then . . . well, *anything* then. Anything antigravity
and faster-than-light. It's based on the one, the "real" one
in the TV show, that had a "radium blaster" on its sleek nose.
This one, too: a sky blue plastic blaster the size of a toothpick.
When he'd thought of it the last time, he was with a woman

—*thirty years ago!*—and running his tongue along
the butter of her thigh when, very gently, but assuredly, she
stopped him with a single finger set against his forehead,
to explain the scar. It was, she said, a surgical scar.
She had cancer. All they could do right now was plant
a kind of "seed" (that was her term), a radiated capsule,
into her leg and hope for the best. For him of course it isn't
a seed: you know, now, his own metaphor of choice. He sees it
taking off, *fooming* through the cosmos of the body,
her body, that easily seems to be worthy of the theorizing
of Einstein and of Hawking; maybe everybody's is.
She died, by the way. There was never anything after
twenty-five for her. But he lifts her out of his memory now,
unwrapping her with something of the quiet awe he felt that night.

Across Town

For the rest of the day, the lover lifts his fingers
to his nostrils and smells her.

Here he is in The Corner Cafe. Her pungency
becomes the redolent steam of his split-pea soup.

Outside: traffic, bleared by the window.
It's winter and the snow is like a second city on top of the city.

It's winter and ice makes walking a dangerous dance.
And even so, the *shul* is filled with old men come to pray.

The Torah gets paraded and they touch it
with their prayershawl fringe, then kiss the fringe.

I've seen them do it: lifting the fringe to their lips,
like bits of bread soaked through with the Glory.

The Two Parts of the Day Are,

first: I'm driving home when BOOMER cuts me off
with a tidily clipped illegal left at Central & Oliver.
The Age of Lizards, the Age of Mammals, and now the Age
of Vanity Plates. AGNESJ appears from out of a cloud
of briquette-gray exhaust, and GRANNY, and KSSMYA.
A blond woman in a T-shirt proclaiming her NATE'S
is piling her car trunk with monogrammed luggage, E;
her keychain flashes out DICK. It's depressing. And

———————

second: Skyler greets me with the news that north
on Woodward, someone rode around the blocks this morning
shooting down people at random—pedestrians,
other drivers, nine in all who won't be coming home today
or ever. He was found with a bomb, an axe, and a beheaded
goose in his backseat. Nine people. Now they're just
the names being grieved in a few raw throats in this city;
on this planet; through the flux called Outer Space. The third

———————

part of the day isn't day at all. It's night; and everywhere,
in the least of its creakings and beetle-jaws,
in the infinite zip of lepton and of quark
through what we like to think is "sky" but is burning and
emptiness, emptiness and burning . . . the night is saying
itself, in its language. I can't sleep. The moon makes silver
lace of my wife's unsheeted shoulder. And: SKYLER, I'm
whispering suddenly, like a fifteen-year-old at the fresh cement

—at the air, at the dark, at the thin lunar light,
at whatever of this world might read me.

Own Recognizable

They bound the foot—they shriveled it like a salted persimmon
first, to specification, then fit it into its slipper.
Alien, to us: there are planets in science fiction more familiar.
And yet they wrote *The white plate is broken, now is the time
of the yellow plate*—of summer, they meant, our own
recognizable summer. And elsewhere they mummified
9,000 temple cats in a burial shaft, and
elsewhere slit the penis skin at puberty and sewed
a jangling bell inside, but everywhere *The seasons turn
like a pot on a wheel, my roebuck, my Nile flower.* I
was watching you sleep. How far were you? If the animal brain
is far, if gender is far, then astrophysics couldn't measure it,
not in human words. You woke, you said *Listen: I had
a dream. We were two birds on one branch, singing.*

The Saga of Stupidity and Wonder

The history of the world could be written
in anything's history: native gourds; meteor rubble;
the capping machine at bottling plant number 7. . . .
I'm convinced of this—how anything,
gripped right and studied long, contains the telescoped
story of everything, the way our protein coding holds
the germ of the lizard we once were. It's so

tempting to start the saga of stupidity and wide-eyed wonder with
us, in bed this morning, waking into another
day of our individual lives and our life together; but
any unit would do. Say . . . oh, say birds. In
1497, in Zurich, the citizens tried and
hanged for sorcery (truly) a rooster
accused of laying an egg. Or then

there's the tale Odoric of Pordenone brought back
from his travels "on the farther side of the sea.
I beheld," he tells us, a man who journeyed
with a faithful cloud of 4,000 partridges following him.
His journey was three days. When he slept, they
gathered like one solid object around him. When he walked,
they were his constant weather: the air was 8,000 wings.

27,000 Miles

These two asleep . . . so indrawn and compact,
like lavish origami animals returned

to slips of paper once again; and then
the paper once again become a string

of pith, a secret that the plant hums to itself. . . .
You see?—so often we envy the grandiose, the way

those small toy things of Leonardo's want to be
the great, air-conquering and miles-eating

living wings
they're modeled on. And bird flight *is*

amazing: simultaneously strength,
escape, caprice: the Arctic tern completes

its trip of nearly *27,000* miles every year;
a swan will frighten bears away

by angry aerial display of flapping wingspan.
But it isn't all flight; they also

fold; and at night on the water or in the eaves
they package their bodies

into their bodies, smaller, and deeply
smaller yet: migrating a similar distance

in the opposite direction.

[Untitled]

Because of their fossils
Leonardo understood the tops of mountains rose into light

from the mangled floor of the sea. How far
have we come every morning, from how deep away,

to dig out from the corners of our eyes
such amber fragments?

The Two Directions

Carlyle had gone to take an initial survey of the neighborhood, to make it, by the act of vision, his own.

—DISCH AND NAYLOR
Neighboring Lives

Lucretius, too, attributes to the eyes the power
of actively extending—sending invisible beams
that grab the world and drag its nonstop images into our heads.
His busy, crisscrossed ancient Roman air
grows more familiar every day, from cell phones
to the SETI signals shooting our good wishes
and coordinates to otherworld receptor dishes we can only
guess at. One could come to think that all
we do is generate an outward radiation. But that would be
wrong, of course. It's as valid to posit our bodies in sleep,
my wife's and mine, as objects being worked upon
by time. I have a picture of an elderly Eskimo woman softening
leather in her mouth—for hours, saliva and tongue—until
its length of difficult grain can be shaped to the use she requires.

There, Too

I'm not the dapper man in the lambswool overcoat.
I'm not the woman unfolding the mail, lost
in a lozenge of light by the vase of roses and ferns.
I'm not the man with the cocky swagger
and fresh dirt under his fingernails.
I'm the triangle—that's right, I'm the triangle

that they make, the way it's made every day
in movies and cheapie self-destructo novels:
steamily, greasily, and I protest this
smutting of my self. I was there

with the square and the circle, originally,
when shape was something pure
and transcendental—long before
the borders-smudging confusion of human affairs.

Whenever you're with another person
—even with who you think of
as *the* other person—I tell you
that the mind and the heart are too bountiful for fidelity,
and I'm there, too.

Civilized Life

She moves like smoky honey, like electric smoky honey, and
if he weren't married he'd beg right now for a taste of it,
he'd flick the old charmola switch to *red hot,* then
the story of crazy, enervating longing could begin; but
he's married. And she?—would be amenable to that
explosive wooing, she likes his grizzled good looks,
she likes his need; but the management frowns on anything
more lingering than a table dance, and so, in a pro forma
set of gestures, she accepts his dollar tip, then shies away.
It might be more exciting writing of their furtive trysts, but
this is a poem called "Civilized Life." She leaves for home
so late, it's early: kids are out on the playground already.
Their wild energies given a shape by the bars of the jungle gym.
Their animal hollering given containment.

The Waltzers

Fire and water. Cat and rat. Snake and duckthing.
"Moongoose. Snake and *mongoose*," said the mother, and the father
stared a slow hole into the ozone layer.
"Let's not forget . . . what? Woman and man!"
—my eighth-grade teacher, unit: Evolution. Although,
as the father said, the Cretinists would be up in arms.
Or Holmes and Moriarty: in each other's arms like waltzers,
down to the rocks at the bottom: getting, at last, each one
to kill the other one. "Creationists,"
the mother corrected; "I *know,* Mrs. OED,
it's a *joke.*" Oil and water. Cat and dog.
Man and whale: inseparable in Melville,
down to the rocks at the bottom. Let's not forget
that Kipling story, about the mongoose
Rikki-tikki-tavi and the snake. "Oh I thought it was
Rin-Tin-Tin," said one, and the other one hooted
in derision until the stars in their black aspic shook
and the sun came up, destroying the stars. And in that story
who caught whom? It doesn't matter,
each one was so caught by his own nature.

The Dating Report

Don calls, to tell me about a woman he's dating.
He likes her—though her psychic therapist says she

drowned in Atlantis. "So many small things push us apart."
His tightass opinion of television . . .   her kids . . .

the first cracks in the city ramparts . . .   panic . . .
grabbing up coins and some earrings . . .

the waters pouring in between.

Branches

A vagina in the center of the pomegranate
Dante Gabriel Rossetti paints in the hand of Jane Morris.
And the pomegranate that holds the name of God
in a cursive swirl of its tissues and seeds.
Those two would be enough to tell us that the world
is not monocular. The woman saying look at this,
meaning the thing. The man saying look at this,
meaning its shadow. And from that,
if conjectural physics is right, the universe branches
into two. Exalting, on the level of cosmology.
On the level of communication across a bed,
it's a dauntingly wearying day. Remember
the linen strip inscribed with a fragment of ancient
Roman poetry? They found it in a mummy,
in a scrim of crackled oil under the chest.
A treasure—rescued from oblivion! To someone, once,
it was rubbish to wad inside an empty heart-case.

Various Ulia

Did we say it out loud? Eventually
we said it. Cancer. Somewhere someone else
said AIDS. But only toward the last,
near the end, when the dying was
the fear—and not the dying's being invited.
For such is the power of utterance.

Susie says that even ten years since the divorce,
she refuses to drive alone at night
—that's when the words come back.

Although the infamous Mercury Theater production
of *The War of the Worlds* (October 30, 1938)
was intended to horrify, still,
"CBS cut the cries of the invading Martians
('Ulia, Ulia, Ulia') as too frightening."

A song comes on; she won't say why, but
she needs to turn off the radio.

Thermodynamics / Sumer

Heave-and-buckle, the furnace warbles its heat up
out the naked living-room window. The new house
shrinks and its occupants shiver; we need drapes.
Not now, this isn't time for anything
thinking accomplishes. You say you saw your sister
leave her grave that way—a wavery and elemental rising

up the dug shaft, and then skyward, as if heaven
and our long approach were a matter of schoolbook
thermodynamics. Maybe. What I know is, your face,
pale at the graveside, turned to clear glass you
half left through—following her out of love,
I imagine—and all week you haven't completely

returned. In this—in death, that is—as in so much
of life, the ancient peoples did it to a literal completion
our subconscious dramas symbolize. Beneath two quilts
and a blanket, I'm reading about the Sumerian
burial pits that Woolley discovered: always,
the royal personage in a stone room, then

the sloping ramp leading down to it, filled
with the bodies of men of the royal guard
and ladies-in-waiting—sixty-seven, in one case—each
with the small metal cup for the poison alongside,
all of them having ritually lain themselves in ordered rows
while the harpist provided theophany music

until her nimble fingers also woozied, cooled, and fell.
It's something I would share with you tonight but you're
all shell; and if part of you isn't, it's somewhere
beyond our describable planet of physical objects
and simple needs. For the length of the stay, for some while at least,
I'll be losing your warmth to that other world.

Swan

Not just as individuals, but also as a couple, they
were so demure . . . no, not "demure" exactly, but a sort
of gracious quietude attended them, and *then*
at the end—and everyone remembers the night of alternating
operatic solos of confession over drinks at The Italian Gardens—
something seized them, something like a sudden lyricism
so demanding of its vessels, that it used them up.
The Greeks of course said the same of the swan: its whole life,
mute; and then that single one-hour flower of fine
coloratura. What's a Geiger counter if not an ear
for how the ticking death-song of uranium echoes faintly
over time? "I heard" the speaker says in a novel of Clifford Simak's
"the tiny singing of the tiny lightbulb and I knew
by the singing that it was on the verge of burning out."

The Way the Novel Functions

In the s-f story you read then dream, a person is
an inch. And so a flower is a monstrous thing,
an insect monstrous more. Out rooting, Unkh
and Titi-bara and seven others of the Tribe were caught defenseless
in the open by a Tiger Wasp—and eight were never found but
Tuska's body was, injected with that waxy stuff
the wasplings eat on hatching: nobody would touch it now,
it wasn't fit for proper Tribal burial and, from the sun,
it swelled to deep sebaceous-yellow in a day.
There's also pleasure here: the wedding night is ritually spent
in a full-blown rose, the couple tussling in that overfolded
tissuey embrace; or simply keeping watch by night,
the ring of fires making ingots of the acorn husks
the rest of the Tribe curls sleeping in. . . . Though
mainly it's fear, it's guardedness and fear, it's every minute
under attack. The Hornets will dive in a pack or by ones.
The Mantis is three-men tall but blends in all too greenly.
It will devour a child with horrible motions of etiquette,
its leg can be used for a saw. And at night, the armor-plated
Stalker Beetles, heavy, yet so quick, their jaws
can slice a throat like aspic. One is breaking
through the slats right now, is gripping you. . . . You
wake. It's day. It's only a day. It's only the common
enormous day to get through, the day with its six
invisible legs and its feelers, the day on your chest.

The Theory of Absolute Forms

It isn't easy to picture an infinite universe,
a star that's traveling through an infinite universe,
but think of how far pain can go in your bone,
in its marrow. —Forever, I think. When Plato
clutched his side and moaned, he knew how this world's
hurt is only the light from its star Generic Hurt.

———————

Say I have a wound like a flamenco beauty's horrible
red camellia set in my flesh. I think the doctor's
whole career has been for this moment. The wound,
my wound, it's only been with me an hour.
His hands are exact. They lift it and dance.
He's been intimate with this wound for years.

Comparative

On TV—a documentary—they were clubbing
a penguin—mute, of course—clubbing it
with only the naked sounds of wood on flesh
—when from the window—the yowl of an alleycat
lifted my skin—a kind of happenstance
ventriloquism

is it "better" for pain to sound like *this?*
—or like *this?*—or like *that?*

and your pain—*your* pain—
is like what?
your pain—
what's good enough?

finally, simile only goes so far—
the stickweed burns as savagely,
as brightly,
as the tulip.

[Untitled]

In science fiction, in a giant glass tube the size of a body,
they freeze a body. On Planet X it thaws. He's alive. One hundred
years have passed and he's alive and twenty-two. He remembers
a story: they send a man faster than light. FTL-drive, it's
called in that story. And when he returns, the people who live
by Earth's speeds are his grandchildren. Twenty-two, and he has grandchildren.
He remembers a story: once they had something called photographs,
they froze you in light. The other you went on, dying.

Architectural

When the King of the Gypsies was buried
they lined up picnic tables for three city blocks
through the cemetery, eating roast pig
and downing flagons of wine, and trying to hustle
the contract for paving over the cemetery main drive.
And there's that tombstone in Paris: the dead man,
cast life-sized, and women wishing
to be pregnant visit to rub his bronze crotch.
Ghosts appear in every culture,
terrifying the living with cliché chains or
aiding the living with cliché moaned advice,
but one was reported driving a rose-pink Caddie
up the interstate: I like that.
Angels. Sphinxes. Admonitory skulls.
Whatever. I'm trying to think of death
a new way—as something not final,
as something to face
that does have a face of its own. You know
the way that children believe if it isn't visible,
in front of them, it's ceased to exist
—is dear, but wrong.
I'm trying to see in the other rooms now.
"Afterbirth," we say, though
that's completely wrong of course.
In one of the other rooms it was there long before.

The Route

*For several moments he was lost in thought and then he straightened
up and looked at me, and his eyes burned with demoniac fire. "I can be
master of a world," he said; "perhaps I can even be master of the universe."*

—EDGAR RICE BURROUGHS
Swords of Mars

Five a.m., and headlight-eating clots of fog
the size of cars approach my car the whole way
from Columbia, Missouri, to Saint Louis.
In Chicago, my mother is being carried by cancer
over the threshold of a next world,
and she fights it, but she goes
an inch a day, and with such pain
as only miles could measure, only an odometer
of suffering. By noon or maybe one I should arrive.
By 7 a.m., the fog is rising from the trees,
is like the huge ghost of a raptor
trying still to lift its prey. "Igor,
fetch me a nice fresh brain," is what you'd think
to hear in this grim landscape—and, as if on cue,
the radio seizes on a wretched drama of medical genius
foully mushroomed into megalomania: "I hope
to rule the world with an army of such as these!"
then a trail of nyeh-heh-hehs. I punch it off. This
simpy play at horror pales next to the real
familial thing. By eleven, I'm into
the sprawl of outskirts smokestacks
—sweating, with the car a.c. on *freeze.* My mother
dwindling in her danglework of tubes.
My mother monitored at the tip of a needle.
If only the morphine does its job. If only
there's one more good day left. Now
that would be hope, that would be goddam hope
and mad science enough for me.

The Sonnet for Planet 10

My mother is dying. Nothing
halts the cancer's steady spread;
despite some talky knee-jerk optimists
in the family, she won't leave from the nursing home
for *her* home, ever. *I'm* there, though,
in a sad half-zomboid try to sort its recent scraps.
A pink note double-magneted to the fridge, *call Ruthie Lakin;*
an appointment at the oncology center
(never now to be kept); *Remember Livia's b'day;*
last week's unthumbed *TV Guide,* and last month's
crossword-puzzle magazine, with its untenanted squares
—a life's unfinished business,
far more eloquent for me than even
those incomplete statues of Michelangelo's,
always breaking and never breaking
out of their origin stone. Do you remember
the excitement over word that a new,
tenth planet was thought to exist? There wasn't one,
of course, and yet by now the very possibility
of its being with us—the promise of it, the weird allure—
orbits up there anyway, and is one of the century's
famous unkept deadlines. *That's*
where I'm going to dump the rummage-sale announcement,
and the reminder card from the dentist,
and the leftover Swiss in its strip of tinfoil wrap:
on Planet 10, right next to the meadow of graven monuments
that feature the text of everything
she and I have never said to each other. This poem
was going to be a sonnet—unfinished, diminished,
burial, funeral, etc.
But I'm weary, and I'm leaving it undone.

The Gold Star

Elaine's job on the geriatric ward included encouraging
the constipated to loose their stingy, gnarled marbles
into the bowl—by hand: there wasn't anything more tenderly
conducive than an orderly's gloved fingers.
There's nothing redeeming in this. Simply: she
needed the pay, they needed her excavating
(literally: *from out / of their cavities*) help.
The rest?—"an alien stink that followed me home,
under my toenails, in my hair." But surely we'd do it
willingly for someone that we loved . . . yes? Even
gratefully—for someone that we loved. And then
we'd clean the pad, we'd rinse it free of its gobbets
the size and color of cornelian cherries . . .
gladly, yes? Gladly and changed. Better;
tested. Even when my mother was dying,
shrinking, growing hard rosettes
as if her lungs were tanks in an experiment . . .
didn't I tend to her? and wasn't it the way
it always used to be?—that with precision instinct
she'd arranged this just so she could prove
to relatives and neighbors that her son
was so caring, her son was the best. I'd wring
the compress, set it on her forehead again.
What a good boy I was!

Coin

When the surgeons slit into my father they went to Jupiter
they went so far, to a barren red moon of Jupiter's.
I'd never been there. My mother had never been there
in him, to a cave on that moon, to the runaway vein
that snaked some inner wall. And even this they slit
and entered, with their Geiger counters that fit in a pore.
They needed to hear its half-life keening wildly. There's
one red anti-meson in everyone—here, at this, even
they stopped. Here, at this, my father turned them back,
as all of us were turned back, and he stayed
—as everybody stays, no matter the opening up—
alone in his pain. The microlasers won't usher you there;
or love. In everybody, there's this final landscape
only capable of supporting a population of one.
I was thinking of this as the bus pulled up,
the last bus of the night, at the hospital stop.
It must have been the amber window squares of buslight
in the 3 a.m. pit-dark—I saw that painting of the eighteenth-century
doctorpharmacist Michael Shuppach, studying
a beaker of a patient's urine, meditating, empathizing,
making the late Swiss afternoon light do great
disclosing swirls around that honey and its sediment,
more intimate in ways with this woman than any
deep sexual splitting-apart or any kneeled confessional
admission . . . down to the single citron valence-of-her,
in its nakedness, in his crystal. There's
one golden anti-meson in a life; and here, even he stopped.
There was only one passenger riding the bus: one face
staring out of a window. Someone
needing a bus at 3 a.m.with a story of why
—for a second, before I stood to board and then
decided not to board, our eyes met,
starting a common exchange.—Then
the face shut like a change purse, over
its single coin minted on Jupiter.

Even; Equal

Snow all night. It fills whole gullies
as easily as sidewalk cracks.
Finally, nothing has definition.
Last winter, at the first real thaw,
they found two schoolgirls under half-receded ice,
the bruises frozen
into lustrous brooches at their frozen throats.
Whoever did it is out here still, is free and maybe
needing more. The word "injustice" doesn't include
the choking gall that burns through me—something like being
here tonight, at my father's grave,
where even the shitty winter weather seems to fall
in the white weave of those off-the-rack, sagged suits
he wore so a few saved dollars could buy my education.
On the cemetery's other side, the tailored graves
of college deans and oil barons. What do I know?
Maybe he's playing poker with them
all night tonight, while January piles up
in deep banks, and the elements
of their own sloughed bodies skirl and reshuffle.
Death—the way snow makes the ditch
and the windowsill even; equal.

Wings

I always wondered why they called them wings.
—Perhaps because somebody always waited in shadow
in them, with a rope.
With a rope like a great braided nerve,
and while some sweet singing or bloody melee
completely filled the central light, this person
would raise or lower the god.

It's summer. Hard summer; the land enameled.
I find the bird already half-dismantled
by ants—the front half. It's flying
steadily into the other world, so needs to be this still.
Do I mumble? yes. Do I actually pray? yes.
Yes, but not for the bird. When we love enough
people a bird is a rehearsal.

In the X-ray of the Sarcophagus of Ta-pero

of the Twenty-second Dynasty, we see the skull
is fit inside its gilded wooden covering-face
as perfectly as thought is, in a sleeping brain,
or music is, in a radio that's *off*
—it's waiting to flower from this
body-of-the-moment. You ask me:
what do *I* know of ancient Egypt?—

almost nothing. A couple of coffee-table books.
A couple of lecture series with slides.
And that at night sometimes, in the zero of night,
I've felt the weight of another head
inside of my head, leaning its skull
against my skull as if to rest—it's traveled such a long,
long way and still has so far to go.

Shawabty, Ushabi, or *Shabti* Figures

Some are lumpish terra-cotta cylinders little more human
than bud vases. Others are gem-set
gold over detailed cedar musculature. The afterlife was life
continuing heightened—there would be groves of palm
belonging to the gods, and date, and lotus, requiring
heightened care. So these would represent
the deceased, these were obliged by magic text
and contract: *O shabtis go quickly to work*
with their inch hoes shouldered like muskets, inch
irrigation-picks, inch plows *Say "we are ready."*
One deed of sale (not rare) is for a set of 365 shabtis
"and their thirty-six overseers, all: 401, to my satisfaction."
In Mesopotamia, statues worshipped the gods nonstop for their owners.
In Tut's tomb they found 1,866 separate fine-toothed inch tools.

———————

TV tonight: a pseudo-documentary on Coleridge. Just
now he's enlisted in the 15th Light Dragoons,
a cavalry unit, although he sneezes near horses and
can't ride fifteen yards. Kerosening the dung-tubs clean,
he sets his clothes on fire. He upchucks supper so
dependably, it's requested he dine in the stables.
Saddles fly off. Swords snap. Whole cannon collapse.
So they allow his brothers to "buy him out"—that is,
purchase a substitute. You could do that then. They
eye each other a moment, then a commercial comes on. . . .
The gofer wheeling in lunch, the set's vet checking
the wire-tripped horses, "Coleridge" resting behind a door
marked *Star* while the dangerous scenes are done with,
his stuntman wrapping up good in asbestos.

Stationed

It's the other ones, who soon enough return
to being happy after the funeral, that are nearest
to their own deaths—in their gaiety
and everyday distraction, they're so open

and unguarded . . . *anything* could enter them;
could claim them. It's the ones who weep
incessantly that are saved for now, the ones
who have taken a little of it

into their systems: this is how
inoculation works. And sorrow is difficult,
a job: it requires time to complete.
And the tears?—the salt

of the folk saying,
that gets sprinkled over the tail feathers
and keeps a bird from flying;
keeps it stationed in this world.

About the Dead

The wooden leg obviously = a prosthetic leg.
The man with a seed from a tree
on his pants leg = the prosthetic sex of a tree.
The glass eye = a prosthetic eye.
And a telescope lens?—the dream life
of the glass eye when it's closed.
The car?—prosthetic speed.
To someone blind from birth
who has no way to context blindness, never having known
its opposite—silence is prosthetic blindness.

If the world's the "web of life"
my high school bio textbook employed as a phrase
to refer to a global ecosystem, *everything*
becomes the viable, artificial enablement
of something somewhere. Everything
—and everyone.

Nathan and I are discussing Keats—the late
autumnal dolor of the Odes; we're lightly
arguing, then somehow we're regluing our opinions
into a single admiration, we're reciting grand
collaborative swatches of his language
and our beer breath, and (there's this about the dead)
he's here, he's more here every minute,
almost crowing with delight now, almost dancing
between us—no, not "almost": *dancing*—
on these two crutches of his.

#1117

From here we can see the combination smoke as it ascends
from a field over to the east: a greasy column of fuel on fire,

and incinerated human bodies. One wing still is intact,
it angles up and shines with schizophrenic cleanliness . . .

the sirens . . . an odor of death on the wind. . . . And once
again, we're ashamed to carry the small weight

of our day's complaints to the edge of an actual tragedy.
A thimbleful of ear-bones stained by office innuendo . . .

a pebble . . . a gram of sexual jealousy . . .
we bring them to the brink of this wound in the earth,

and they're inadequate, even as tinder, even as salt.
Our language fails: "tinder," "salt," and we're ashamed

to use our metaphors in the face of this literality.
"A thimbleful." "A pebble." "In the face." Although

the marriage *did* crash. It died. It lost its way,
and it died. At night sometimes

when she lay in the bed, I know that there were thoughts
inside her skull like the voice in the black box saying

whatever they say as the flight goes down.

Some Common Terms in Latin
That Are Larger than Our Lives

From a description in a catalogue of rare science-fantasy titles: "Involves a utopian society in Atlantis, war with giant apes, prehistoric creatures, dragon-like beings, etc."

Mutant-engineered bloodsucker djinns, invisibility rays,
lost civilizations, past-life telepathic romance
—anything, finally, can fit in *etcetera,* even in
its abbreviation; much as in some story

out of Borges, where the world is the same as a library
holding all of the books in the world, and one book
holds the sentence "This is all of the books
in the world," so is, by itself, sufficient. Or

this woman on the streets of Manhattan, September 11,
2001: the look in her face is a gene
of the entire holocaustal event; fast-forward to it
any time you need to construct that whole

unbearable day. And other people are huddled
under girders, shrieking out as if to angels somewhere
at the edges of this, to presences outside of the human
—gods, and demons, and beings of the supernatural realms,

et alia. And others are too dazed even for that;
they're empty now of everything except a stare
at the incomprehensible shape of things, the sky,
and what's beyond the sky, and beyond that, *ad infinitum.*

Astronomy

It dies. And a gazillion years in the future
the sight of its dying reaches Earth.
—Computed in dinosaur years, that's three days
from the brain's death to its being recognized as dead
in the far frontiers of the tail.

———

Night. A party. "Come out here for a minute."
Dina told me: she'd miscarried. But
her body hadn't registered that yet, it kept
preparing for a birth. And so we sat on the porch
in silence for a while, in the light of that star.

. . . one of whom had apparently died in childbirth;
  we found the skeleton of an infant within
  her remains.

—ZAWI HAWASS, OF AN ARCHEOLOGICAL DIG

—it was, in its way,
a pietà.

And the pictures in the planetarium gallery
of a star in all the stages of its last progression,
dying—first a "white dwarf," then a "black dwarf,"
then a "black hole," that the composition
cradles in the milkiest arms of the universe.

One Continuous Substance

A small boy and a slant of morning light
both exit the last dark trees of this forest, though
the boy is gone in an instant. Not

the light: it travels its famous 186,000 miles per second
to be this still gold bar
on the floor of the darkness. I suppose

that from the universe's point of view
we do the same: a small boy and an old man
being one continuous substance.

We were making love when the phone rang
saying my father was dead, and the sun
kept touching you, there, and there, where I'd been.

The Winds

These are the nights when I think of the housemaid
cleaning that woman's cubby. First
she empties the basin of water and the chamberpot.
Then she returns, the sheets as usual are caked
with use, and these she changes, making sure
the new sheets like the old ones have a lace hem.
Under the bed, amid a circus of shoes,
of Roman sandals, and saucy mules, and furled Oriental slippers,
she finds the packet tied in twine, which she undoes
and, after the first brute shock, removes
the ear. She holds it in her palm
until it looks just like her palm, but swirled a little.
The whorls have brittled, and the lobe is blue
with paint, from where he tugged at it, in thought,
while working, listening hard to the cry in the wheat
and the cloth and the plate and the night winds.

Dürer

His natural fidelity and honesty caused him to approach reality direct.

—MARCEL BRION

The dessicated flukes of a whale. A leech so
green it's black, and is the jewel being worn by a long
pink finger of pig meat. Below that,
twelve chanterelles. One is sliced in half, so is the window
to a sunset on a ridge with one unbreakable pine, all
done from the color of mushroom, by a mushroom, in a mushroom.
A roc's egg. A geode. A walrus tusk. The planisphere
of cherrywood and cedar, with a fistful of planets
of particolour Venetian glass, and token stars like anthers
on fine wire stalks—nearby, the ornate ivory key
for its employment. Fox-fur robes. The shell of an ocean crab
as wide as a child's face. A length of linen, hard and
modeled into difficult garnet twists by someone's
month-blood; it had been around and in her for a day.
A suit of armour. Beside it, the detailed, dour
sketch of a rhinoceros. A vast green lace of seaweed
over the mantel, and a bagpipes like the hellish genitalia
of some creature from the sea. A jar of brine.
Inside it, the rough nub of a fifth leg
from a stillborn sheep. A linnet's wing. A radish
in the shape of a couple rammed headlong in sex.
A radish in the shape of Christ on the Hill
with even the nails in depiction. A slice of
cat placenta, in lemon juice in a bright blue plate.
A knucklebone. A ferret's skull.
An oar. A horn inkwell. An owl's claw.
Is this what he needed to study, to draw
the clear, true, crosshatched portrait or self-portrait of a man?
This is what he needed to study, to draw
the clear, true, crosshatched portrait or self-portrait of a man.

The Sciences Sing a Lullabye

Physics says: go to sleep. Of course
you're tired. Every atom in you
has been dancing the shimmy in silver shoes
nonstop from mitosis to now.
Quit tapping your feet. They'll dance
inside themselves without you. Go to sleep.

Geology says: it will be all right. Slow inch
by inch America is giving itself
to the ocean. Go to sleep. Let darkness
lap at your sides. Give darkness an inch.
You aren't alone. All of the continents used to be
one body. You aren't alone. Go to sleep.

Astronomy says: the sun will rise tomorrow,
Zoology says: on rainbow-fish and lithe gazelle,
Psychology says: but first it has to be night, so
Biology says: the body-clocks are stopped all over town
and
History says: here are the blankets, layer on layer, down and down.

Lullabye

sleep, little beansprout
don't be scared
the night is simply the true sky
bared

sleep, little dillseed
don't be afraid
the moon is the sunlight
ricocheted

sleep, little button
don't make a fuss
we make up the gods
so they can make us

sleep, little nubbin
don't you stir
this sky smiled down
on Atlantis and Ur

The Fossil
of an Omelet

a few poems excavated from 1972–1983

First Ride & First Walk

Finally my heart stopped murmuring.
They lifted me from the glass case
in my week-old sleek pink skin.
Daddy Irv was shnookered already
on good news and better *shnapps.* They
say he fixed me in the carriage's
boy-blue swaddle and then took the snakey
paths in Humboldt Park with his
left hand a bountiful humidor, his right
on the handle supplying whoopsie
steering, and my name angled bright in
his breath like a swizzle stick. Mommy
found him, hours later, by then the
cigars invisible but offered with equal
panache. I was gooing. He was singing
Hey Theodora, Don't spit on the floor-a,
Use the cuspidor-a, That's what it's for-a.
Grandpa Louie led him home. A diminishing
trail of for-a's through the dark. I
never pleased anyone that much again.
The park was safe in those days; Mommy
Fannie just stood there, watching me cry,
then lifted my plum face soft to her nipple.
What a day. I dozed, then. And she
left the carriage there—it could wait
for tomorrow, those days were full of time—
surrounded by grasses and me at her breast.
Walking home in the deep green silence, a cow trying
hard not to waken its bell.

Watch

There's a pleiosaur at the Dallas-Ft. Worth airport, its bonesnout jetstyled by the earth's work. I'm from the dawn of time too, having wakened at 6 for an 8 a.m. flight, the alarm having excavated me from the ground floor of sleep. It was found by the construction crew. Then pieced long and low bone by bone. I bumbled through the bathroom's few ablutions, everything blurred as if the world were caught on film set to a different time than mine. I wound up the heirloom. Its face, despite the sleek lines, is anachronism; crowds form, something like runway crews helping a jet dock into a later time zone. It was Grandma Rosie's, filigree gold from a time of dented chickensoup pots every gray ghetto day and parasol Sunday evenings. My father gave it to me just a week ago, passing it down, I could feel the individual bones in his handshake move minutely through their element. 100,000 years ago; the steppe must have shook when it crashed. So early, and such a fog—of course I dropped it. The crystal broke. Everything shook light sharp on its edges. Of course I would; when I was thirteen, a truculent manchild being groomed for bar mitzvah, didn't I snicker at the Passover table? They went from a great ton winch to tweezers, and here it is now silent and commanding while, outside, motors shiver the air. You'd have to know Daddy Irv, his salesman's bluster, his smile set in like a fixative: so that, when he suddenly wept, the first time ever in public, our whole table smashed like a plate. It wasn't much later, she died—though I gave her at least the gift of seeing her only grandson bar mitzvahed. Everything stopped for a moment, I ran across the room and cradled his head. What would be flesh is something plaster-looking—the skeleton, though, is true, and awesome, and makes its own flesh around it: the power of architecture. Time reversed a moment: he was the child. Light in fragments down his cheeks. And so I stood there, holding the broken face. That's what it is really—a stopped clock. Dead, it says its life forever. Says gneiss, says coal, says crystal forming. Here I am, with my baggage. You can't stop time but you can stop *a* time. This time, this one. I've never been good with faces. I think it forgives me, this looking thing with the motors far behind us, its empty eyes, its story full of repairwork.

The World of Expectations

What starts with F and ends with U-C-K? starts
another stupid high school joke. We also
snapped the thick resilient straps of Maria
Alfonso's bra. I don't know what we expected.
Annoyance, perhaps—though a kind of annoyance
that opened the way for attention—then maybe
intimacy, though we wouldn't have phrased it that way.
We called it F-ing. An alarm goes off,

the expectations are serial and easy: the clumsy
effecting of fire-drill practice, arrival of miles of hose.
And maybe Dennis or Leo or I would get to stand
near Maria, and maybe she'd even bend in her
provocative way that showed the first shadowy
rampway into her cleavage. When I finally did get
effed, of course it had nothing to do with the world
of expectations we mapped round and flat

where the condom ate wallet for years. Now I hear
Leo's divorced; drunk enough, it's as if a large hand
crumples him like a Coors can. The point is, even
Dennis's happiness, what kids mean and a sexual
axis, never struck our daydreams. The point is, not
even sex, necessarily—what did they see
in Station 19 when the bell went crazy? Flames
like cartoon devils? Their heroics, axe and ladder,

tested successfully? Glory? Pain? Some calls to glory
and pain are real, of course. But back then
we pulled levers for hijinks, for stupid jokes. And it came
long, red and clamorous. Firetruck.

A History of Civilization

In the dating bar, the potted ferns lean down
conspiratorially, little spore-studded
elopement ladders. The two top buttons
of every silk blouse have already half-undone all
introduction. Slices of smile, slices of sweet brie,
dark and its many white wedges. In back

of the bar, the last one-family grocer's is necklaced
over and over: strings of leeks, Greek olives, sardines.
The scoops stand at attention in the millet barrel,
the cordovan sheen of the coffee barrel, the kidney beans.
And a woman whose pride is a clean linen apron polishes
a register as intricate as a Sicilian shrine. In back

of the grocery, dozing and waking in fitful starts
by the guttering hearth, a ring of somber-gabardined grandpas
plays dominoes. Their stubble picks up the flicker like filaments
still waiting for the bulb or the phone to be invented. Even their
coughs, their phlegms, are in an older language. They move the simple
pieces of matching numbers. In back

of the back room, in the unlit lengths of storage, it's
that season: a cat eyes a cat. The sacks and baskets
are sprayed with the sign of a cat's having eyed a cat, and
everything to do with rut and estrus comes down to a few
sure moves. The dust motes drift, the continents.
In the fern bar a hand tries a knee, as if unplanned.

The Lost First Decade

Without a caption one might never know Mickey
for a mouse, the tail and lack of finger
not making him human any less; or, more,
the smile, knowledge of how to gum up
tin cans into a submarine, and faith
in how "the Desperadoes will wind up bee-hind bars!"

make him a better man than I ever grew up into.
I've still the hat: and don't I feel silly now,
a bearded twenty-five, with huge black plastic ears
for a yarmulke. Except I *want* to whistle
on the el as if the whole rush-hour jam would nod
in time on its way to work and easily break

out harps strung from suspenders, drums
from gutted attaché cases, or the girl in the corner
blow a ragtime clarion on her prosthetic leg.
There's a thumb in my lover's nipples
I suck. And in the dark, though I've never said it,
haven't I gasped around something, it's Minnie

undoing her blouse for the glass of warm milk.

Hard Times

1.

Faucets
hover over the sink
like the short sleeves
of an amputee
remembering what it was
to wash up.

These are hard times
in Chicago, darling.

2.

Winters like this freeze
anything shining
to anything unbuttoned.
Hard times.
The lonely man's neck
must wait for spring
to thaw the knife-blade
out of the cut
across his eager fingers.

Ice. The infant gums
and tongues some warmth
about the blue ankle
trapped
in the frozen baptism,
beats his head against ice
for the foot bloated
belly-up within.

———————

Hard times. Ice. You could claw
a hole in the tear
glazed over your cheek
and fish
with my heart on a hook
for your sorrow.

———————

Ice in Chicago. Darling,
hard times. Anything wet
becomes monumental.
The lonely man
haunts the streets with an egg
of semen
cracked in the palm of his hand.

3.

I need you. By the way
my fingers travel
over the swells of you
like refugees
leaving America
I know. The thumb
is blind from birth.
It bends
its head to the ground
and moves
by what it hears there.

A time of need.
Voices in a telephone cable
twine without touching.
Lovers too
have been known
to keep rubber between them.

Ice:
words in a wire
die of cold
waiting outside
for their ring to be answered.

I need you
to say: to a herbivore
the whole world's a salad.
You're silly
like that. I need to feel your breasts
burn like bulbs.
And we need the bulbs.
They make their own light

———————

and we do with them,
in a hard time,
for cherubim.

Scar / Beer / Glasses

You can always tell the badguys on TV: they sneer.

—MIKE KING, IN CONVERSATION

They only have an hour: they have to.
Some keep noxious pets, or finger
scars while talking. They all have music
around them like a black cloud. This
is also the lesson of language during sex, or in
a capsule NASA-boomed around the moon, in fact
in any boundaried time . . . we need the clarity that needs
a single saying. This as opposed to the bathroom
mirror, morning and morning again. Who
knows if that face is horrific or good?

And so in a frontier lumber town, its
citizens illiterate, the bar might have a beer
the size of a yearling colt above its door; the
barbershop, a pyramid of cream like a pharaoh's blueprint. . . .
Neruda speaks of a street in Chile like that: "an enormous
saw, a colossal boot"—2 by 4
vocabulary. And every morning, lumberjacks heading
into the world of what those workable boards were
first—like men who enter the place their
codified symbols come from. A vast, dark woods.

In this fourteenth-century painting of St. Peter, he's
wearing glasses—that early kind that look like handles
of scissors astride the nose. Anachronism
is an homage here: the easy, loud notation
meaning *learnèd man* has been sent back in time.
And there are paintings of saints in deserts, or
forests of stupefying gloom, who in their wandering
are calling to the heavens for direction, some
show of being heard: lightning, the track of an angel's wing. . . .
They only want what everybody is looking for, really.

They want a sign.

Village Wizard

(1200)

Begged by a novice-wizard to display the secret
of his craft, Waziri demonstratively
kept silent.

Asked to perform at the Merchants Bazaar
a feat never seen before, Waziri came
with a dozen coins in his purse and left
with a dozen coins in his purse.

Requested by the husbandless maid to conjure,
Waziri concocted three gifts: a flask of lotion
scented with spice; a beaker of potion
made with grapes; and a potent amulet
wrought with pearl to wear on a necklace
between her breasts when she bared her breasts
to the waxing moon. Even her husband
called it magic.

Paid to recite a spell for sleep, Waziri
began his life story.

Told to foresee the Emperor's future,
Waziri closed his eyes.

Ordered to exorcise evil influence
from the royal heir at his birth,
Waziri cut the umbilical cord.

Commanded on pain of death to provide the impossible
virgin speculum for the Queen, that fabled mage's mirror
so pure, it would have imaged nothing—not its maker,
not the air, and not the darkness—before her face
reflected there: with pity's stare, Waziri, wizard,
wept that tear.

Still Lives

What is it about this draped arrangement of green batiste
with Chinese oranges glowing like coals in its folds.
This grapefruit open for business: a pink motel
of tissuey rooms. These plums looking dusted with talcum.
In the long sad line of egg and avocado leading
up to the dented tureen, what is it that tells us they'll
be made to suffer the singing of hymns before supper.
What is it. This spoon that holds the whole blue ceiling
but says a story of emptiness. The way that sack of kittens
caught in stasis becomes a potato. The way a potato leans
outside of its own deep-umber definition, into
the hump of another potato, which is shaded
off into haze. The sharing of confidences. The calling
of body to body, two lute squashes hung as if
in facing pawnshop windows. This peony.
This vase. That bug-eyed bass with just a comma
of its entrail juices, as clear as springwater. What
is it about them. What is it about the sweet
accumulation of meat, of wedge of meat
on wedge, in the rooms of the grapefruit hotel.
What is it about the dented moon
in the chill of the dented tureen—we know
by inference she's working tonight, she's pulling the seas
and the crazy high blood of wolverines, she's earning
so her husband the sun, the great Talmudic scholar,
can spend his days in the study of glory.
What is it. What is it ever. There's a dirty glove that requires a step
away to be a mallard. And a group of bings is tilted
as if waiting for the duck's enormous limp body to be placed
in the stars. The bings, the near-black, clear, fat
caviar of a tree. The chilies. The cocoa beans.
What is it about this lusterware ladle of Dijon mustard
folding the light so it looks like van Gogh's ear.
It's near the little apple knife, it's frightening.

Or is that tiny silver blade by the delicate spirals of appleskin
a sardine. What is it. This is the light from inside
a pearl, and it's hard to tell. This is the border
where radishes meet—the small red dwarves, the long
arthritic blacks—and talk like second cousins
with different languages, talk beyond translation.
What is it. The cheap ceramic kettle with chartreuse willows
on its round side bended back by an invisible wind, so
giving the kettle the look of motion, giving the thick, the almost
spongy, steam the look of a railroad engine's flag of speed.
The leeks. The ewer. The rum. There is a legend
of a saviour appearing in days of mighty travail, that must be
what the ample-buttocked burgher pears are congregated to buzz
about, such is their obvious gravity and intimate
disposition in a corner of silk with dove-and-tulip borders.
That must be. And if it's not, it must be the symbol of it,
for us, for someone. The suck-button arm of a squid. Its
curve as eloquent as an architect's stencil, at least.
Its slippery texture, its length. Its horizontal run in front
of the spherical singlemindedness of grapes, and what that means
of apposition and love. What does it mean. What is it.
The grapes are green. The other grapes are a purple only known
in the bellies of certain dragonflies and shellfish, and an outer
constellation of them lightens into the pure emphatic
red of a borscht. What this does to the green grapes. What
does it do. This sprig of mint. That garlic. What is it.
That Spanish onion, peeling its purple
flophouse wallpaper of a face. These lovely kidney beans, the insides
of our bodies must look like this in their dreams. The jazzy
juiced drupes of the blackberries, of the raspberries, and the bland
sweep of a crockery cup of cream—it's newly risen
to the top and gleams as tough as an ivory pendant.
Yams. A single, languid, yellow rose. The thoughtful intervention
of a yellow rose amid a uniformed squadron of yams.

What is it about disparity, about whatever binds.
How many medals for valor and savagery might be
these beads of water on an eggplant, with the nickels
of light at their centers. The milkweed
choir in its golden bottle, white-robed, unperturbed
by anything fleshly. And the sexual enthusiasm of one
buff, blush-bodied peach for another, for anything,
their velvet clefts, the single hour the clock
of a grapefruit-half counts off, the cheap rooms and the sixty
sweet pink minutes. Yes, and of course the censorious
pointing of a celery. Why, and what of it. These assumings
of our attributes, this easy way of saying the egalitarian
meetings of bananas, the smooth crude blueprint of a human hand
that's a true-drawn bunch of ripening bananas,
what is it. This is any artichoke
in absolute cross-section, with its heart like a cast-bronze
Buddhist god in its temple niche, its heart like a dancing
green flame god! This is the candle; this,
the gelid slab of hogfat just gradations away from
being a candle. This is their agreement, in a special color
shared by them, a wonderful waxy pastel. What
is it. Let me introduce the tomatoes, some done as
if early, with patches of yellow like an infant's soft spot
making you want to weep for what you were. And so
they're on the sill. The grain of the sill. The exact
crack in the plaster. What is it about. The breast of flour.
The cruet. A peppermill. The impossible commune of corn.
An orchid. What is it about an orchid. Why can't I say
I see these things in them. The calling of like. The anther
and the radio. What is it about
the spill of milk brushed blue and gray but it's white
against the hickory, the lean-to and the spire
and the temple column of simple carrots simply placed, the parsley's
green mantilla of lace, the tongs, the towels, the smallest

of the rumples in a towel, the poem of the heel of bread,
of pigtrotter and of brie, and of Swiss, and of veins in the blue,
of wheat like a rain,
of salt like a snow
of enormous hard
cartons of weeping.

Object Functionsong

Let me see my face in the mirror
Laugh, just once, when I'm not able
To laugh. Let objects be my teacher.
/the mouth of a jar, the neck of a bottle

Let the grill of the radio, the crosses-shape
Of the calendar page, be a jail
Music and time escape.
/the spine of a book, the eye of a needle

Let my lap fit well the lap offered
By wood chairs. Let them be a durable
Stencil about me—definitive, hard.
/the head of a pin, the legs of a table

Let the spin of the phonograph show
How I in my rut, how I in my circle,
Still can sing, if the point is true.
/the chest of drawers, the cock of a shuttle

Let me learn from the shapes of things.
/there, in the corner, the hinge wings

Animal Functionsong

Make me a place of peace, and leisure
>   *spider, beaver, masonwasp*
Teach me pain's more beautiful gesture
>   *oyster, salmon, eiderduck*
Let me survive past Time that bred me
>   *lemur, tapir, coelacanth*
Lead me into the cared-for family
>   *lioness, dambear, pelican*
But if I pray too huge this morning
>   *buffalo, mountain gorilla, white rhino*
Asking one gift too outré
>   *tusk, milk, civet-musk, panther-silk, ambergris*
Thieve me a least sweep scrap of fatback
>   *packrat, jackdaw, jay*

Things I've Put in This Poem

1.   1972

The top line is sea-level. Here, a girl dances the black flag
her hair makes in wind, over green leas fleecy with primrose.
She is out to dig for potsherds, shells in shale, pebbles veined
pied and peacock enough for rings and pendants, something
spaded up from history to shine between her breasts.
And splitting one hillock, her hands undress red earth
from around a skeleton: yellowed, at peace, a bullet
packed in red dirt where the heart was.

2.

Long weeds of lantern-light seem to sprout
from the night soil; looking closer, through those bright cracks
splitting a farmsteader's shack in the dark of the 1870s:
one man, pallid and spread on the checkered quilt, twitches
under the flame-cleaned knife and forceps
the county doctor poises an inch above his chest.
The goal: to pry an arrow out of flesh. The advice: here,
bite on this. And the gray veins at the temple bulge
into a world without anaesthesia, from the wild try
of a dying man to chew a lead bullet in half.

———————

(The outcome: he doesn't die. Barb out, the farmer lives,
breeds, and whistles whacky orisons in the bull manure,
thinking: when I do die, let them lower me in my grave
wearing this memento, this tooth-marked pellet of birdshot
that is all the suffering in the world.) The scene:

———————

skin split, forceps pinching in muscle, doctor's breath
a cloud above his face, the farmer clamps his jaw
till its bone hinge warps. And in that moment
before his troubles tumble out of him into the shadowy sack
of fainting: he feels the fever go into the sweat, and leave.
The pain goes into the bullet.

3.

So I've put some special things in this poem.
The girl whose hair is a small night sky star-specked
against the ordinariness of my daytimes
I put in so this poem will make me think of Syl.
She is Syl. She brings a primrose home to me.
The grass and flowers are here to remember
greenery by, in the forthcoming days of its disappearance.
Let those lines symbolize chlorophyll.
The jewelry I put in to be those circles of beauty
human hands shape for human hands,
to glint against the twilight.
And the quilt, and the shells, and the lantern.

And the bullet I've put in to make this prayer real:
    All our pain, go into the bullet.
    All our pain, go into the bullet.
    And bullet stay buried in the bottom line.

Houdin

*. . . succeeded very well in his first attempt, with the exception that he
ruined a gentleman's chapeau, while performing the trick of the omelet
in the hat.*

—MAGIC AND ITS PROFESSORS

Sometimes, summer rain makes sky a closing
iron maiden. You know it, you've been there.
Remember?—Your lover's whole body a
great reproachful finger; then, later, your
eight hours as a Grief Tester goes into overtime . . .
and just to get through a day unbroken is

a real trick. So now you understand. I've
done my famous The Hippopotamus
in the Bathtub, I've done Zeus's Nosegay,
once I even did Ten Hundred Gnats
and the Floating Crystal—all without a hitch!
So? Look, it happens. You who have done

The Man in the Woman, The Burning
Crepe, the well-loved The Child
Out of the Flesh, and The Dawn Sun
Doubled in Your Eyes—I know you'll forgive
this sodden chapeau. Besides, I promised you
something marvelous. There is an omelet in your hat, sir.

Human
Beauty

new poems

Voyage

At night I wake up with my sheets soaking wet.

—BRUCE SPRINGSTEEN

The banditos of the inner region would take not only
your money but, with little provocation, your throat
—their dogs were said to love that tender delicacy
especially. Other menaces that Darwin met
with equal calm were from the land itself:
volcano; earthquake; and the jaguar's swipe
will tear a man open as easily as an envelope.
Those dicey moments shrivel up and blow away in the gale force
of his zeals: "I am today red-hot with spiders,
they are so interesting!" A loveliness is everywhere: "The haze
became a most beautiful pale French gray." And the Earth,
of course, was just beginning to open herself for him: *here,*
like a lover, *here,* and he could look inside, down
geologic forces unimaginable. And so we're always a little surprised,

remembering that the background for these five years of adventure
was—this, from a letter—"one continual puke."
His correspondence home provides us with a face for his heroics
that the published versions turn aside: "I hate every wave
of the ocean with a fervour, which you who have only seen
the green waters of the beach can never understand.
I loathe, I abhor the sea and all ships which sail it"
—then upgorged, for a vivid proof, all over
the brass and mahogany. This display from someone
who could stomach "the disgusting black bugs of the Pampas,
about an inch long, crawling over my skin, and in the act of sucking
they changed from as flat as a wafer to globular."
"So curious," he called the experience. Something
in his ocean-going frailty, then, is heartening as I picture him

with my friends in their various sleeplessness:
Serena, my student, zero insurance, the lover-father
long absconded and Donnie, nine, "a call from his school,"
in a corner with one arm's belly slit like a fish,
"he'd used *my* razor he stole," his hug around her leaving
a high-tide line of his own red misery on her skirt,
or Ron from one block up, "was just an annual physical" and
so what, please, was this tiny squid-thing doing inside
his X-ray with its tentacles squirming greedily around
the gray-tone shoals, "and now we're waiting to hear," and now
let these two stand for every one of us awake
all night in a private hell on Her Majesty's Ship *Insomnia*
until we simply surrender and let the sickness
at the pit of us be the entirety of us. All night

—a voyage. And when the bed has reached
the shore of another morning, that's when I often see him
holding to the rail, somewhat weak—a little
porridgey in the face, if you want to know the truth—
but already deeply inhaling something amazing
from the horizon. He says: Get up, go out.
Go out and see what's new today with the species.

1124 into Wichita

Some of us are heading into funerals, and some of us are heading
just as evidently into the morass and molasses of love.
(Each has its detectable aura.) Some of us are money. Some
are flutes. A few are moneymoneymoney. Some, trombones.
I think that one or two are delivering an apology
on an invisible silver wafer—if it's not too late. Another
is repeating to herself the script of a wonderful proposal,
a ring-tailed zinger of a proposal—if it's not too early.
Some are asleep: the adrenaline shift in their bodies
has just punched out for the day. A few are fueled
by hate: their flight, a slow and patient bullet.
Someone is lactating: there's a dark rose over the light pink
silk of her blouse. We're here. We're so high, we
don't even own a molecule of shadow. Down there, now

too small to see, a tree—a willow, a crazy philharmonic maestro
of a tree—is conducting the wind: those owl pellets flying
all around in the air could be notes. And somewhere else
a tarp that's half-undone on top of a farmer's rick is repeatedly
lifting and dropping, all day, like a woman's hand on her breast
in a worried self-diagnosis. Down there, everything keeps on happening.
Gusto. Failure. Slithering boas of light dry snow. And
sudden wedges of sun driven into the darkness. Everything—
waiting for us. Some of us want it, some of us don't,
but down there somewhere every one of us has a destination.
There's a case lined like a casket, for the flute; there's a purse
as pink inside as a vulva, for the money. All of us
know this. All of us now in a changed awareness.
All of us heading down in a locked and upright position.

Human Beauty

If you write a poem about love . . .
the love is a bird,

the poem is an origami bird.
If you write a poem about death . . .

the death is a terrible fire,
the poem is an offering of paper cutout flames

you feed to the fire.
We can see, in these, the space between

our gestures and the power they address
—an insufficiency. And yet a kind of beauty,

a distinctly human beauty. When a winter storm
from out of nowhere hit New York one night

in 1892, the crew at a theater was caught
unloading props: a box

of paper snow for the Christmas scene got dropped
and broken open, and that flash of white

confetti was lost
inside what it was a praise of.

"All totaled, the sunlight that strikes the earth at any given moment weighs as much as an ocean liner."

—FROM *The Book of Useless Information*

Another day when work crews in the rubble discover
the feet of a child—three years old, they guess—smashed
by a fallen lintel, as flat and dry by now
as two corsages from a tomb. Another night
and small explosions: small, but—big enough: a kind
of strong caffeine by which the darkness keeps itself
awake. Let's have the sun negotiate a peace
with war-torn nation-states like these. I think the sun
might be successful. After all, its light is neutral:
it will limn a line of spider silk glued loosely
in the wind, without the stinting of one wavelength
that it also gives to the jumbo edge of a jetliner's wing,
to the tiny homuncular bead of itself that floats
inside a pineal gland. The sun: it rises

above our partisan enmities. It's perfect
for the brokering of armistice: this hemisphere right now, and soon
the other: one bedraggled weed and needle of glass
at a time. One dawn in Victoria, Texas, I saw it
lave its gilt along the throat of an opening lily,
with the pinpoint glory an artisan monk would bring
to his embellishing of a letter beginning a page of scripture.
That was on the lawn; inside the building—Oak Grove Hill
Assisted Living Center—Reese's parents started
one more day of their diminishment. Ninety-one and -two.
"Yesterday you had an *anniversary!*" says Reese: the overemphasizing
gusto of the visitor. "*Fifty-nine!* Did all that time go fast for you
or slow?" His mother considers, then out of her small,
gray-veined translucence, answers "Fast." His father

adds: "And now it's done." There's silence, then;
there's silence, and the color of finality appropriates the room.
And even here, now, in the drab-tone wash of this get-together,
light won't be denied: as if its presence is obliged
in these grim corridors as equitably
as in the bright expanse of spendthrift pollen and voluptuary flowering
—obliged by forces of governance in the structure of the photons themselves.
It will crack its way inside, around the drawn shade;
it will wait inside our deepest tissues, reemerging the way
it does in the green, green chemical storage of the leaf.
"Here, there, and everywhere"—the Beatles song. And
everything: arguably, my own day's small displeasures are a part
of a uni-field that also holds the war, and the lintel
that falls, and the child-cadaver under its weight: accumulated

details of a single, solar system. When the circus steamship
Panama Beauty foundered in the shallows off the coast,
they dragged two camels through the waves, to shore,
"the balky creatures exhibiting scant gratitude"; and
an elephant ("that needed seven men to pull her continuously,
like Pharoah's slaves with a Pyramid stone"); and one
daft hippopotamus ("there aren't any handholds
on that beast"), which kept attempting counterintuitively
to return to the ship. The day was 102 degrees. At noon
one man at last collapsed, with three
of Doctor Romulus's Dancing Mice in his hands. It *looked*
as if the mice were the problem. We know better.
Reese knows better. There are times
the light brings too much for the strongest of its stevedores.

"Assisted Living"

makes of her a chameleon: in a week, she looks
like someone who does need assistance. Some require
the use of a rubber-footed metal walker, some
require a bingo game. The elephants bring leaves
to their afflicted ones: can we do less? And other
animal metaphors appear here. Especially I think
of the cries of the woman in room A2, the reverse
of a bat's. Oh, not because she can see; she's blind
all right. But because she's strapped to her bed, and hers
is an echolocation for staying in place, not flight.
When the krill-rich water is strained through the whale's
baleen, it's already as good as lost to digestion.
That's the way his mother entered the doorway here,
a self on the way to being transubstantiated self.

Versed*

A story about the girls out playing
a game of Naughty. They have two dolls they make do things
they can't themselves. Today, they're at the village's great
manure heap, with some loose idea of getting
little Greta and Mooshkin all besmeared. It's summer,
it's the worst in many decades: so the concentrated heat
in the dung has exerted a special pull, a small, insistent
upward gravity. Out of the earth
it's come, this splayed thing they discover there
—is it a starfish? is it a fisherman's glove?—
in the middle of their laughter. Out of the earth,
out of the clay and the coal, against the texture of history.
A human hand. Leathery and twisted, but—
a human hand. And the rust-edge of a blade.
The village had almost forgotten those stories
about the torture chamber a hundred years in the past.
But not the earth. It remembers the dragons.
It remembers when we had fins.
And if it doesn't remember (see? the mist . . .
the gnawed bones in the ash pit . . .)
still, it doesn't forget.

———————

Then they released me.
I was wheeled back out, from the cloud of not-knowing.
I was fine—my wife said I was fine
and the orderly brought me a cola.

*pronounced ver-said, the drug; commonly used in "procedures"

The fish of those days have disappeared,
the armored fish with a crest like a ninja throwing-star;
the chainmail length of the proto-eel.
They no longer weave the waters. And
the hominids who took the first, faltering steps . . .
the original "people" . . . they
no longer skitter across the land.

And then? . . . and then the day continued on, this day
that took the look of any day, with lunch
at the corner tamale joint, a browse
through Barnes & Noble, and a long read
into sleep. Oh, maybe a "twinge";
maybe a minute of "smear of blood"
—from where? Almost, I couldn't have told you,
so efficient is that drug, and so familiar
the slide into slumber.

In 2003, the deep-sea research ship the Tangaroa
explored the Tasman Sea. Among 500 species of fish
it snared is the "unicorn batfish," one that walks
the ocean floor on fins which work like actual legs
—as if the sludge-and-shale hands of time itself
uncupped, releasing this deeply implanted, incredible thing
into human sight after millennia. Or tell me
how amazing to see those photographs of footprints
of an ur-ancestral upright ape,
that the bed of a layered-over riverbank wouldn't give up
to erasure, any more than the moon allows itself
amnesia of its craters.

But I didn't sleep. A wrongness
had been entered into me, earlier, on the procedure table
—a presence. And the print of it remained,
disturbing the standard patterns, it rustled in there,
in the gray meat, in the gnarl. It stirred
despite the wave of blankness
when the chemical hypnotist whispered, "You will awake.
But you will not remember."

———————————

A man can scream like a rabbit
having its legs snapped one by one.
A woman will scream like a horse, will shit
where she stands like a horse,
in a stall, on filthy straw,
if the right things are done to the right,
the delicate, places. There is an expertise
to everything; and the torturer,
should he be among the best of the class, has his.
It happened here, in these chambers, underground.
With whatever was handy, at first: a lug of wood,
a blade you would otherwise use on a pig's
soft cheese of a belly. Later, of course, the tools
were specialized: there are books about them now.
The screams began, and the screams continued,
over years—for a generation. And then one day
there was silence. It was cool,
the rains began. There were strata of gneiss,
and rock with lichen, and then the little bell-shaped
wildflowers hanging in brightly shaking staves
in the spring air. Somebody opened a pastry shop.
Somebody cleared the field. It was a farming community,

mostly, and its rhythms and various pungencies
and gossips were those particular to a farming community.
Everybody contributed to the manure heap
out in the overgrown field, over by the miller's stream.
One morning, two girls are playing there, with dolls.
You know that story. You haven't forgotten.

In the nascent science of archeoacoustics, experts test
the ancient sites for locations of "sonic intensity":
echoes, rocks that gong when struck, etc.
For shamanic trance, for oracle, for ritual enhancement
as a sacrificial throat was slit . . . these places
may have been chosen in part for the sounds they bounced
—sounds we can recover. That night,
one girl has a haunting dream:
she clutches her doll, with her ear to the ground,
and, just below the spongey, everyday soil,
the earth releases a scream.

———————

And occasionally the filament in the bulb
of my bedside lamp emits
a brief, thin, high-pitched dirge of a noise

—remembering the knives that cut it
out of its vein, in its mountain.

Fourteen Pages

*"I am Raoul de la Roche Pierre de Bras, whose father writes himself
Lord of Grobois, a free vavasor of the noble Count of Toulouse, with the
right of fossa and of furca, the high justice, the middle and the low."*

—ARTHUR CONAN DOYLE

Sir Nigel

A "mini-stroke": and now Amanda's father
was a little figure of schoolroom paste
left overnight on the sill:
a sudden rain had turned him general
and blurred. This was the same year
that her mother disappeared, one thread of thought
a day: that doesn't sound like much, but
in a month the unweaving is terrible to see;
it leaves you talking to the rag left
at the end of the shift, when life is mopping up
and ready to go. This is the common theme
of common poems in every generation, and it still asks
to be said in ours: *how quickly!*
The rank and lineage that Raoul de Bras unfurls
is like a banner of scarlet and inset gold
the length of a coach-and-six, and equally
weighty. He is a squire and the son of a knight,
and in love with the Countess Beatrice, and an even bloom
of courtliness and valor is as natural to his manners
as is clover to a meadow. It's on page 192 that we
initially meet him; and he's dead on page 205, the bolt
of a crossbow "driven to its socket" in his neck.
Is that a unit we can take away and use
in application?—*fourteen pages.* Not that this
provides much comfort or illumination: "Wasn't
Amanda's father four-times-fourteen-pages?" etc.
Even so, we'll try whatever terminology we can
in our attempts to understand the body

swallowed up by time. The prep she did the day
before her colonoscopy, my sister said, "was just
like shitting razor blades"—as accurate
as anything the doctor's instructional pamphlet says.
And really: what else *can* we bring to the brink
of our lives, to the line where the darkness starts,
if not our language? When they rolled me into my own
procedure (that's the pamphlet's word: "procedure")
what did I have?—they'd taken away my clothes,
and the tether I use to keep my brain from floating
into anonymity. But a voice survived,
inside somewhere, a voice below
the bullying of the Demerol, and it said
"I am Albert Goldbarth, whose father signed the rent check
'Irving Goldbarth' with the fake gold pen he earned
for over twenty-five years of service with Metropolitan Life Insurance,
he of the genuine heart—and the salesman's overbearing laugh
that never represented the true heart adequately;
and he gave unto me the lug nuts and the hubcaps
of the north side of Chicago at my birth, as well as the candle
that lights the menorah, and the shockingly sexual pink
of the lox at Sunday brunch, the skivvies
and the quilted winter longjohns, and the prayershawl,
and the secret naughty coin for 'heads' and 'tails,'
and the American right that even an insignificant man
and his insignificant family have, to go to bed
with their honor intact, to walk the dog
as if the night were as good in their nostrils as anyone's."
It was small, as I said—a pipsqueak voice,
a match that burned for a moment. And then,
like any match, it was tossed to the pile
of billions of matches preceding it.
Why do I write? It's what I do
with the portion of carbon I am, before it returns to the universe
of carbon that the trees created even before there were people.

Some Leaves from the Permission Tree

List

He drilled a hole in her head
and could at last see what was there,
he wrote it down: a worm bug thing,
a writhing pin, a shiny angel
—in his dream,
he drilled, and he saw, and he wrote it down,
it was so clear to him. That
was yesterday. Now, in the "real world" of everyday
commercial hype, political wiggle-room halfass facts,
divorce retraction, newspaper-headline stew, and the usual
nullifications, secret doublespeaks, and simple sloppy
penmanship . . . who knows? He looks at his list in the sun
a warm hug thing   a writing pen   a skinny angle
and looks at her and smiles   /or is it *smites*/   who knows?

Breath

"*He's* got erotic pizzazz"—I heard. A stewardess,
on a steward deplaning. Yeah, but I'm the guy who heard
"The Oranges and Spices" as the famous title
of Darwin's book. It also wasn't
"Hitler and yon" in the handwritten poem
a student turned in, it wasn't a permission tree
in the middle of persimmon season. Some of this
seems mildly comic, all of it says that serious things
go wrong at times, in even the tiniest turning over
of breath from a mouth to an ear. How could we *ever*
fantasize we'd understand the alien needs of saucer people
beamed to Earth? Or: really, what was she *thinking*, knowing
everything about what he was like, and keeping on dating him anyway?
—that steward, who's got a rod up his ass.

Snow

The letter arrived. It bore a typo, "nex" for "new":
"I hope you like my two nex books in the spring." But
at the moment it was fall; the leaves were dropping,
green to a kind of sucked-dry brown. Or a "t"
was dropped: it should have read "next." The word,
that winter, came close to becoming a mantra: *Next
time? Trust me, there won't be a "next time"!* (overheard
in the throes of the "perfect marriage's" sudden dissolution)
and *Oh Jesus, shit, what* NEXT? (as a couple who claimed
they hadn't loved each other in years found out she was pregnant).
This was the lesson of winter: nothing is sure. The snow
slurred hard, familiar shapes to a paste. Then
it was spring. One day, a package from my friend the former
priest, as he'd promised: two sex books to read.

World

That night, his dream: Maureen had entered
a convent as a novitiate . . . which was "true," that is
in "real life" she *had:* this worldly nineteen-year-old artist
did decide to consecrate her earthly life to things unworldly.
In the dream, though, she had disappeared through a door below
a blinking hot-pink neon sign that said . . .
not convent, COVERT. "What?!" he said, and in the dream
his "what" took shape in the air like the oily and orange
letters out of a can of sentient alphabet soup. The sign
responded, GLOBAL COVERT CENTRAL COMMAND,
in giant throbs. That makes no sense, that self-implodes,
he thought. But what *did* make sense? "Muse" or "nurse"?
"Inflam-" or "infor-" mation? "Help!" he said, and the letters
in the air said: What A Crazy Whirled.

Completing the Things

And even after he'd donated one of his kidneys
—not to mention their rampant and rabbitly frequent

sex, on the lawn; in the mens room once at Tia's Margarita Bar;
at zero-gees in a rented space-flight simulator,

their juicy extrusions afloat in a colloidal nimbus—
even so, it wasn't real, tactilely and permanently real,

until the word was spoken . . . "love" . . . and that took three years:
something like the way, in a vastly different arena, the lab technician

said it . . . "tumor" . . . and then, and only then, did the true
finality end its month of invisible overhead circling and settle

its claw-grip onto the rim of that looted sarcophagus,
my mother's lung. And while I hold no theory that

experience means less to the prelingual . . . still, I know this:
for my friends the journey often isn't clear until

some word declares itself the destination . . . yes, so *now*
we see how all this while we were really traveling

up the sensitively wind-whipped, spinous ridge
of a "frisson"; or how that year you spent in crazy love

(and how you acted, ditsy in your deepest cortical self,
half-dreaming every convoluted step

of hurt, and withdrawal, and reaching out,
through banshee-shrieks and lust-engorgements) . . . this,

a "hypnagogic" time. Surely, that New Guinea tribe
the Asmat . . . they can enter realms

denied to us because *they have* a culture-term
like "soul ship"—words, in part, are pegs

that fasten our conjectures to a grounding of validity;
the sailings of such vessels through the mist-lands

of the ancestors are credible, skin-prickling historical ventures.
"The subconscious," "jihad," "Eden" . . . don't

these designations let us live inside ideas
as truly as if they were rooms? And if we did possess

a way to say that state between the angel troops of Lucifer
and those demonic things they turned to, once

consigned to Hell . . . then we'd possess a new domain—of incompletion
and transition—and might find its signs

explaining our own actions. "Tumor": and then we could weep.
"Love:" and then they could register for the anchoring accoutrements

of love, the silver dinnerware, the matching rosebud bedsheets.
All this week, my wife and I have been quietly bickering

and everything that isn't a part of this steady demand
on our attention fades off at the edges. By the end

of the day, so many familiar objects and events
are an inconsequential smear of smoke and ions; in the morning, we need

to recreate the world anew. I watch her stretch her arms
in bed, studying the bone arc of a peacock's fan

her outspread fingers schematize, as if this little
miracle of flex and anatomical design is the fulfillment

of a promise evolution made, in the days of the caves.
Meanwhile, I'm looking around and thinking how the Word

completes the Thing . . . as in the legend, Adam carefully
naming the animals on their first day here: *the chiffonier,*

the drapes, the high-hipped Japanese lamp,
the stack of paperback books on the floor.

Whale and Bee

Earl called today: another fight with Thelma.
Who would doubt it?—evolution *wants* our marriages

unlikely. We're experiments, in search of further
alloys of the human genome. Fair enough. And yet

their sadness seems a brutal price to pay
for that. By now—ten years—their daily love is so

entangled, it's like hearing that the marble
is at war with its own veins. And lately,

any indication of the ways the world is one
holistic organism, melding and dividing

in its small parts, is a wonder that surpasses
my ability to comprehend. That "cloud"

once meant "a hill" . . . what was it like
when they first separated?—one remaining

earthbound; and the other in its new life:
vapor, whim. There was an ancient time

when "melody" and "tragedy" were one.
In the nineteenth century, Her Majesty's Navy

manufactured a brighter and more durable candle
by wedding the heavier oil of the whale

to the wax of the bee.

While Everyone Else Went Starward

In a thunderclap, the Rapture arrives and rises
into Heaven with the saved inside its pockets. And
us?—we're here, we'll writhe and die like fish
in the puddle a river left behind. The whole Earth
may be that, according to one new
science-fiction novel: residue, with its resident life,
while everyone else went starward. If it's dire, this

abandonment . . . let's not forget the half-rhyme,
"dear." Perhaps to *really* understand what's dear *requires*
absences and loss. Down here, a remnant beauty
flourishes. The ones who come to Stonehenge with their flowers
and candies, centuries after its makers' disappearance.
That woman in Sydney, Australia, who had her husband's
ashes sewn into her breast implants.

The Muse of Invention

Noon: they were happy. One o'clock: they had hurt each other
again. As if they couldn't tell which atmosphere
they breathed in best, so needed alternation. In this,
the clock complied: seemingly, the machinery of the day
can grind a new emotion hourly. The bedroom sun, compacted
in the gel in a jar, to the look of a shrunken head. . .
the bedroom sun, a patient, golden hand
at rest on top of the conga drum. . . . They know
that some year later on, in retrospect, the proper combination
of these everyday components will be obvious—*this here,*
and this: resentment; minus the ottoman,
and with the heavy X of two crossed wrenches
like the design on a crest: forgiveness—but the muse of invention
is wary of committing herself too readily. Darwin,

encamped on one of the southern islands of his five-year voyage
—*embosomed,* he wrote, for he loved this place—observed
a sudden amplitude of color as the flap of flight
revealed it and framed it, for a moment, on the underwings
. . . again, and then again, and then again, in what
his eyes saw as a sequence of these units
as they almost, *almost,* blended unbroken into a ribbon
of indigo shine. And even so, he didn't
foresee cinema. Nor did Leonardo
give the world the printing press. Amid the twigs
and stickers of the forest floor, amid the city's colonnades,
and especially amid the itch of the flesh, and the warring oaths
that rive a human heart, they did
what they needed to do, and the future took care of itself.

The Song of How We Believe

Thomas Edison . . . tried to invent a machine for communicating electronically with the dead.

—WENDY KAMINER

Give us an incisor, and we'll rationally conjecture
an entire prehistoric head, to the glint
in its eyes and in the light along its scaled skin
—but first, we need that tooth, that seed
by which the flowers of our waking dreams can feel
tightly tamped in a logical soil. No doubt Edison
and his backers were emboldened every time a wire sizzled
with another blue effusion from its tip, or an electrode
danced, for the blink of an eye, with its tiny geyser of power . . .
this was *real,* not the goosey, gassy mediumship
of a biddy in a muumuu squinting weird and talking
half-an-octave lower; no, this was something even
a financier investor could touch and measure and imagine,
therefore, owning: *gears* for powwows with the dead! We need

one promissory rivet to roll in our fingers, as real
as any coin or lucky charm—just one, but then the whole blueprinted
river-spanning bridge will rise inside our heads with a gritty actuality
you could spraypaint your initials on. Already we can see
the ribbon-cutting and the years of use and rust. And he?
—rolled up in grief, in bed, can he believe a bridge exists
between his life now and his parents' recent deaths?—the one
to cancer in the spring, and the other later that summer as if
a swimmer who couldn't resist the pull of the sinking ship?
He curls to an insular ball. And she?—beside him, she
can sense this fraying length of marriage thin another micron
off itself, and shiver in the chilly flux of chance. She wakes
up early enough to see the tearose smudge of dawn, she asks
the sky or the gods or the future for . . . for what

initiating doodle toward a strategy by which they might survive
this parlous time? What nanospeck? What fossil bacterium?
"If you laid out all the acknowledged hominid specimens, they
would barely fill a tennis court"—but offer just one knuckle-chip
to guide us as a base line, and we'll build up to the thoughts that once
soaked slowly in their cranial compote, and we'll compute
digestion quotients for the marrow licked from every last cracked-open bone
like a jam. And likewise every last anachronistic wonder
of the faux-colonial village will take shape and be solid and covered
in a beckoning seventeenth-century verisimilitude: every "witch jar"
filled with urine and pins, every post-set pen with its redolent
population of pigs, and the circle of happily chattering thatchers
in the Massachusetts sun . . . but first, one artificial wormhole
in an oak shelf, serving to germinate things. Edison

already (1891) had patented the radio; and proved
the human voice could be stored up, like a soup, in a cylinder,
for future use; and was well on his way to the 1910 "kinetograph feature"
Frankenstein (and Edison's was arguably the first true movie studio) . . .
how easy it must have been then to believe
how, on that bedrock, we could tinker into creation a river
of such adept electroconversation, it would carry us
into the realm of the shades (where even brave Odysseus shrank
in terror) to speak, with a clarity, and with an equal clarity
be spoken to in turn. In this same way, that woman thinks
they have a bedrock: hasn't each of them been married once
before?—they have a history of errors they can learn from,
and can learn *away* from, into something stronger. So
one afternoon she accompanies him to the cemetery: here,

his parents: okay, let some razzledazzle healing start.
And can we imagine its taking place? If we're given
an early pebble or photon or chromosome of its taking place.
In ancient Japan, the emperor had a "dream hall" in his palace:
he would sleep there on a special polished stone
and then "the voices"—often the dead—would advise him
on matters of state. Can we believe it? The stone itself
is a first step in believing it. The stone is a technology;
a sign; a link. And even now, the dead may be ready
to offer our couple their best idea on compromise and closeness
in a marriage. Can we picture it? If we're given
a symbol for picturing it. If they stand there and hug on the verge
of those graves and, just as in some comic book's scenario,
an electric lightbulb beams forth over their troubled heads.

The Too Late Poem

Nothing in the room can go back.
The ashes couldn't be paper again,
the paper couldn't return to its parental linen rags.
That arrow doesn't reverse: the linen
could never again be a possibility
waiting, alive, inside the field of flax.
Whatever's recently happened
in the room is beyond the boundary of this poem,
but we know this: its people can't go back
to who they were before. And the light,
here, now, or any light as the day goes forward,
yours, or mine . . . it can't regain its first existence,
at the start of things: an innocence.
For once it touches the world, it becomes complicit.

———————

She's left the room. He stays in the bed,
below the covers, and when she exits the house
—the door is audible—he curls up, bean of sadness
that he is. Her travel is greedy, it needs the miles (by now
she's past the city limits). His is weaker, but ambitious,
if by fetal position we mean a desire to travel
the whole life-corridor back to its insular source.
I'm sorry, but we can't: nor can the photons of the cosmos
do a U-turn and reconstitute the Original Field of Energy
the size of a barnyard egg. They're going to scatter outward
over the edge of zero. *Barnyard egg* . . . he remembers
his grandparents' small, hand-labor farm . . . the horror when he first saw
a decapitated chicken running crazy in the grit, to flee
the fate that had already happened.

Stepper

How long is the day they argue through?—a week?
is it a year of a day? is it the abrasive, millennial haul
of a glacier of a day? It leaves enough ground-down, mysterious
debris in its wake to be as slow and thorough as a glacier:
a powder of grievance, with the occasional undigested
choke-bone sticking out. How endless is this? Her ire
with the stone by stone authority of Chartres
(*if* its rose window were replaced by the secretive face
of the Sphinx) . . . how many generations does it take to build
this monument to choler? It couldn't be dismantled
even over a lifetime. And his own vendettas,
unveiled today: they must have required all of the spleen,
all of the hardening gallsores and conviction, of the forty years
of wandering the Sinai desert, under the watch
of those living pillars scribbled inside with a writhe of fire and dark.
What would the unit of measurement be for such contention?
Not a stroll around the block. A pilgrimage trail, maybe;
maybe Lewis and Clark. We think the hands are the tools
of a scribe; but certain stories are told by the feet,
and by a weariness in the third eye. Alexander brought
—in addition, of course, to warriors and generals—"steppers"
with him on his expeditions, to count the paces, and so
add to our topographic knowledge. Every day . . .
the dust of Asia Minor caking in one's hair.
All night, for 1700 miles of nights . . . the cold slopes
of the Hindu Kush against one's cheek,
until the flesh takes on the feel of rock. Some
never returned as themselves. This
is evidently what needs to be done
if you're going to conquer the world.

Bundh

"The spyglass, then, presented a challenge to even the most sympathetic or expert observer simply because it was the first instrument to extend one of the human senses. Unlike spectacles or magnifying lenses, the optic tube offered not just a distortion of what was already there, but more. *It revealed evidence that was different from what the naked eye could see, evidence that* wasn't otherwise there. *And if you raised it toward the sky, it revealed—with 'all the certainty of sense evidence'—evidence that contradicted what was otherwise there. And the two views of the universe couldn't both be right."*

—RICHARD PANEK
Seeing and Believing

Oh yeah? says Shay (a stage name) as she cashes out
for the night from what's a veritable lettuce-head
of singles. Finished "strutting ass," it's fling
the skimpy whisper-of-a-thong and killerdiller do-me heels
in her gym bag, then she's out and on her way
to the observatory: sloppy jeans, and sweatshirt
saying *Heavenly Body,* Anna (real name now)
being red-eye shift this month as she completes
her PhD in astronomy. "Look *here:*" and she pointed
to a textbook chart, *Alternative States
of Elementary Particles* as they binked, undid,
and rebinked into being one another. At first
I didn't get it. But then I saw
how this was her biography.

———

The boy is also a king—a pharaoh; the pharaoh is also
a god. And on a Persian vase, a warrior-priest
has raised a thick, sufficient wing from either shoulder: almost,
we can hear the thwack of wind in a harbor's sails.
Goldbarth's Rule of Confusion (and Unexplainable Beauty):
Any one thing : two things. Some, an easy
equipoise. Some, the schizoid urgency
of Jekyll sensing the lava of Hyde beginning to form
inside him. There's a serial murderer currently working
my neighborhood with duct tape and a butcher knife; presumably
he stands in line to buy his milk like anybody else.
One Jewish legend is the *lahmed vov,* the "hidden saints"
for whose sake God refuses to destroy the world.
A tailor maybe, a one-legged baker, a laundress . . . even *they* don't know.

The Pope's sun is as smooth as a yolk,
and it orbits the Earth. The other sun . . . Copernican;
and *blemish all upon it.* Only one can be
definitive, and so Galileo is shuddering in a coach
on his way to the Vatican. How many suns can one sun be?
*O Mistress Sun, O Mistress Sun, Don't heat up my cheek
like a bakery bun!* The Bible's was as still as a coin
in an album, over Jericho. So many . . . Galileo
readies himself to explain his choice of these
simultaneities. And Drake? (because we're back
in the twenty-first century) . . . Anna is home now
from her late-night astral scanning, and drops heavily
against him in bed . . . the only man she's ever married,
and so (her joke) her best husband and worst.

And wasn't Drake a jerk at first?
Yes, but he changed, he rose to the occasion.
Is it possible, then, for person-A to be person-Z?
The "sky" is also the "atmosphere."
Can you prove this? Can you provide an example?
Yes: you. See?—you're my "other" brain.
Does this explain how a head on Earth can also have eyes on Jupiter?
And that sad old man recanting in the Vatican's cellars once surveyed the skies.
Don't Drake and Anna often argue about her job, until love dies?
Yes; but destruction can also be a vehicle for preservation.
Oh? Provide an instance of this.
In 2300 BC, marauders set the royal palace at Ebla (Syria)
on fire. Today, the palace records still exist:
their clay was baked that permanently.

———————————

One night she dreamed: she was stripping
a gauzy sarong from her hips: and it became a cloud
of nebular fur, and there below it was the surface of a planet
she peeled as easily as an orange: and in it
a man was looking up at the sky through a mighty lens
and calling to her through the wide, wide blue,
"Anna! Anna-Shay! I love you!":
and when she awoke, each layer was true. A single heart,
by itself, is a cohabitation. A single word . . .
take *Bundh,* the name with which a British company
christened its line of curry sauces.
Only six million pounds of advertising later
did they learn that it means "ass" in Punjabi.
(In Hindi it means "to merge two things together.")

The Novel That Asks to Erase Itself

But perhaps that couple sitting in the corner booth
in silence *isn't* working out some bitterness

in what got said, but working on not saying it:
a sturdy and impressive Taj Mahalian construction

that we'll never see, which of course
is the point—as if inventing anti-matter

or zero: something immeasurably important
although beyond our witnessing senses. They might be

the lesson of *Frankenstein,* incarnate
in this neighborhood bar. The genius wasn't

in making the monster; and certainly not
in killing it; but would have been,

invisibly, in not making it to begin with.

Walleechu

What would we have offered then, in those days,
as she wasted (it seemed hourly) like a movie of death
at triple-speed—a year of our own?—an arm of our own? What
lacquered box of a happiness would we have gladly given,
to reclaim our mother from what she'd become
on a sheet that, after a night of pain and leaking,
was a butcher's tarp? A leg?—a leg
of us for a day of her? Although the heart is not
a bivalve, it can be spaded out of the chest
and given away—would we have done that, say
a month of it in exchange for a month for her?
Would we have hung it on the kind of tree that Darwin saw,

"the altar of Walleechu," on the high and empty plain
approaching Bahia Blanca? Here, on the leafless branches
of that solitary presence, the local Indians had attached,
"by numberless threads," their various tokens of beseechment,
"meat, bread, pieces of cloth, cigars, &c."—and "poor people
not having anything better, only pulled a thread out
of their ponchos, and fastened *it* to the tree." But
a luxury ocean liner, with all of its orchestras
and silver champagne buckets, is only a trinket
to the gods—how could they want some little knot
of a child's hair? And yet they do, it seems. What
wouldn't we abandon for their favor? In the days

of my love-troubles, I might have offered my tongue
on a salver for what it had said. Or my eye—would
that do? On a fish hook and a swaying length of nerve?
Another bit of human glitter for the jackdaw sensibility
behind this tree. Here, take it, let it dangle
and gleam in the blanched sky of this country.

Context

Miraculous *objets*—and all the more so,
when they're first uncovered in reverent hush
and with a flourish bespeaking their rarity, eased out
from whatever pearl-and-jasper cask or angel-hair cocooning
is their fittest concealment. Somewhere,

in an emperor's famous cabinet of wonders
was a roc's egg, fully as large
as the head of a calf, and the color of ocean spray
in a drizzle of almond liqueur: the major-domo
would exhibit it for special guests while wearing gloves
of velvet trimmed in moleskin. Somewhere else,

a brooch of gold inset with two thick snips of hair,
the one from Byron and the other from Augusta (his half-sister),
and initialed by both as a sign
of sexual consummation: you tell me
how many layers of richly scarlet swathing
is commensurate with this,
and is the one right curatorial response. Somewhere

a length of ectoplasm
from the spirit realm, around
a ruby spool. Somewhere in an emerald urn
in an ivory case in a secret room in a monastery:
two of Jesus' petrified tears.
William Beckford wrote that once, in 1787, in Spain,

a prior showed him an angel's feather. There it was,
"stretched out upon a quilted silken mattress,
the most glorious plumage ever beheld
in terrestrial regions—a feather from the wing
of the Archangel Gabriel, full three feet long, and . . ."
something. I'm going to save that last descriptive bit
for a later place; so much depends on proper presentation.
For example: in a class last night, I taught Toi Derricote's

clitoris poem: the gorgeous "purplish hood" of it,
the "pale white berry." She says: "How shy
the clitoris is, like a young girl /
who must be coaxed by tenderness." Surely I've heard
my students in the laundromats and bar booths of the world:
fuck this, and eat me out, and up your ass,
and just as surely none of them—above a page
in a university room—would say one word
(I mean that: not *one word*) about the opening

intimacy of her carefully shepherded language.
Nor would English writer W. H. Mallock consent
to purchase "special photographs" from someone
who approached him on a cruise; and still refused
a moment later when this same all-purpose huckster
simply segued into his second pitch: "'Perhaps,' he went on,
'you would like a piece of the true Cross.'"—we're

reminded how the aura of the stewardship is crucial;
how a "rightness" must attend and lift
the veil, or its force is lost. The Torah
in a silverplated shield. The burlesque queen
in her dozen ounces of glittery flounce. About those
"special photographs" . . . I've seen them too, of course,
and I've enjoyed them, on their own terms,
in their own way, for the need that they address.
But nothing matches when the entrance to that universe

is heralded, the first time, by the urges
and the hesitancies and the ritual locutions
of the first time . . . when that deepness
is a gift (as William Beckford says
in somewhat different context) ". . . of a blushing hue

more soft and delicate than that of the loveliest rose."

"The famous Catalan Atlas of 1375. . . .

[I]n an impressive act of self-control, the cartographer actually left parts of the earth blank."

Like vertigo: over the canyon rim, or down
the "plunging" neckline . . . you *don't want* to look:
but look: and are lost in a where
beyond any- and else-. And so those maps
that end in unmap, in the way
this ancient Chinese scroll is of a fishing village
that debouches, on its left edge, into
—Nothing, into artfully unpainted space
that says it's from before the world
defined itself as separate from the Void,
it says *Come closer, I'm only a scroll, you
won't fall in, come here, come closer.* Such horror.
And purity. Not one atom. Not the nucleus,
not the cloverleaf of orbits. *Here, look into me. . . .*

Even as it lures us, we recoil.
Every marriage knows—we risk
the damaging word, to break what's more
unbearable: silence. Into the barren dark
of the grave—we speak, we sing. And if the cave wall
is a flat blank—not for long; soon
it's a depth of leaping umber-bodied beasts.
Or think about the endless desert wastes
the gold-infatuated forty-niners suffered through
as cattle died, and wagon wheels
burst, and canteened water dwindled. *Go Back Now,* or
Coorage, Oaysis Ahead!—they'd find these written
on the skulls of steers, small messages
in an otherwise maddening emptiness.

———————

My sister patted my mother's head; and then
they closed the casket. Look at it this way:
the amoeba—and later the labyrinth
of the human brain; the book
—and later the World Wide Web; the Earth
—and later rockets to Mars. The universe
wants itself (and so, its "us") to move
toward ever-greater density of associational links.
It wants the Entirety of What Is
to be one simultaneous thought. And so
it wants my mother's bones
as yet another tiny message, on the way to that conclusion;
wants her scattered,
to be signs through the unknown.

Emblem Days

The weasel slinketh; and also the marten and the ermine; and so
these bear the stamp of perfidy and betrayal, and Judas Iscariot
exults in them. The supple muscle of storm
a panther is, is Christ the avenger. The nightingale
is the sweetness of a human life: its joy the size of tiny wings,
its death the size of bones like elfin cutlery. Even a child knows
how crows among the rubble is a portent. This was the age
of signs: an herb . . . a mineral . . . everything bespoke
a larger system. It was an earlier time, and simple:
not the way *we* think, at all. And yet . . . in the difficult days
of my father's health, which were also the difficult days for me
of love, its sting, its promise . . . I entered a field and there
was a single tree, and on it a single, deep red
apple alive with a cardiac fierceness.

The Western Frontier

It turns out that I *hadn't* written "reads down
to the grave": no, that was my slanty scrawl
for "reaches down," a note done in the days
of gray haze after my father's funeral:
I'd waved in his direction, or I'd thrown some farewell
fist of gravel . . . now I see how lovely it would be

to read to him, who never in his life had time
for books: to once a month approach that patient
and resonant elsewhere-space, sit tailorwise
at the lip of it, and begin in the faith
that my voice was heard: the way it was
when someone stood in the rose-stain light

that washed across the sanctum where
the Virgin's milk was restless and attentive
in its ruby-gewgawed tube
(or hairs from Noah's beard;
or specks of dung from Job's scraped pile,
set inside a tiny silver urn) . . . and at the utterance

of kvetch or pledge or simply sharing everything
unshoulderable that day . . . a conversation starts up,
easily, as if the width of death were one cell thick,
and these—the pilgrim and the milk
(or hairs, or shit, or finger steeped
in time's strong teas)—become electrolytic messaging

across the void: this dialogue, of negative
and positive . . . this morphing-in-and-out-of,
of the physical and non- . . . is what we see in even early
[ur-ly?] stories, when the spirits
and the worked stones of the caves become
the same one living presence, stones that seem to throb

beneath the touch like hearts: and also later,
in the story of the ivory statue, Galatea, stepping off
its pedestal with the pliancy and metabolism
of any live Greek beauty: and later, a marble
figure of Jesus shedding tears, a wooden Jesus pouring
as copiously as a spigot from his side: I like particularly

the story (this is from 1311) of when the carven image
of a Vishnu icon is pillaged out of Tamilnad to Delhi,
and the sixty Tamil elders who come to petition for its release
discover it (him?) in the chambers of the sultan's daughter,
"rubbed in musk and adorned in beautiful jewels
and keeping her company at night in human limberness":

which isn't completely dissimilar from Marcus's remembering
the times he'd go at the close of the day to a low hill
by the silo, and he'd watch until the ember-color
last light of the lowering sun seemed suddenly
to gather itself corporeally in the one high open window
"and inspire me to keep on in this crappy lifetime—really,

almost as if it spoke": and yes, of course, we *don't* want
to be courting schizophrenia, or any
of the other disassemblers of the psyche, but
we need to be open . . . we need to be open to welcoming
our small (and safer) version of Ezekiel's
shake-and-roar, four-wheeled, wingéd, zoöfacial

traffic from out of a cloud of fire; open even
to our own come-hither syllable or two of the voices
that, in a greater and overwhelming clamor, swam
without cease in the cochlea of Joan of Arc, a kind
of pretech nanobioengineering story, and a kind
of glory amok in the blood . . . we need to be open to this,

if potentially only, let's say one-fourth only, something
like the way that six of the thirteen original colonies
considered themselves three-sided: on the west,
they still were open—"all the way to the Pacific" was the claim—
and it's this promise, it's this airy and unmapped terrain
—this anything frontier—that has me thinking walking

west today with book in hand, to read him—what?
who knows? . . . it may as well be what I'm reading for myself
right now, a science-fiction novel where the spaceship
pioneers a mysterious nebula-arm of stars, and as
my voice begins the long, long haul, they
beam themselves onto an unknown world.

The English Rat

Brioche. Barouche. And one of them you can still buy, by the dozen,
at the sweets stall in the weekend farmers market; the other
hasn't been seen in a century (although they tend
to blend, to be conjoined twins, in my mind).
In a Victorian story I'm reading, a barouche conveys
a scalawag apothecary (baggaged up with plaister glop and leech jars)
to the bedside of some rummy doxy dear to the heart of a magistrate . . .
these words are only here with us by a lingering atom or two
of spoken breath. That this barouche has been instructed
"at the strictest adjuration" to proceed "with all alacrity" . . .
this language is a snick of time away from lying down
in the dust with its brothers and sisters: Scythian, Etruscan,
1940s proto-hipsterspeak. This disappearing language
and its world. On his Galapagos excursion, Darwin

witnesses "red scoriae"; the lizards "are not all timorous,"
and in their parted stomachs is a seaweed—"foliaceous."
He assures us this is all "well ascertained." *Bone
voy-ah-gee* to words like that, my father would have said in his
own corny jocularity: *Arriver-dair-chee. Adióses, Moses.*
(It's a miracle the *real* 1940s proto-hipsters didn't beat
the living shit from him, in his sweet, misguided attempts to "belong.")
And now?—he's down in the earth-roofed streets where
corner drugstore Sumerian gets spoken. (You'll have noticed how I slipped
a secret "bye, bye" into the first line.) Darwin knows that language
stays in place no better than the English rat: he sees how,
in the islands, it's been "altered by the peculiar conditions
of its new country." Come down to the shore: there goes the *Beagle,*
over the azure-crested horizon. *Toodle-oo.*

The Song of Two Places

Even when we're gone, we're here. The ashes
of Franklin Berry in their plastic urn
were stolen and held for ransom: as a "presence,"
he was in his sister's life as indisputably
as if he commandeered the chubby recliner chair
in the living room, still, and filled
their shared apartment with his repertoire
of misremembered television jingles: every contact
from the perpetrator, every interview with the police,
was only further contribution toward a kind
of simulation-him, and when the facts
said "gone," her heart heard "here here here."

———————————

At Hillside Cemetery in Auburn, Massachusetts,
"superintendent Andy Shreve was surprised to receive a bill
from telephone company Sprint demanding that Danny Yeckup
pay twelve cents, including ten cents for a call on February 16,
five years after his burial." *Even when we're gone,*
we're here. "A Chinese couple offered 75,000 pounds to a man
if he married their daughter, even though she had died
at twenty-eight the year before: the mother had dreamed she was lonely
without a husband in the spirit world." *We wiffle away*
through a pore, we snip our tendril of attachment to the surface
of this sphere, and yet we're here. Between the solar systems:
emptiness. Between our neurons: emptiness. *And yet we're here.*

———————————

The wonder and frustration of that fifth-grade question
won't abate: if zero is nothing . . . how does it make a 10
by sidling up to a 1? Ah, but the power of nothing is not
to be underestimated! Jason's parents have given their lives
to him, to his nothing. He drove the big-fin junker Cadillac,
sixteen and drunk, off the fishing pier into Lake Keargill.
Now the car's still in the bottom muck; and he's
the Jason Nieva Foundation, the Jason Nieva Scholarship Fund,
and a spotless bedroom as frozen in time as a Paleolithic robin's nest
made perfect in the blue hold of a glacier. *Zero* . . . what
was it like, in the head of that man who gave it
its shape, and taught us how to value it?

———————

It doesn't require more than a sprinkle of delicate stitches,
no more than you'd use in sewing closed a bag of sachet . . .
just that, and certain herbs, and a chicken's twitching heart.
And the corpse, of course; and then a zombie walks the earth
to do your bidding: maybe it carries your load of firewood,
maybe it strangles that man who cheated you at poker.
Something conjured from the very grave: truly *ex nihilo*.
And we all do this magic, in smaller ways. What service
would I want from *my* dead people? My father's small advice.
My mother's small forgiveness. There's a sweet and homely rightness
in the tiniest of afterlives. That Caddie
at the bottom like a five-and-dime Atlantis.

———————

And the opposite, too. By that I mean I've seen Aunt Sally
make her face a lens—that's right, a great, industrial, burning,
lighthouse lens—through which her whole self tried to beam out
into Morrie's open grave on the day of the funeral; and I've seen
a not dissimilar transportation, out of the eyes,
and on the breath, at the completion of sex: it left
the body emptied, for an hour, of its immanence.
And yet it can be more casual than either death
or lickerish usage. Certainly a committee meeting will do: the focus
wanders, and the eyelids shed attention like the falling
malt off the wings of a moth. The mind can be Mars.
The now can be flying. *Even when we're here, we're gone.*

Atmosphere

In the comic book, Atlantis sinks . . . so slowly,
the throats and pulmonary systems over generations
keep pace: scales; gills; and dainty fins
at shoulders and elbows as if butterflies have landed there.
Is it credible? No; although it happens
in a fingersnap when the fetus exits
its all-surround nutritive swaddle, and inflates its lungs
for the first-time oxygenating rush. Otherwise,
without that mechanism, it would drown, like the fish,
in air: those slits that keep on sucking
death across their membranes. In Chagall, the sky
is filled with goats that float like dirigibles; wingèd cows;
and ectoplasmic human lovers . . . teasing us to believe
all these countless lives share a single effluvium.

———————————

In the story (there are dozens of versions) the children
follow the piper into the heart of a hill,
a solid hill, and when they return years later
(maybe a hundred years later) they're still the same age
—*the same.* And yet not quite the same, how could they be,
who have learned such alien respiration—thriving,
somehow inhaling the earth and exhaling the earth
as if it were any Saturday afternoon. As for
the rest of us . . . our mouths can only take in
smallest portions of the matrix that we came from,
even the beckoning of cunnilingus, even
the pleasure in feeling the words of ancient languages
anciently shape our mouths. . . . And then we rise back
into the breaths of our everyday element.

———————————

There are numerous tales of war like this one
coming from the bloodiest of colonial days . . . when American troops
and Britain's Hessian allies wound up resting
for the night in their respective encampments on either side
of a valley. As the stars came out, a bagpipes started up.
From the opposite side of the dark, a voice joined in.
A drum. Another voice. They made a single
invisible lyric presence cupped between those hills.
They were drunk on that music, together. And then
dawn broke, and the day grew clear, and the sword
demanded to be taken up, and the musket,
and the cannon, and the thirsting bayonet. As if . . .
the atmosphere was different now,
so it called to a different part in us.

And the Rustling Bough As an Alphabet

Like anything else, the air in motion
is schizophrenic . . . or anyway, is modulated
over an extensive range, that starts

at the gentlemost fingering of the lingerie
out drying on a backyard line
—a subtle lilt of those acrylic petals—

and ends at the hurricane-force destruction
we once saw: a row of ten-floor buildings
flattened to the ground, lined up like bodies

in the hands of a gang-style execution.
Could *anything* be in charge of all this,
of all this simultaneously? A God,

a blind God. He would read the world
by exactly that braille.

Burnt Tree

And after my poetry reading . . . there was Sam! and
Darcy with him of course! I hadn't seen them in
—well, no, not Darcy; someone else, new, Sue,
"a lot can change in ten years." Yes, but: ten?
Could it be *ten?* And it was my fault, I'm the one
who let our Kansas-Pennsylvania friendship fizzle
into nada. Why? I couldn't tell him why,
I didn't know. It's just. . . . I didn't know,
I still don't, I was ashamed, "we liked the reading,"
it's that one day when I glanced up
at my rearview mirror, there—with the guitar
my parents bought to shush my nagging, and it stayed
unplayed beneath my bed, a stillbirth
with her mouth wide in an O of rigor mortis; there,
with my three-year marriage in Texas; there with the gods
of the Inca empire, and the one-time long-gone
boisterous, raffish soul of Yiddish theater, and the theories
of the homunculus and the effluvium, and cribbage,
and the cakewalk, and a pair of ratty running shoes
I swore that I'd be buried wearing—there, with these,
receding at the speed of onward travel,
on the roadside with the rest of history . . . there
was Sam, his sweetly klutzy smile
and mismatched shirt and pants, for no good reason,
waving good-bye.

———————————

A dream: the corpse's eyelids lift
completely off the face, and float away
among the other loosened petals of the world. . . .
A dream: the corpse's fingernails—ambered, thickened—
clatter loudly to the floor like a hand
of dropped Scrabble tiles. . . .

This afternoon—as *every* Wednesday afternoon—
a woman in the green shirt of The Plant Girls is appraising,
with a brusque but understanding eye, the square
of potted flora in the foyer of our student union,
watering if needed, adding soil if needed, and always
snapping off the wan and the brittled . . . today,
as she's doing that latter, she throws me a look
of coolly defensive authority, as if she thinks
I silently condemn her for those necessary yanks.
I don't, though. Who am I to say she shouldn't
feed an every-Wednesday bag of cullings
to the winds that, even now, are bearing
unraveled lengths of player-piano rolls
and Confederate currency in a colorful gust,
and the tusks of the woolly mammoth,
and every microorganism and pope
of the Ptolemaic universe.

Darcy phoned me: did I want a drink with her
at the one upscale bar in that pitiful three-bar
Pennsylvania town? It turned to seven drinks.
I think—although this was never overt—she wanted, somehow,
to explain herself, the new "her," what it required,
how it was worth . . . well, Sam was never mentioned by name.
He was an abstract concept: "sacrifice." In the ancient of days,
a book that I've been reading claims, "a class
of Hindu men believed that marrying for a third time
was unlucky: it provoked the fates." And so they would marry
a tree: there was an entire ritual,
singing, vows. The man and the tree

were husband and wife. And then? So simple:
the tree was burned, and the man was free to wed
the next woman he yearned for. This is how it is,
a fact; a law of physics; a religious tenet.
In every day, some thing must die
for the day to keep on living.

Buchenwald:

originally, the beech woods of that area.
They have a quiet grandeur, when we edit
historic associations out of them. Bole after bole:
a quiet and recurrent grandeur. There was a copse
not far from my childhood neighborhood, the sun among the trunks
like clear, sweet speech and punctuation. I also
think of these sluggish summer evenings lately near the highway
where the mill pollution veils the lowering light
in especially glorious drifts of smoky tangerine and deep, seared rose.
—How even appreciation
of beauty becomes a betrayal.

Unforeseeables

The authorities imported certain rabbits
to the island, as a remedy for a certain obnoxious weed:
they'd graze it, easily, to a reasonable number.
It's why I thought of Frank and Dorrie and when
their marriage had entered its deep plum moment of melancholia
—none of the usual mood enhancers helped her—and,
at Frank's insistent pleading, she began to see a therapist.
I gave the plan a thumbs-up too. But maybe
you've already guessed: in just a fingersnap or two
of human sexual time, the rabbits overran the countryside,
and rats were imported to check that growth . . . so one year later
officials were offering goat-herders up in the steppes
a bounty of one cent (which was reasonable pay for then
and there) for every rat tail brought to a magistrate.
The lesson: some solutions only add another problem.
Dorrie started to sleep with the therapist.

It's a bit like astrophysics . . . once the answer to the question
is "dark matter," the answer is really another and even
weightier, stickier question. Once the second honeymoon
has used up feeling like the first . . . it's everything else,
all over again—the promises that wear away
at their edges as if from silverfish; the false incriminations—
only now exacerbated by the size of a cruise-ship cabin.
You can see, we're back at the story of Frank and Dorrie.
How could we *not* be? "Plum," I said in section one: the way
the sweetness of the meat inside beseeches us, and the color
of bruise on the outside is appallingly familiar. It's their story;
and it's your story and mine. Once evolution's answer to time
is the human brain . . . well, here we are, with all of our burrs
and webs and unforeseeables. Up in the steppes,
a constable uncovered caves where the locals were busy
breeding rats, *adding* to the population. Of course; a penny a tail.

Stomackes

*"We know far more about the philosophical underpinnings of Puritanism
than we do about what its practitioners consumed at countless meals."*
—JAMES DEETZ

1.

Yes. So we must reconnect
ideas of God, and the definitions of "liberty,"
and the psychology of our earliest models of governance, with
oyster peeces in barley beer & wheet,
chopt cod & venyson seethed in a blood broth,
hominy pottage, also squirell.
Their heads might well have brimmed with Heaven
and its airborne personnel, but still their mouths were a mash
of *white meat* [cheese] *and a motley collation*
of eel leavings, a fine samp, and a roast Fowl.
Worshipp first, then after—butter Biskuits!
David Ignatow:
"seeking transcendence
but loving bread"

2.

And it *is* too easy to get lost in abstraction,
as if smoke, and dream, and quantum ersatz-states
are our proper environment . . . it's easy to conceptualize in "politics"
and not in the clack of the black or white dried bean
we drop in the voting bowl. In some tribes, there's a designated
"reminderer," and when the shaman novitiate—or sometimes
simply a mournful family member—follows the star trail
into the country of ghosts, and lingers there, this person tugs
the wanderer back home: perhaps a light thwack
with a broom-shock, or the rising steam of a broth that one
can hungrily shinny down to Earth like a rope.
In the Mesopotamian Inanna myth, it's water and bread

that resurrect the goddess and allow her
to begin the long ascent out from the craters of Hell.

We can spend all day, and many days, and years, in theorizing.
"A Computer Recreation of Proto-Hominid Dietary Intake: An Analysis"
. . . we'll float off, through these foggy lands of argot,
in the way that someone else might dissolve in the blue cloud
of an opium den . . . no wonder there's such pleasure in uncovering
the solid fossil record of those appetites, and in emptying out
its evidence grain by grain, a stone piñata. How often
the stories bring us back to that grounding! In 1620,
a first exploratory party from the *Mayflower* went ashore
on the northern Cape Cod coast. The weather was bad
and disorienting: a half a foot of snow, in air
so thick as to be directionless. But we sense they recouped
their spirits that night, from "three fat Geese
and six Ducks whitch we ate with Soldiers stomackes."

3.

And it *is* too easy to lose ourselves in cyberthink,
untethered from the touchable, from even the cohesive force
suffusing through one atom. "What we keep,"
reports an archivist at the *New York Times,* "is the information,
not the paper" . . . everything e-storaged now.
A thousand years of pages, *pffft:* dismissiveness
as obliterative as a bonfire, in the long run. Oh yes,
easy to cease to exist as an actual shape, inside the huge,
occluding mists of legalese: we say "repatriation
of native archeological remains," and we mean
human bones, that's what we mean: hard and dear
and contested. We say "ritual signifier of threat," but
what the Narragansetts sent to the colonists at Plymouth
was "a bundl of thair Arrows tyed about in a mightie Snake skin."

I died. And I was stolen
into a land of strangers—of not-the-People.
I floated all day, many days. And here
the ribs of my cage were empty: always
I was hungry, for the things that People need.
But this was not the sun, and this was not the soil,
of the People; and I was restless, I had no one
for between my legs, and no drum in my chest.
There was much war from this: the People
desired me back, they said "this one
is part of many-ones," and after words and words,
their word was so. One day the breezes sent the fishes
and savory beaver parts, and I knew at last
that I was home: my mouth of my skull watered.

4.

"When hegemonic identity-structures systemize cognition—" whoa.
There are times I think my friends might flimmer away in that
high-minded mush . . . and I concentrate, then, on the names
of those people from 1621, names that are true, specific
labor and specific, beautiful common things. Cooper.
Fletcher. Glover. Miller. Glazer. Mason. Carpenter.
Cheerfull Winter.
Oceanus Hopkins.
Lydia Fish, Nathaniel Fish and Steadfast Fish, of Sandwich.
Zachariah Field, father, and daughter Dutiful Field.
Pandora Sparrow.
Who wouldn't care to meet Peregrine Soule?
And who could wish to let go of this life
when faced by Countenance Bountie?

Astronomy / A Pulitzer Prize Winner's Statement That Bears Upon Early American History / Cakeology

1.

It's a stunning idea in any case, but I really *was*
at Tastee Donuts sampling their "new hot meltaway glaze"
with the other 7 a.m. habituees of that accommodating place
—the mumblers; the flirters; the absentminded over-stirrers—
when I read in the *Times* that, while it isn't likely, still
it's *possible* that the universe is limited, and shaped to wrap back
into itself . . . "like a donut." Light would travel
a tubular, circular track; if so, the stars we see
on Earth are stars we'll see again, the way a carousel horse
[a racing greyhound / a boomerang / *fill in your own*]
returns, with its web of association. This might go some way
toward explaining not only the nature of so many of our beliefs
(say, reincarnation) and our patterned thinking (seasons
as a "round"; the way that sound repeats in poetry
and song; the standard form a sundial or clock face supplies
to the shapelessness of time), but also our everyday
adventures and inanities: the man whose second wife
is his first, except ten years younger; the woman who somehow thinks
another pregnancy, at forty-five, is going to reset her life at *start*.
This cosmotopography offers a sort of rationale for 3 a.m.
—an hour after the bars have evicted the wobbliest
of their denizens. Here I am, in the 24-7, nonpartisan welcome
of Tastee Donuts. Here I am, and here they are: the mumblers,
the flirters, the ones who stir their order of joe in a blitz-eyed daze,
here now at the counter as they were then, in the grace of a wattage
that's stale and simultaneously evergreen,
and not changed by so much as a photon.

2.

But the light of our own and only lives—the light
that wears our eyeballs' irises intimately, like finger rings—is always
felt as a singular thing. The setting sun of a day in June, in New York,
in 1790, heightens the strikingly bright white handkerchiefs
some citizens are wearing as masks against the influenza
of that especially muggy season: they look like a fleet of square-riggers
bellying out of the murk. The sun in the dust,
in the puddles, the sun that gilds the tiny chambered nautilus
of an infant's ear. The sun that falls on a cart of corn-fried squirrel
for sale, and gives those skinny haunches the glimmer of scepters.
All of this says *now,* it says *this very instant,* and it surely says
this instant is important, as James Madison nattily picks his way
through the droppings, to Jefferson's quarters
at 57 Maiden Lane, where he and Alexander Hamilton will meet
to argue Hamilton's plan for having the federal government
assume—that is, consolidate within itself, and take
responsibility for managing—the debts of the individual states
of this newly created Union. Well, for Madison
this is anathema: the specter of so centralized a governmental power
is all too reminiscent of just that arbitrarily wielded,
monolithic strength the English monarchy had exercised
over its colonists' lives. It was, says Joseph J. Ellis, "the fear,"
the *now,* the *here,* "that the states would be absorbed
by the federal government." Then he's savvy enough
to go on to say, "And at a primal level it suggested the unconscious fear
of being swallowed up by a larger creature, the terror of being eaten alive."
—Because, when the sun is finally set
on Maiden Lane, and over the prairies, and at the stone lips of the caves,
a darkness comes, and it fills us,
rises inside us and moves us as if we were puppets it uses
to mouth the most ancient ideas.

3.

It's not outrageous anymore—the way it was
when I was growing up—to get tattooed. The lady lawyer
and that dear man from the Heart of Jesus Charities,
for instance, have their secret epidermal art; the chaplain's wife
is comfortably public with the twining line of ivy
she uncovers when she reaches for the top shelf,
though when I was seventeen, it was only a whore,
a smashfaced dock hand, or a sweaty carny roustabout
who'd dare to flash such skin. Nor is it "weird"
to see a shaved head—not when foreskin pins,
and labia rings as thick around as impressive Victorian drawer pulls,
fill the pages of body-modification zines. And yet
the combination—Ace's shaved head tattooed
with a flamingly detailed scene of all four horsemen
of the Apocalypse on their galloping ride from ear to ear—
is still enough to shock one for a moment, as the stark light
here in Tastee Donuts seems to deepen the tangerine-reds
of the flames of Destruction even beyond their original
acid bite. Ace: one of the mutterers. Lacey D.,
just off the second shift at a nudie club called Front and "Sin"ter
is normally one of the fellowship of coffee-stirring-and-staring-and-stirring
repeatoids (is it zombiehood? or Zen?), although if she's pharmaceutically
wired, she can be one of the flirters, along with Dirty Bob,
and The Dwarf, and Angelo-From-Jersey. It's 3 a.m.,
and they're here. It's 5 a.m., and they're here. And when the sun
is fully up around 7ish . . . everyone's here,
you, me, and every yawning neighbor of ours
on this clarified half of the planet. There was no such thing as "3 a.m."
in ancient Rome, and even so . . . the time is the same,
and the hangers-around are the same, in this *popina*
as the watered wine is poured—a kind of clock to measure
the passage of night—and Valesimus mumbles

his gnat-itch grudges and shopworn hopes, and Apollonia
zones out over her rough clay cup of beverage, oblivious
even to the leers of the muleteer across the couch. "Ho,
one more plate for me!"—Marcellio, who shares
his order of delicacies with the rest of the group. He loves
these little round cakes that the management
sweetens with honey from up in the hills.

Talk with Friends

"... it wasn't only my great ancestors, the ambassadors and statesmen, that people were recalling, but the loony ones as well."

—SAUL BELLOW

His grand-uncle, Ash says, started a weekly newspaper
up in Ashley (no connection), Kansas. "He didn't have
any experience. He just started it." One fumbled
handset letter at a time—this was the 1920s. "Gossip,
dumb jokes, local announcements, screed around election years:
everybody loved it. It was all they had up there,
and third-hand copies were read around the entire county."
Then came the time he made up—"no one ever knew why,
I'm not sure *he* knew why"—that the circus was passing through
between two larger Kansas cities, on a given day, at a given o'clock,
and because they'd be needing to water the elephants anyway,
they'd also do a free show, "he described it
as 'the Most Glorious Superganza of the Ages,'" for the good and noble
citizens of Ashley. "People from out in the hills
and as far away as Slaterville were driving in, a full day in advance,
with their children and tents." He left town
under the mound of hay in a hay cart, and didn't return
for over a year . . . "and even then, for his first six months
he relied on a set of sorrel-color mustachios he'd purchased
at a sundries shop in East Moline." My friends,
your stories: packed inside yourselves as infrastructurally
as molecular lattice inside of a crystal.
Lil, whose dog was kidnapped once
as part of a neighborhood drug war. Red,
whose ex drove drunkenly smacko into the side
of the Little League stadium, wobbled out of the van
and into the field, upchucked nonchalantly
onto home plate just as if it were an everyday part of the game,
then bent to hug his slugger son with such
a fierce paternal passion, that the crowd was suddenly moved

from violent anger to supportive cheering. E.,
who has, she tells me, two vaginas: *lots*
of stories from the late nights of her dating days.
My friends: our lives are carbon. We'll be diamond one day,
all of us, from the pressure of time—and that beautiful bluish
gleam inside will be the last trace of our stories.
In her book *Kooks,* a rambunctious and seminal study
of American home-grown wackos, Donna Kossy says
that after Supreme Head Alfred Lawson died in 1954,
the national scatter of churches that bore his name
"soon disappeared." *But* my friend Derrin
blundered into one, right here in Wichita, Kansas, in 2003,
on an otherwise standard Sunday morning of garage sales:
"Three men probably in their seventies. I imagine
they're the absolute last of their tribe." There was some amiable
chitchat, and then Derrin left them alone
to their Lawsonian service, including the dynamic ways
of Zig-Zag and Swirlation in the universe, and how
the Earth is hollow and the home of fellow beings,
and that our planet "feeds at the North Pole
where the Suction is at its highest, and excretes
from out of the South Pole; and the same with atomic particles,
which are alive." Meanwhile, Derrin returned to *his* life,
helping raise Felice, and sometimes playing electric bass
for the Wrangleroos, and managing (his 9-to-5 employment)
Oak Grove Cemetery, where, in fragrant records books
that date back to the Civil War, a determined reader can follow
the parallel changes in commonest cause of death
and handwriting fashion—those elegant grape-brown arabesques
of an earlier day degrading into a lazier,
perfunctory scrawl. My friends, your stories are clamoring
to rip out of your bones like a pack of bats.
Your stories are Remus's tar babies, Venus's flytraps,
addictively sweet and Scheherazadian nougats. Simon

tells me that he improvised a condom
from the shrinkwrap off a paperback New Testament
when he worked in the stock room at Good News Books; but
Simon is *always* aswarm in women, "the marrieder,
the better"; meanwhile, one night over Irish whiskey seven, Neil
says—and Neil is forty-nine—that he's never been *touched*
by a woman. "Never?" "I mean it. *Never.*" And his face
begins to dissolve in the poured-forth acid of that statement,
right there in the bar, it softens and drips to the table
—as if it could bear that terrible knowledge
only when it was interior, but not once it was out in the light
of the world and became a story. My friends, you're "noise"
in the intelligence community's sense of the word, and somewhere in it
is a "signal": the story. My friends, I'm here
for the intercept. We'll be diamond one day,
we'll be narrative strung across the breasts of the future.
Every one of us: the star of a story
being played out in a grain of sand, a story sung
by the dust in its floating chain gang. Thomas Jefferson's
wooable cutie—the lithe and cultivated twenty-year-old
Martha Wayles—attracted dozens of suitors, but
(the story goes) when two of his rivals arrived at the Wayles residence
simultaneously, one richly umber autumn afternoon,
they automatically stopped in the hall outside of the drawing room
where Thomas played the violin and Martha played the harpsichord
and, faced with this near-perfect harmonic convergence,
they turned to one another, shrugged, put on their hats,
and retreated in silence. So imagine this delicious bit
of anecdote repeated, friend to friend, until it's still alive
now over three centuries later. That's how time works:
it's a story, and it arcs ahead from aleph to zed. If not for stories,
my friends, we wouldn't know how to measure the passage of time.
My friend with the tale of hiding from Nazi saboteurs.
My friend with the schnauzer that requires a nightly suppository.

When Nick grew sick and needed to recuperate,
he entered a Tokyo hospital, where he found his roommate
—a middle-age, graying business type—in quiet conversation
with a young man who was introduced as "Son.
Truck driver. Good boy." Then the father was wheeled
out of the room to some invasive moment, and the son
made an elaborate show of closing the door. He stood
in front of Nick. He lifted his shirt off, and he turned there
in the clinical glare of the room completely naked
from the waist up, so that Nick could see the extraordinarily
intricate, all-over tattoos of chains in inky blues,
with vividly red-and-saffron butterflies that gusted
like a wild hope among the heavy chains: these, the tattoos
of the *yakuza*. "Ah! Truck driver!" And he laughed then
for a single measured beat, redressed, and exited.
My friends, I think we've had it wrong: there are maybe a dozen
stories in the world, and *they* tell *us*. The story of Want,
of Fill-the-Hole-in-Me. The story of shattered glass
we carry in our heads all day and tumble there all night
until it becomes a fine, bright pollen.
The thumb of salt we each suck: that's a favorite!
The story of Glorious-Stars-in-the-Sky, as well
as the story of Electrical-Sparks-in-Our-Bodies . . . twins
who were separated at birth and raised in different houses.
Ash's daughter died at twenty: a vibrant, talented woman.
Now some vein of that death always shows in his face.
She was traveling in South America, as part of a college
summer program. She went for a swim: she never returned, the water
wanted and wanted her. Now all we have are stories of her,
and her own poems. I've used fake names all throughout this,
taking Robert Louis Stevenson as my guide, who wrote:
"There was a man of the islands, whom I shall call Keawe;
for the truth is, he still lives, and his name must be kept secret."
But Emma's poems I couldn't invent. These lines are hers:

"This is all the world, and in my sleep
there are older ones . . .
how many people I have been and how much
each of them has cost."
And she wrote:
"If there was ever a river drawing its carriage of little lives
to the sea, I am in it."
And I wrote, many lines ago, about "molecular lattice
inside of a crystal"—easily grabbing an image
as if I truly knew that domain. But who
could have predicted such heartbreaking beauty
in *any* crystal ball?

Grahamesque

"[Choreographer Martha Graham] repeated some transparently obvious fictions throughout her career, insisting that dancers have more bones in their feet than normal people. . . ."

—EMILY CHRISTENSEN

Some have more. Or anyway *claim* more.
In his autobiography, Davy Crockett gilds the boast
that he "can whip my weight in wildcats" by adding "and
if any gentleman pleases, for a ten-dollar bill
I can throw in a panther." Don't you think
a single snake uptendriled from a scalp
and hissing aggressively in the air should be enough?
—and yet Medusa displays a luxuriant *corona* of snakes
(although a pittance compared to the giant Briareus, he
of the fifty heads and one hundred arms).
It's all a load of hooey, of course: he may have seen a golden wall
of hula-shimmy lava (excuse me: *wheat*) and seen the cobalt
and viridian print of a billion Buddhas' brain waves
(and for that, read: *sky*) but the whole of that shuddering glory
and phantasmagoria entered Vincent van Gogh through only
the usual duo of eyes; nor did the sawed and rendered brain
of Albert Einstein hold an extra hill of zippy neural gigabytes.
And still, we understand the wish for a tangible proof
of supracapability. The Rock of the Prophet,
rising out of its thousands of prostrate pilgrims
like Gibraltar from its sea of kowtow waves.
The Cross: the wooden, historical *thingness* of it.
What would we do, if the numinous *didn't* have bones
like those, to throw down to the level
of our human needs?—like colors that the universe concedes to us
from beyond the visible spectrum, so we're willing
to believe in it. Or: Mindy, in the children's ward.
Just last year she was thirteen, at her ballet lessons

like all of her friends . . . stumbling coltish clumsiness;
a springy coltish grace. And now she's waiting to be wheeled in
to the deep procedure of bone-marrow work. How extra large
a teddy bear will it take, to say her mother's love?
How many balloons? How many supernumerary
Eiffel Towers and Noah's Arks of balloons? Here,
in the precincts of the ordinary, where most of us live, it must be
that the finger Davy Crockett squeezed the trigger with
—impeccably ricocheting his bullet off a hanging skillet,
a bar's brass rail, and a coffee urn, before destroying
that shot glass on the moose's mounted head—depended
on extra bones, a snake's-spine length of extra bones,
but ultra-tiny and fitted together like millefiori.
It must be. As little as 1%
of the three billion "chemical letters" in our DNA is laboring
in ways we comprehend; the rest is what geneticists call
"junk DNA": as of now, "we don't know why it exists," a cellular
parallel to the astronomers' "dark matter." That there's extra
amok in the cosmic whirl—confoundingly, exaltingly—is old news,
and we fold it into our thinking
without even thinking about it: "oodles," says a friend
in her retro-colloquialspeak. A dozen,
no, a baker's dozen, the whole shebang, the whole nine yards,
from soup to nuts, the everything-but-the-kitchen-sink,
and then the sink, and then the microlilliputian life
in its sponge and its S-trap. As for Graham . . . I've seen videos
of her dancers doing steps so quick, so tight, it looked
like darning. Like a hundred pounds of body trained
to work its channeled power as a thimble. And I know
if we could see the foot that Martha Graham sees
as a matter of faith—if it were glass, or even only as translucent
as a molded shape of aspic, with its contents on display—
we'd see it isn't an anthropometrical matter of how many more,
but how best used: a filigree

of focused expertise. I entered the kitchen that night
as Mindy's mother was staring at and past
the ragged stacks of dirty dishes, into . . . the future?
The weave of the human heart? She saw me. "I want," she said,
"her surgeon's hands to be like dancer's feet."
I knew what she meant. Then she started to weep,
and ran out. And I was left alone, admiring
a single bead of water that hovered immovably and nimbly
at the faucet's tip: a symbol?
A Grahamesque symbol?
The entire kitchen sink
en pointe.

Cock

Chile, 1834

A month before his dinner with the visiting Spanish lawyer,
he had "set out for the purpose of geologizing,"
and rode back over the ridge of the Chilecauquen
with a huge jute bag of living shells
from the sandy flats at the coast, and with another,
as full, of dead barnacles scraped from the rock.
A few months forward from that dinner
—on the island of San Pedro, where the *Beagle* was anchored
awaiting him—he would be sneaking up on a fox
"of a kind very rare" and donking it stoutly
"on the head with my geological hammer." (The fox,
he'll write, "is now in the Zoological Society.")
So what does he think, when the Spanish lawyer expresses a disbelief
that the King of England would be so loco as to bother
to ship to this sensible, orderly country a man
"to pick up beetles and lizards, and to break stones"?
No, the whiff of something "off"—like suspect meat—attends
eccentric stunts like these. "I do not like it:
if one of us were to go and do such things in England,
do not you think the King of England would very shortly
command us to leave his shores?" Renous,
another student of bugs and rocks, from Germany,
is also there at dinner, and he mentions then
that once, in a house in San Fernando, he'd been discovered
contemplating the transformation of caterpillars to butterflies.
He couldn't deny it: there they were,
the writhing green proof, in an open box!
"The Padres and the Governor consulted, and agreed
it must be some heresy"—and so Renous was arrested.
Darwin can only shake his head in a quiet bemusement
as his guests converse. Those inchling creatures
crawling over their chopped-up foliage, heads as blunt

as thimbled thumbs . . . *heretical?* How
could *anybody* believe that the innocent jumble
in the baskets and flasks of a naturalist is dangerous?

————————

And Lillian Colton—the woman in Owatonna,
Minnesota, who for forty years has avidly collected
the seeds of that state and, with them ("poking them
into place with toothpicks and gluing them down"),
has portraitured "American presidents,
movie stars, country musicians, rock and roll legends,
scientific and religious leaders (including Mother Teresa)"
—what suspiciousness might seize the Spanish lawyer
if he saw her on her rounds? What edgy wariness
would grip him if he chanced on Nellie Staves,
"at 87 perhaps the most famous Adirondack trapper,"
out in the summer to harvest shell-shaped fungus
off the dead trees of those shaded, spinous hills?
—she'll work for twenty hours straight on one,
with the point of an old school compass, stippling it
into the scene of a great alert-eyed ram
or a sunrise, watching as the fungus's own interior,
brown juices dye the image into permanence.
Who would these represent, for the Spanish lawyer, what
forbidden Other?—a girl in the corner, walling her attention
away from her sisters' strident hiphop, by reading
a fanciful tale of witches? a girl on a dancer pole
at Sturgis, strobing her tits for the boys in a quick 1-2-1
semaphore of fuck-the-work-week revelry? Surely
not. Surely these are no threat to his world. And yet
for nothing more than positing a newly ordered
sky map, Giordano Bruno was led in chains
from his cell in the Roman prison of Castel San'Angelo, there

where he'd spent eight years as the Inquisition hammered
at his ideas and his calm resolve. It was February 19th,
1600; he was tied to an iron stake; a wedge
was stuffed in his mouth, to prevent any final
utterance of blasphemy; and he was burned alive.
The leg skin bubbled off of his body like a Christmas pig's.
It turns out that a redone sky implies
a redone God—and a God is intolerant of this,
a God is jealous of any counterclaim to the pedigree
of His cosmos. Yes, but . . . surely not
this mushroom picker? not this boy who simply speaks
to invisible friends as he wanders around the alleys?
Oh but that would depend on the given Spanish lawyer
of that given day and circumstance. In Ghent,
a cock was put on trial and sentenced to death
for repeatedly disturbing the peace of the Lord's day,
Sunday. It had been warned; so now
it was just, to lead this beast to a chopping block
—restoring the sanctified order.

Kansas, 2004

Ah, for a witty transition from "cock"
to my neighbors Suzette and Edie!—lesbians, now
in love with each other for over a decade and wanting
only to declare their love in a marriage vow,
"like anyone," as Edie says. Not that
my schoolboy humor would find favor
in their reading life . . . although we get along;
some shared affinity enables The Church
of the Gay Girls and The Orthodox Congregation of Guy
to coexist with an amiability. Still, I've witnessed

other people pass them by with the slitted,
ophidian stare of xenophobia. Suzette and Edie
—are *they* the new apostasy? are they our own
Anne Hutchinson? In 1638 she was found guilty,
after a two-day trial, of heresy—of being "a woman
not fitt for our Society." With will, she had embraced
doctrinal misinterpretations, "some of them blasphemus, others
erroneous and all Unsafe, and of the Devill of Hell,"
and she was excommunicated from Massachusetts Bay Colony
"evermore." Her actual crime?—a claim
"the Holy Spirit illumines the heart of every true believer"
without the need of a minister intervening.
For this, she was harried into the wilds
—it was called a "hiving-out"—and set at the mercy of wolf
and of winter, "and it were Death to return." Her *other*
actual crime?—that after a pregnancy, she had been delivered
"of thirtie monstrus Births or thereabowts at once,
some of them Bigger, some Lessr, some of one shape,
some of An other, few of any Perfect shape, None at all of them
of Human shape"—which perhaps is what you'd expect
from a woman of "nimble Witt and active Spirit and verie
Voluble Tonggue." At the Republican convention,
it was, indeed, the voluble tongue that Edie always flapped
so saucily (and too, I'd guess, her rainbow-hue
WE'RE ALREADY BEDDED . . . WHY NOT WEDDED? T-shirt)
that (on her side) led inevitably to the violence.
A surly officer suggested that she move. She pointed out
how *she was already in* the caged-off square
allowed for free-speech protest, and had no intention
of leaving. There were "gestures they exchanged" . . . and then
a stun gun's 50,000 volts were suddenly alive inside her,
just enough to crumple her into helplessness so that,
when the panic began, she was trampled by friends and police
alike. A lung was crushed, and when I visited

three weeks later, her skin was still a nightmare
Turkish rug of bruise. (For a moment, I saw in the air
around her the first disabling gust of snow in the woods
at the border of Massachusetts Bay in 1638.) To be fair,
I should add that the confrontational officer doing crowd control
went home with *his* head little more
than a pocket of blood and neural damage. Do *not,*
I warn you, ever lightly cross a Wiccan bowler.

Terms I haven't yet used, from my pile of notes:
separatist, sedition, dogma. Finally, though, when those clouds
of abstraction open up, it's always one specific
ordinary rainy day, in Chicago, in 1961. I'm thirteen,
squeaky-voiced, and with an Adam's apple popping
from my thin throat like a doorknob—while my father is large,
he fought the neighbor's crazy German shepherd
to a standstill once, and behind him are generations of him,
solemn and knowing. We're standing there
in front of the house, in a dim autumnal downpour,
and it wouldn't look to anyone else like an even match,
my scrawny shouts, his thousands of years of righteousness;
and yet, in emotional terms, I have the upper hand.
I won't believe in his God. I won't believe
in any God, in any synagogue, in any mumbojumbo
or rabbinical teetotum, and I'm screaming this
and screaming this and screaming this, until I see
the rain become his face, and for the only time
except his mother's funeral on a similar day
of wet and chill in a shivering mix,
my father cries in front of me.
And God, if He's there, must write my name down
on a list that He'll turn over to His deputies on Earth

—His Spanish lawyers.
There are many terms for this,
but only one rain. Now it's falling, grayish twill,
on a hill along the coast of the Chonos Archipelago islands.
1835. A mound of seals in the distance, "huddled together,
asleep: they appeared to be of a loving disposition;
but even pigs would be ashamed of their dirt,"
which is picked at by the turkey-buzzards. Terns,
gulls, black-necked swans. A deposit of sandstone.
"Four great snowy cones" of the local volcanoes.
He couldn't be happier. He has computed the number of eggs
in a tenth-of-an-inch of a sea-slug's potent slime,
he has suggested how "a great volume might be written,
describing one of these beds of sea-weed." The otter.
The spunky Chilean mouse. He has read
"a most interesting discussion on the history
of the common potato." He couldn't be more mesmerized
in the grand salons of Paris than here, in the rain,
with his sodden insect net. And who
would complain? He isn't any rooster. He isn't
going to rudely wake anyone from a long sound sleep.

Coda

Field

". . . there was always a spot which it was forbidden to touch, or to walk upon. It was dedicated to the gods—and especially evil ones—in return for their implicit agreement not to stray into provinces where they might molest mankind. The same idea obtained in parts of Scotland. Uncultivated pieces of land were left fallow, and termed the 'guid man's croft.'"

And this is that poem. Not much happens.
There are countless possibilities. I imbue
the poem with a solid man, and a hint
of woman (sometimes the reverse is true).
Not much happens. There are images,
small everyday ablutions, that are potential
strategies and symbols: he wanders
under moons and comets, his lungs full
with biological processes, fish, fruit,
or the probability of their disappearance,
the gesture of a pianist's wrist peaked
like a thoroughbred's foreleg, a dance
troupe in ritual circle (this is the female
entering the poem), the funeral, the children,
the mosque, the mask, the map, the home.
Not much happens. Anything can;
but this one I leave for tattered health,
mistallied votes, financial misfortune,
the ups and downs of sexual deprivation,
undernourishment, and overcaution:
unworked. Let this be my guid man's croft
that I will not finish or furnish or sign
with any name but my true name.
I leave it: propitiatory, begun, benign.

Albert Goldbarth
1972

About the Author

ALBERT GOLDBARTH was born in Chicago in 1948 and since 1987 has lived in Wichita, Kansas. (*The Georgia Review:* "Goldbarth has deliberately and doggedly established his own writing counsel far from the so-called literary centers of the country.") He has been publishing poems of note for thirty-five years, in journals that range from the *New Yorker* to *Gum* and *Hearse* and *Kayak;* in many textbooks and anthologies, including numerous appearances in the annual *Pushcart* and *Best American Poetry* series; and of course in his books, two of which have received the National Book Critics Circle Award for poetry. Among other honors are a Guggenheim Fellowship, three fellowships from the National Endowment for the Arts, the Center for the Study of Science Fiction Theodore Sturgeon Memorial Award, and awards from *Ark River Review, Beloit Poetry Journal, Black Warrior Review, Northwest Review, Iowa Review, Poet Lore, Poetry, Poetry Northwest, Prairie Schooner,* and the *Virginia Quarterly Review.* He is also the author of a novel, *Pieces of Payne,* and of five collections of essays, including *Many Circles: New and Selected Essays,* winner of the PEN West Creative Nonfiction Award. He *could* have gone to med school—what was he thinking?

The Kitchen Sink has been set in Adobe Garamond, a typeface drawn by Robert Slimbach and based on type cut by Claude Garamond in the sixteenth century. Book design by Ann Sudmeier. Composition by Prism Publishing Center. Manufactured by Maple-Vail Book Manufacturing on acid-free paper.